PRAISE FOR *REINVENTING VIRTUAL EVENTS*

"Passive listening will allow you to transfer information. But if you want competency, you must gain experience. Justin and Julia have innovated an experience that leads to real learning with the potential for a faster path to competency."

—Anthony Iannarino, Keynote Speaker and Workshop Facilitator

"I have been to a lot of virtual events over the past three years and seen most everything—from polls to fancy platforms—but GTM Games was different from the start. Not only did people engage virtually before the event, but they stayed engaged afterward. That is the Holy Grail for online events!"

—Carole Mahoney, Founder, Unbound Growth

"New empowered buyers are demanding accurate and timely information from trusted sources in their network on demand. Gone are the days when they will wait for a sales demo, travel to a legacy event, or cut through online noise and clutter for answers—they are looking for their ecosystem to offer them highly customized virtual and hybrid events specific to their industry, segment, job role, location, and business outcomes."

—Jay McBain, Chief Analyst—Channels, Partnerships and Ecosystems, Canalys

"While the concept of the Metaverse and its application in business may seem a distant future away, Justin and Julia provide a compelling case for why it should matter to your business now and what you can do today to prepare you and/or your company for this virtual shift! While this book is about the 'meta,' the strategies in this book are anything but meta!"

—Victor Antonio, Author, *Sales Ex Machina: How AI is Changing the World of Selling*

"As a coach on these games, I can tell you firsthand they are a whole new world of interactivity for B2B. I was impressed by how hard each contestant worked to apply the unique skill I taught them. This book is a primer for unlocking customer-centric events for your organization—and another step in growing like a weed."

—Stu Heinecke, Author, *How to Grow Your Business Like a Weed* and *How to Get a Meeting with Anyone*

"If you need better customer acquisition strategies, then you need to get inside Justin's and Julia's heads. Truth is, you need access to insiders who know what is working today and how to combine tactics and strategy for results. Justin blew my mind in our last meeting, and I know he'll blow yours."

—**Oren Klaff**, *New York Times* **Bestselling Author,**
Pitch Anything **and** *Flip the Script*

"In Reinventing Virtual Events, Justin and Julia challenge the status quo by presenting a fresh, innovative approach to designing and conducting highly effective online events. If you're looking for cutting-edge insights that will elevate your next virtual event, this book is for you."

—**David Hoffeld, Bestselling Author,**
The Science of Selling & Sell More with Science

"GTM Games has been a key community to amplify my message of MOVE that unites sales and marketing with RevOps. I enjoyed being a coach twice and bringing my unique methodology not just to marketers but sellers also. HYPCCCYCL is elevating GTM in B2B."

—**Sangram Vajre, CEO, GTM Partners**

"The world changed in 2020, and so did 'events.' For years, the tech community lived off and thrived on the connections made, content shared, and the learning that happened at live events. In an instant, it felt like it was gone. However, the hunger for connection, learning, and camaraderie didn't go away. But given the risks associated with potentially hosting a spreader event, people had to find a different path for growth. Then along came HYPCCCYCL. While the name was confusing, the concept was genius. Live, gameshow-like experiences that drove deep learning, connection, and community all done in a virtual environment. Once I watched my first battle, I was hooked, as was the rest of the world. If you want to learn how they've changed the world of virtual events, you should read this book."

—**Doug Landis, Growth Partner, Emergence Capital**

"Reinventing Virtual Events breaks the mold on how to perform captivating events. Julia and Justin solve today's most vexing business problem: how to grab hold and keep the attention of today's overwhelmed consumer. While most books tell you WHAT to do, Julia and Justin provide the HOW by revealing their proven step-by-step process to help win the hearts and wallet share of today's consumers. Groundbreaking, innovative, and cleverly written."

—**Shari Levitin, CEO, Levitin Group**

REINVENTING VIRTUAL EVENTS

"These unique, interactive events challenge professionals in new ways and showcase the interdisciplinary skills and coordination needed to thrive in the modern world of B2B buying and selling."

—Mary Shea, VP Global Innovation Evangelist, Outreach

"Like going to the gym to get stronger, HYPCCCYCL is a safe space you bring your reps to so you don't have to practice on your prospects."

—Josh Braun, Founder, Josh Braun Sales Training

"Learning from others is not new. Learning from experts is not new. Even coaching is not new. But having a framework of learning simulations with immediate, real-time feedback by real experts is a game-changer."

—Rosalyn Santa Elena, Chief Revenue Operations Officer, Carabiner Group

"As a sales leader, I provided sales training to every new hire regardless of function. I'm a firm believer in role-playing to build skills quickly. VPs of Sales should leverage active learning models like HYPCCCYCL versus the more passive workshop approaches."

—Scott Leese, CEO and Founder, Scott Leese Consulting

"The best way to get true alignment around the customer is to throw away the silos and start over. Build it from the outside in with each person understanding their impact and the impact of the others on the customer experience."

—Alice Heiman, Founder and Chief Sales Energizer, Alice Heiman LLC

JUSTIN MICHAEL + JULIA NIMCHINSKI

REINVENTING VIRTUAL EVENTS

HOW TO TURN GHOST WEBINARS INTO HYBRID GO-TO-MARKET SIMULATIONS THAT DRIVE EXPLOSIVE ATTENDANCE

WILEY

Published by John Wiley & Sons, Inc., Hoboken, New Jersey.
Published simultaneously in Canada.

For general information on our other products and services or for technical support, please contact our Customer Care Department within the United States at (800) 762-2974, outside the United States at (317) 572-3993 or fax (317) 572-4002.

Wiley also publishes its books in a variety of electronic formats. Some content that appears in print may not be available in electronic formats. For more information about Wiley products, visit our web site at www.wiley.com.

Library of Congress Cataloging-in-Publication Data:

Names: Michael, Justin, author. | Nimchinski, Julia, author.
Title: Reinventing virtual events : how to turn ghost webinars into hybrid
  go-to-market simulations that drive explosive attendance / Justin
  Michael, Julia Nimchinski.
Description: Hoboken, New Jersey : Wiley, [2023] | Includes index.
Identifiers: LCCN 2022036314 (print) | LCCN 2022036315 (ebook) | ISBN
  9781394159253 (cloth) | ISBN 9781394159277 (adobe pdf) | ISBN
  9781394159260 (epub)
Subjects: LCSH: Teleconferencing. | Business meetings. | Special
  events—Planning.
Classification: LCC TK5102.5 .M465 2023 (print) | LCC TK5102.5 (ebook) |
  DDC 621.382—dc23/eng/20220914
LC record available at https://lccn.loc.gov/2022036314
LC ebook record available at https://lccn.loc.gov/2022036315

Cover Design: HYPCCCYCL
Cover Image(s): © Ricardo Gomez Angel/Unsplash,
                © Simon Lee/Unsplash

SKY10037998_110722

Contents

Foreword

By Mary Shea, Ph.D.
As a former Forrester analyst and Outreach's current Global Innovation Evangelist, I have the role of identifying emerging trends, connecting the dots, and preparing the market for changing dynamics.

Analysts and evangelists challenge the status quo. They keep their ears to the ground, make predictions, spark dialogue, and provide space for discourse—so their community of business leaders can grow, innovate, and set up their organizations for success.

Although we have never "met" in the real world, I have known Julia and Justin professionally for several years. I rely on both to vet new ideas and theories about the future of business-to-business (B2B) marketing and selling. They always push and extend my thinking. Very few marketing and sales experts have the depth of knowledge, creativity of thought, and generosity of spirit that these two have. At Outreach, we coined the term *revenue innovator*. Revenue innovators are a new cohort of leaders who put buyers at the center of their strategies, arm their sellers with the most innovative technologies, and who over-index on data rather than intuition to inform their business decisions. Julia and Justin are quintessential revenue innovators.

In the fall of 2021, as Covid-induced Zoom fatigue fully set in, I predicted that the "webinar was dead." This was a controversial call that panicked B2B marketers who have relied on this demand gen workhorse for years. In the spring of 2022, when Forrester Consulting conducted a B2B buyer study on behalf of Outreach, I found that prediction was overstated. The study revealed that before accepting a remote or in-person sales meeting, 55% of respondents attended a supplier-hosted webinar, and when searching for a new product, solution, or service, 57% of respondents found webinars to be valuable.

But as it turns out, I was on to something with my prediction. While the webinar was alive, its traditional static supplier-centric format was dying. That is where Julia and Justin come in. With the launch of HYPCCCYCL's Go-To-Market (GTM) Games, where community members become active participants and content creators in the virtual event, they completely reimagined the webinar.

Reinventing Virtual Events is an examination and celebration of new and more innovative ways to structure virtual events by making them interactive and customer centric. In addition to creating more engaging formats, GTM Games use role play and simulations to break down business function silos. They do this through cross-training such as having sellers engage in simulated marketing drills and vice versa. The GTM Games focus on revenue operations (RevOps), product-led growth (PLG), or account-based marketing (ABM) drills. In the second season, you will see challenges around a diverse array of revenue methodologies like SPIN (situation, problem, implication, and need-payoff), MEDDIC (metrics, economic buyer, decision process, decision criteria, identify pain, and champion), ValueSelling framework, Challenger Sales model, and others.

I'm eager to see how Julia and Justin innovate next, but I am most excited about the transformational power this book will have on the digital/virtual event industry. It's more than time for entrepreneurs, founders, event marketing teams, and startup companies to embrace this model and put on bold, interactive, and engaging events. Even though Julia and Justin have big technology chops, you don't have to. Remarkably, much of what is expounded upon in this work can be pulled off using Zoom, social media, and your company's website. Excited yet? I am!

Foreword

By Seth Marrs
In my role as an analyst at Forrester, I live at the intersection of execution and innovation. My job is to help companies grow by constantly challenging the clients I work with to solve real-world problems with new and innovative solutions. This is where I met Julia and Justin. In my constant search to find innovative solutions to real sales problems, I kept running into their innovative content and practical solutions.

The biggest long-term challenge businesses must deal with coming out of the Covid pandemic is delivering growth numbers in a world where a company's buyers and sellers no longer value in person at the same level they did in the past. Even as we return to normal after Covid, we have seen 50% of in-person meetings replaced with virtual ones. How can companies generate the same results or better with the increased importance of virtual engagements?

The initial attempt led to a significant jump in webinars and online events. This is great for buyers because they are getting more access to information with less friction in the buying process. Unfortunately, this additional access to information doesn't come with more time, so while many buyers signed up, a much smaller number end up consuming the content. Turns out the intention to watch is still limited by the busy life of a buyer.

To get true engagement, companies need to do something different. Julia and Justin's concept of go-to-market (GTM) cross-training has provided a new and engaging way to drive online engagement. Solving real-world problems through GTM Games that had sales and marketing leaders trade places educated potential buyers by helping them understand and better collaborate with their sales and marketing counterparts. Doing this also exposed buyers to solutions they can invest in to help achieve their goals.

Julia and Justin have a deep understanding of sales and marketing technology, so understand what is possible, but have also done these jobs in the past and so also know what it takes to deliver results. Combining these two things led to a concept that produces real value. When I led my GTM session, I could show the marketing leaders competing in the game how much value they could add to sales if they went beyond engaging at the lead level and started working with them to show insights to sellers that they can use to win more of their opportunities. The fact that solutions like Chili Piper and Outreach could help enable this became obvious as they thought through what they needed to better collaborate. Buyers were learning and companies getting business in a way that is a win-win for both. This is what we all want from a buyer/seller interaction, and Julia and Justin's "cross-training" concept was valuable to all involved.

This book is a must read for anyone looking to drive growth in this new post-pandemic environment. It will give you a practical guide on how to generate more value through virtual engagement by using a proven concept built by top thought leaders.

Foreword

By Mike Bosworth

In the words of Sam Walton, echoed by Justin and Julia in *Reinventing Virtual Events,* "There is only one boss. The customer."

From my perspective, "the customers" of *Reinventing Virtual Events* are the same people who have frustrated me in my work as a sales trainer specializing in business-to-business information technology (B2B IT) sales for the past 40+ years. Frustrated as I attempted to get human beings working in the sales and marketing silos to work effectively together—to *integrate.*

I now believe the primary reason I struggled negotiating these agreements is that both silos are set in their ways as product-focused rather than *customer-focused* organizations.

A product focus causes both silos to unintentionally disable the buying process of their desired customers, and the startup time of new employees, particularly new salespeople.

I have observed many product-focused organizations that end up with sales and marketing doing their best to ignore the other silo and operate independently from each other. Too many CEOs enable this behavior because they have experienced the emotional exhaustion of trying to be the referee between two powerful, independent human beings. They typically lack the skill set of a couples therapist.

To reap the benefits of *Reinventing Virtual Events, both* your organization and your customer's organization—the CEO, CMO, and CRO—will have to commit to a series of *agreements.* Agreement on WHO is the customer, WHY they need it, HOW they want to buy it, HOW they will use it (to make or save money/solve problems/achieve goals), and WHAT are the possible results. Note the two *HOWs.*

The best learning experiences are experiential—experiential go-to-market (GTM) simulations. *Reinventing Virtual Events* will guide you to providing two levels of experiential learning. First, integrate your own organization, then get agreements from your customer organizations before helping them reinvent their virtual events.

Introduction: It's Time to Reinvent Virtual Events by Making Them Customer-Centric

There is only one boss. The customer. And they can fire everybody in the company, from the chairman on down, simply by spending their money somewhere else.

—Sam Walton

If you only read the books that everyone else is reading, you can only think what everyone else is thinking.

—Haruki Murakami

© Luca D'Urbino

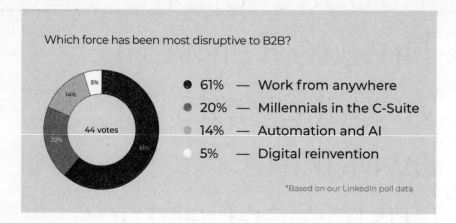

Which force has been most disruptive to B2B?

44 votes

● 61% — Work from anywhere
● 20% — Millennials in the C-Suite
○ 14% — Automation and AI
○ 5% — Digital reinvention

*Based on our LinkedIn poll data

You transform a virtual event by putting your audience in the center versus panelists and an audience alone. We are taking virtual events to a new level by featuring customers as contestants in the center of the action and randomly calling on customers from the audience to make them a part of each simulation. Customers judge, drill, role-play, break into teams, and compete against business-to-business (B2B) luminaries.

We proved this model in Go-to-Market (GTM) Games, the most disruptive B2B event series ever conceived.

Like a virtual Barkley Marathons, it is innovative, bold, and compelling because marketers and sellers finally collaborate and cross-train to solve real GTM challenges through intense simulations. Our proven model of GTM learning requires teach-backs and drills, which produce 90% knowledge retention compared to static Netflixs style lectures.

The GTM Games is a monthly, nine-days-long obstacle course featuring 21 participants. We've been honored to showcase the top 100+ voices in B2B, yet we constantly look to expand our roster. Our mission is to laser-focus GTM teams on the customer so that they can expand beyond their silo.

Now is the time to tailor your events to your customers.

Flashback two years: Julia did an event where the whole agenda touted a Reddit-style design in the promo lead-up. Social media maven Brynne Tillman was the featured expert. Users and potential viewers built the event concept collaboratively crowdsourced, and the questions they asked before defined the event.

There was a landing page with a Reddit-style up-voting system. You—the audience—build/curate the event's agenda yourself versus the last hundred years of: "We are a vendor building an event." Envision potential software users promoting your event for a month leading up to it, uploading questions, and an entire webinar built on relevant themes your users surfaced and ranked. There was no ulterior motive around the topic, just a star speaker and rapt users.

Curiosity Is the Currency of the Modern Event Flywheel

She called it an "Interactive Webinar with a Social Media Expert." The tagline, "Join us in a special event where you can ask your burning questions on all things LinkedIn for Social Selling." Results? The event was super-engaged, with hundreds of questions pouring in. It began to make her think about a new event blueprint: You provide the coach's expertise, and your audience reciprocates with their time and focus. Whichever theme your base gravitates to most becomes the topic, and the thrill of building it this way makes questions fly out of the woodwork.

When we think about throwing 200 events together, one of the most unique experiences was spotlighting CEOs and VPs doing "cold calling." Our ideal customer profile (ICP) was uncommon for this theme, not just sales development reps (SDRs) but VPs of Sales. No one believed that Julia could make VPs of Sales attend an event about cold calling, much less participate. The crowd was skeptical that senior executives would even make cold calls in the age of email sequences.

Behold the elusive trap for any vendor. Vendors believe their ICP is interested in something obvious they want to sell and forget their audience comprises ordinary humans who buy for reasons only they understand. Her research revealed that nearly all roles in sales right up to the C-Suite are still interested in outbound calling.

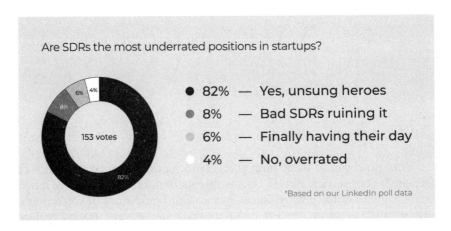

Are SDRs the most underrated positions in startups?

153 votes

- 82% — Yes, unsung heroes
- 8% — Bad SDRs ruining it
- 6% — Finally having their day
- 4% — No, overrated

*Based on our LinkedIn poll data

Despite this, a large cohort of executives believes it doesn't work. It is too expensive. Valid phone and email data is costly and has low contact rates. SDRs have insufficient product understanding to resonate with increasingly technical buyers, and inbound marketing leads are junk marketing qualified leads (MQLs).

There's a whole debate around whether MQLs should even be a metric and a growing insurgency against the SDR-account executive (AE) industrial complex.

Imagine breakthrough results like 2,000+ registrations and getting your customer acquisition costs (CAC) down to $2 for VPs of Sales versus $75+ cost per lead (CPL) best case scenario on the open market right now with ads. Because Aaron Ross cold called against all levels, there was a massive buzz on social media and thousands of likes. It was the talk of the B2B industry while it ran, sucking the oxygen out of the space. You couldn't "not see" this event. Word of mouth was so intense.

As her next endeavor, legend has it that approximately a year ago, Julia Nimchinski approached Justin Michael, "Hey, would you be up to emcee a competition where salespeople did marketing drills and vice versa?" Justin dismissed her immediately, "No thanks, that's the theme I'd least like to do. Can't we just hold another killer cold-call competition? Exactly like we've already been doing?" And thus, GTM Games was born, Julia's brainchild. The thought was Bransonian, "Screw it. Let's do it! No one has done it before!"

And you should follow this philosophy, too, rather than remaining in your silo and silencing the inner voice that scratches away at you to be innovative. Fan that flame and go big with us to reinvent yourself (and your industry) by putting the customer at the dead center of your corporate stage.

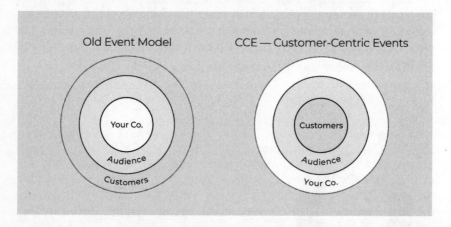

Until now, you've likely built your brand reputation on the bedrock of your product or service. But it's time to disrupt that. Like most, you've relied on your unique value proposition and even your brand story (if you're more sophisticated) to stand out in the ever-crowded marketplace. But we're here to tell you that you're getting it all wrong because your customers are your real "platform," literally and figuratively in a Michael Hyatt sense. You just have to unlock this potential energy stored up since your company's inception. For expansion, there's no substitute for the unlimited power and virality of word-of-mouth amplification that comes directly from the people who value you most. Customers. Execute your growth through the lens of online experiences.

2020s New Reality: No in-person sales, no in-person marketing, and little to no attribution with "dark social" communities that are untraceable and growing like gremlins. We simply don't know where our audience is coming from, and walled gardens prevent us from tracking it or leveraging open application programming interface (API) architecture to integrate with the best measurement platforms. LinkedIn is a prime, front-and-center example of a closed system we all use, but only *they* have access to the complete "customer journey" data.

Persistent Reality: The No. 1 thing every business needs is more customers. To grow revenue effectively, you must become a master at customer acquisition. Paid advertising is just too expensive now. The barriers to entry are often in the tens of thousands, even millions of dollars. The halcyon days of social media 1.0 or 2.0 are gone. When the medium was young, you could amass 5,000 followers or direct connections seemingly overnight. Throttles and controls regulate the information flow of every legacy social network, so if you move too fast, you'll fail over, get your profile shut off, or even end up in LinkedIn jail. We've built experiments to inform your strategy and tactics in this work. The only viable solution becomes growth hacking.

In-person events may bounce back but will never be as robust as in the prior era. The major social networks have moved to a "pay-for-play" model where reach gets cut to 5% of your followers (if you're lucky). Forking over serious capital is often a non-option for startups, founders, nonprofits, and individual thought leaders. We resign ourselves to getting 10 "likes" or need to rely on "bot" schemes to boost comment threads and rig the social algorithm to realize ever-diminishing returns. Sad to see so many gifted executives succumbing to this temptation right now, but we don't blame you. Reach is gone.

Zoom webinars are a powerful means to generate leads organically (even for free), but it's tricky to do this elegantly, and GTM leaders are time-poor running lean. Setting up a "thought leadership" webinar just won't cut it now, no matter how visionary the talent roster is and how ingenious you perceive the theme. You need to be creative and innovative, break the mold to pull an audience once, not to mention sustain and grow it over time.

It used to be enough to parade your C-level executives out like show ponies with some industry experts, crib some pseudo-intellectual questions, and follow a linear format. In the glory days of "Peak Webinars," we all winged it the night before and got away with murder to a packed house.

But now we find our tried and true antics put the audience to sleep. We've even worked with partners that couldn't break out of their silo, no matter how interactive we tried to make it. They insisted on sticking to the script. Hence, they call it "Death by PowerPoint," a distant cousin condition to "Death by Chocolate," the latter a desirable life state.

You can overthink this stuff. Viral social media is real, raw, and unscripted. It's possible to maintain professionalism by being spontaneous and off the cuff. Putting intelligent people in the hot seat to answer questions genuinely is how Barbara Walters built her news interview empire.

Your competition is well capitalized, with unicorns raising $100-million funding rounds. The war for brand supremacy is brutal. They out-staff you, out-spend you, and out-innovate you. How can you compete? Or maybe you're a unicorn who has stagnated and needs to grow faster.

Additionally, you could be facing pressure from new software as a service (SaaS) scale-ups undercutting your pricing or copycatting your features. Then there's the case of the intrapreneur tasked with disrupting a legacy corporation's event marketing plan. Nobody ever got fired for hiring Big Blue. Are you sure you don't need to innovate? Since 2000, over half of the Fortune 500 has gone out of business. Think fast. Think again.

Over the last 20 years, empirically, most deals in sales and marketing came from in-person rendezvous, which drove 90% of revenue. Remember the glory days in enterprise sales, getting on flights, and holding Michelin 3-star sushi dinners in San Francisco, New York City, and Chicago (cue the glass-bottom boat in a lightning storm). Could you build rapport in person to grease the wheels of doing big enterprise deals? Sure, there's a far greater propensity to get a deal done. But this era could be facing extinction as you read this.

Since Covid erupted, B2B teams must generate new business remotely, which has caused a Cambrian explosion of dialer and email sequencer tech. Hence, these products finally crossed the chasm, for example, Sales Engagement Platforms and Revenue Intelligence. Remember when they launched in 2011 and no one was ready? When we all pushed Sales Engagement and (then) Conversational Intelligence so hard? Leading analyst firms finally professed that companies are adopting "Sales Engagement," or they will start considering this tech closer to 2025.

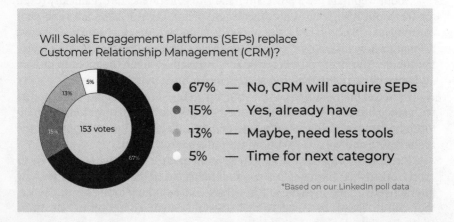

Will Sales Engagement Platforms (SEPs) replace Customer Relationship Management (CRM)?

- 67% — No, CRM will acquire SEPs
- 15% — Yes, already have
- 13% — Maybe, need less tools
- 5% — Time for next category

153 votes

*Based on our LinkedIn poll data

At the onset of the pandemic, ad unit CPMs (cost per mille or thousand impressions) went crazy. The cost to get a quality target prospect in B2B to download one white paper exceeds $175. On Planet Unobtanium for many entrepreneurs, founders, small and midsize businesses (SMBs), and startups.

Human civilization began by pressing the flesh. Offline events became a cash cow and a crutch to get big deals done but are less relevant today. Meeting up at some exotic location, ski resort, or junket in Las Vegas, the martinis flowed, and booths went for upward of $25,000 per sponsor.

Now we can't even shake hands, maybe fist or elbow bump at the threat of a resurgent pandemic. Even though social media releases dopamine hits, there's nothing like eye-to-eye contact or shaking hands to get a deal inked because it immediately fosters trust in a way even the best Zooms cannot. Although human-to-human (H2H) is coming back, the era of cramming into a packed plane, jetting off to San Francisco, Atlanta, or Manhattan, and squeezing into a conference center to sit like sardines in folding chairs looks antiquated, even unsafe. It all comes down to sweeping changes in how business people want to interact with each other. Executives became lazy, thinking, "why should I fly if I can Zoom?" The cost per in-person event effort has shot up markedly.

What is your preferred way to interact with a salesperson?

200 votes

- 50% — Virtual meeting
- 31% — In-person
- 12% — Email — direct message
- 7% — Phone

*Based on our LinkedIn poll data

Mary Shea, Outreach's VP Global Innovation Evangelist, researched seller interaction preferences in 2022 and found that buyers now prefer virtual meetings over in-person ones. Salespeople would rather send emails and social touches than get on the phone, and buyers prefer it too.

Whether we know it or not, we live and work in a new era of GTM simulations because the physical world is slipping away into an intangible "hybrid model." Soon we'll meet with virtual reality (VR) goggles on in VR simulations as the avatars of our choosing, so we *must* be ready.

Evidence? At the *Connect Conference* in 2021, Mark Zuckerberg (Meta) predicted that the Metaverse "will be mainstream in 5–10 years." Venture capitalists (VCs) invested $10 billion in virtual world startups in 2021, according to Crunchbase. Apple's Tim Cook has hinted at an augmented reality/virtual reality (AR/VR) headset.

As promised, this book provides innovative ways to generate explosive revenue growth with virtual events.

We will help you transform static, boring ghost webinars into packed, interactive, must-see simulations. Like most founders, entrepreneurs, startup marketing teams, and small businesses, you're looking at a rising wall of water on costs and razor-thin margins. Although there are 10,000+ vendors to enhance how we market and sell, the technology becomes more expensive to integrate daily. Even basic customer relationship management (CRM) can cost thousands per month once you get all the plug-ins and enable its automated features. We wrote this book for you—the innovators and early adopters—as you look into growth hacking and new ways to get your name and brand out there. As *reach* dries up, competition for eyeballs skyrockets.

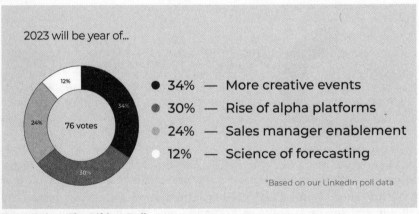

2023 will be year of...

- 34% — More creative events
- 30% — Rise of alpha platforms
- 24% — Sales manager enablement
- 12% — Science of forecasting

76 votes

*Based on our LinkedIn poll data

Zoom. Fatigue. Flat. Lifeless. Dull.

What's become of virtual events in 2022? A graveyard of sameness. When will we innovate the flat webinar format? There are exceptions to every rule. Enter Mary Shea, Ph.D., and predictions for 2022, of which a top trend she's tracking is *Virtual Event Innovation.*

"To maximize the impact of one of their largest budget line items, marketers in 2022 will need to experiment with more engaging, immersive, virtual formats and to differentiate with smaller, highly curated in-person events.

To keep event participants engaged in 2022:

– Forgo the large in-person annual industry conference.

– Deliver smaller, tailored, and exclusive in-person events.

– Leave the traditional static webinar behind."

Please check out GTMmag.com's "The Big Question" for more predictions like this—**GTM trends for 2022.**

Essentially, we will *reinvent virtual events together in this book.* Now a quick pep talk: Remember, you have everything it takes to innovate. We use the term *heuristics* for sales and marketing, which means "mental shortcuts" taken from computer programming, often attributed to David Hoffeld's *The Science of Selling*, who's been a coach on GTM Games.

It's easy to recognize the lion's share of Zoom webinars are "one-note." Think about it. The expected format is a "safe" theme, perennial panelists, an unassuming moderator reading off a script, and some Q&A at the end. It's a linear progression of events with near-zero interactivity. Participants tune in to check out, multi-tasking the whole time. Admit it! The last dozen webinars you were on, weren't you phoning it in from the background while you crushed your inbox so you could "humblebrag" that "yeah, I was there." We're all guilty of this. Imagine how your prospective customers must feel? What a snooze!

Unforeseen global circumstances raised the bar on in-person. People will only travel to Burning Man, Dreamforce, TED, Davos, and other buzzy, high-production-value events. Why make big-ticket investments in travel, crisscross rugged terrain, and endure brutal connecting flights and travel delays? Trains, planes, and automobiles are a far cry from John Candy, but well worth it because of outrageous value delivered in person in a way only events of this caliber can. We all know the legacy "in-person" ROI: Deals get done when you meet at a conference, raise a glass of chianti, break bread, eat a "Great Outdoors" steak dinner, all-you-can-eat Brazilian, and shake hands.

But now your audience has too many options. Couldn't you just watch that keynote online or read a recap? Sure. Attend a local charity masquerade versus head off to Venice? Catch a concert live-streamed? Classic events are here to stay, long live events. *Viva la!*

Business people won't want to return solely to in-person events anytime soon. We've become accustomed to virtual Zoom calls, whether convenient or just Pavlovian. Inflationary gas prices and multi-hour commutes aren't helping us either. Even as Elon Musk bangs the drum for the 40-hour in-office work week, all the research points to hybrid work as here to stay. We predict reducing work to four days will become a new standard.

It's the same for mixed-format events. We have entered the age of "hybrid."

Since the pandemic hit, the fashionable solution to event marketing was to slap together a bunch of uninspired webinars and blast out generic emails and ads to promote them. We are not judging you. Maybe you cracked the code and are doing event promotions better than the crowd. But inboxes clutter fast with identical templates, and creativity runs thin. The more spam a decision-maker receives, the quicker they hire an executive assistant to run interference on their inbox, even inside their LinkedIn.

Companies have started to throw virtual and hybrid confabs (in-person + online) as a cost-cutting measure. Still, they are an elevated art form that can be complex, sophisticated, and highly produced to attract attention you can't get anywhere else. But it's up to you. We will show you how to take them to the next level of innovation.

The average CEO receives dozens of "new normal" invites weekly and hits delete. Trust me; they don't need an Amazon gift card or steak dinner with your reps. They want to spend more time with their family and climb Mount Kilimanjaro. That's why a big part of our Event Reinvention™ (ER) formula is to create enduring themes that are so transfixing and memorable that even the subject line converts and pulls the right audiences toward you. You can't help yourself but click on it! We will show you how to unleash event ideas that attract your optimal ideal customer profile (ICP) and are viral by mere design.

You are the heroes of the global village. Small and medium-sized enterprises (SMEs) account for 95% of the world's GDP and 60–70% of employment; 400 million small businesses are operating in hybrid remote working environments worldwide. Our book can light a spark to galvanize the global economy to recover faster via innovation. It all starts with you, so keep an open mind.

This book is also for the corporate warrior intrapreneurs looking to effect change from within by revolutionizing their GTM strategy by breathing life into a run-of-the-mill webinar plan. Maybe you're part of a marketing team and feel invisible; this book will help you find your voice and flex your power.

If we did it bootstrapped and on a budget, so can you. This book will be your companion guide as you build out your "event" GTM and look to drive revenue more effectively and efficiently derived from existing webinars. It will be the key to sustainable revenue growth fueled by events as a cornerstone of your marketing mix to propel you with confidence through any recession or economic downturn.

Zoom sees a staggering 300 million meetings per day. Per day! GTMers, as we call them, need to generate excitement through online events and often have no idea how to be creative in this new medium. Or how to be commercially successful in converting viewers into customers by nailing their strategic selling motions after the fact. "Just hold webinars" is too obvious and will peform averagely.

Sophisticated marketers—you are accustomed to generating leads digitally but don't dismiss this writing. We have new info for you that we guarantee you haven't seen based on our snap polls peppered throughout this work. If you're holding virtual events today, you compete in crimson oceans of static clones. You can't stand out no matter which topic or theme you assiduously choose. Sound familiar? The problem is the old-fashioned "event" model itself. If we had a nickel for every marketing team in each category that coughs up a brilliant idea for a webinar, but we can see it's the identical "heuristic" to all their peers, we'd be bitcoin billionaires.

While there are new platforms like mmhmm (mmhmm.app), from the creator of Evernote, that allow you to shrink your head into a corner, use virtual whiteboards, or broadcast video behind you like a CNN anchor, new technology is not the focus of this book. Since Zoom came out, its robust roadmap now includes a whiteboard at this writing. Indeed, it will absorb many more features from competitive startups as the incumbent, like conversational intelligence for recording analysis (just added). If it were all about making it look snazzy, why do you occasionally see an under-produced "Indie" event online pull over 1,000 attendees?

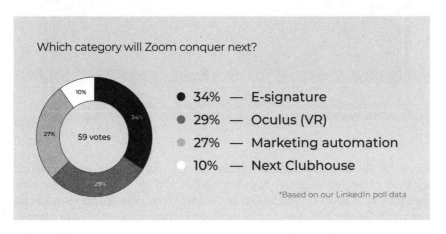

We encourage you to think out-of-the-box with content models and programming formats that supersede the need for visual gimmicks. If you can afford event technology, become proficient with all possible vendors. We are big fans of Prezi Video for face filters, fun captions, special effects, and live video shares behind the presenter. Try out Hopin, which just bought Streamyard (many integrations), and Restream, a strong Zoom alternative that broadcasts live to 30+ platforms. They are fantastic additions with bells and whistles like landing pages for registrations, badging, selling tickets, and accommodating 50,000+ attendees.

We wish we could tell you packing virtual events was as easy as amping up the production value over the top of a Zoom. We all crave a "magic bullet" to nail a virtual event from a tech perspective, but like any software, slickly produced marketing events often struggle to get even 15 viewers. We recently attended a "LinkedIn Live" event with under five guests.

Here's how we tackled an age-old problem of entertaining and educating business people online since the dawn of the consumer internet in the mid-90s. As the pandemic hit, we launched one of the most successful B2B virtual events ever in under a year, entitled GTM Games, generating 50,000+ signups, featuring 120+ elite thought leaders and 70+ top sponsors upending the stale B2B events industry. We achieved unprecedented attendance and sponsorship from inception. Even the first event began at a scale of many established communities 5–10 years in the making.

As the business world bounced back into hybrid mode post-pandemic and even into a recession, we kept fueling demand for our virtual event concept, proving this wasn't just a flash in the pan. One Diamond Sponsor put up a monthly "Super Rep" award that drove even more excitement and engagement. Of course, we chase "knowledge" as the prize along with delivering some bubbly and the top 10 GTM books.

You can follow our blueprint affordably to achieve any scale you desire. We did this using essential tools, collaboration, and teamwork. We prioritized design thinking and hybrid imagination, but above all, customer-centricity. We are strong proponents of finding contractors on Upwork, Fiverr, and arbitraging competent globally distributed teams.

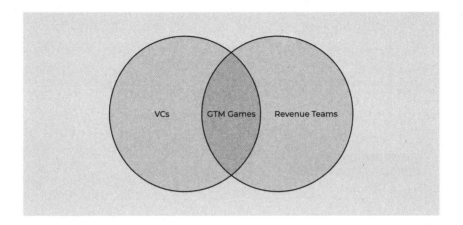

Interacting with the VC community in putting GTM Games together was gratifying as luminary venture capitalists coached our final GTM "Endgame" rounds each month to crown the victor. One of the secrets to building a riveting event is eliminating hierarchies. Influential executives and VCs are generally humble, sharing valuable thought leadership freely, mentoring the next generation of entrepreneurs and giving back, hence the success of seed incubators like 500 Startups and Y Combinator.

In a former life, Julia created a dynamic event featuring a next-level "sales method hunt" and differentiated content from impossible-to-reach B2B luminaries with this give-to-get strategy. She first researched every contributor heavily and then provided a unique platform to enable them to grow their audience organically. She built a cold-calling competition with thousands of VPs of Sales at a $2 CAC unheard of in B2B.

What makes our current event so unique and successful? GTM cross-training, a new event category under the umbrella of "e-sports," Julia invented, featuring salespeople doing marketing drills and marketing leaders doing sales drills. Mary Shea, VP Global Innovation Evangelist, Outreach, former Principal Analyst at Forrester, reacted to the effect, "I can't believe no one's done it before."

And it started a movement.

Emulation is the highest form of flattery. Nearly every new website in SaaS talks about GTM Leadership; the acronym "GTM" was scarce before our launch. Almost every new campaign is black and white or closely themed to mimic our graphics and UI. We even have carbon copies springing up from rival communities to appointment setting shops to marketing and sales SaaS software mainstays. Bring it on! It's all reminiscent of a Van Halen solo. You instantly recognize the original is Eddie tapping away on the fretboard with two hands in a style he invented and popularized. All the rest is just karaoke.

Siloed skills are killing your pipeline

New normal requires new skills. Now's your chance to crack the funnel with the top practitioners in the world.

ACCESS RECORDINGS →

By this writing, we have minted thousands of brand ambassadors that badge their profiles as members of HYPCCCYCL to unlock the archive of past Zoom recordings. They amplify the "HYPCCCYCL #1 GTM Community" message within dedicated dark social communities that have tens of thousands of members in them and growing. We've created a robust niched group of obsessed GTM innovators unlike anything seen since Clubhouse or "LinkedIn Groups" that got deprecated.

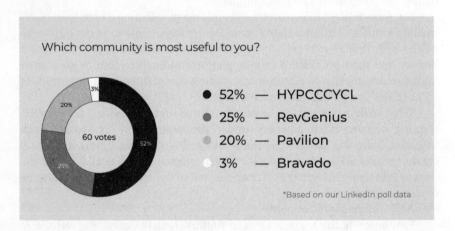

Which community is most useful to you?

60 votes

- ● 52% — HYPCCCYCL
- ● 25% — RevGenius
- ● 20% — Pavilion
- ○ 3% — Bravado

*Based on our LinkedIn poll data

Why it works: The best way to learn something is to walk a mile in another's shoes. Those who can't do, teach, or so the adage goes. You can't learn how to heliski from a guidebook. Can you imagine, *Heliskiing for Dummies?* The minute you drop out of that helicopter, you'll snowball down the mountain and right into the ICU. We've proven that the best way to break down the walls and break you out of your silo is to cross-train interdisciplinary, multi-functional skills. How will sales ever understand and collaborate with marketing caught up in a turf war until they gain respect for how hard it is to do the job daily and vice versa? In our event, professionals traded roles and lives like never before in interactive drills versus languishing on static webinar panels.

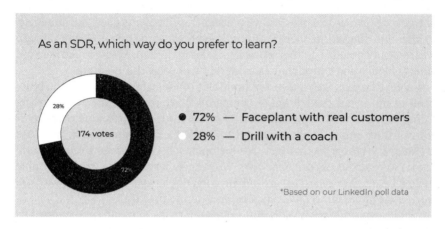

The NTL (National Training Laboratories Institute) Learning Pyramid speaks to achieving 90% retention when participants coach and teach each other in a real-world scenario versus the prevailing static passive webinar model where you just watch and take notes. (Note: In the pyramid, practicing fosters 75% retention.) Few take notes on a webinar. Attendees usually multi-task their inbox, sip tea or coffee, and chat while watching out of the corner of their eye because webinars are generally "boring." Just analyze your own behavior during most virtual meetups and think, what would draw me to be interested in this panel?

In contrast, at any moment in GTM Games, an audience member could be dropped into the drills spontaneously, which our audience loves, keeping the viewer constantly on their toes, at the edge of their seat. Sometimes it's a surprise cameo by someone everyone knows on the call.

Let's say there's a drill on cold calling. In our "GTM Slack," we'd call out for participants randomly and "promote to panelist" anyone who raised their hand with a good reason to do the drill and willing to be coached as a guinea pig. Sponsors pitch coaches, which is unprecedented and rule-breaking. VCs make surprise appearances to judge the event, setting the stage with real-world GTM scenarios depending on their investment thesis: Angel-Seed, early-stage, PLG, Founders, or Series B-D.

We experimented with hybrid event structures that are entirely novel to the industry. Imagine a half-dozen panelists live drilling negotiations in 3-minute bursts with a top coach, then pairing up to drill cold-call openers, email tear downs, and various elements of website analysis like "submitting a lead." We found many of these simulations happen in the real world. Just rarely do we get to see them as laypeople. A great example is that magic moment when a manager does a dry run of a board presentation with their direct report.

When SDR leaders train their teams with role-plays, skills rapidly improve and are cemented. Kevin Dorsey is a master of coaching and skill-building philosophy and is a massive proponent of drilling. All elite athletes and coaches know "we play like we practice," as the saying goes. But strangely, in sales and marketing, there is almost nowhere to go to practice right now. So we ironically practice on the customer—sales malpractice. Stay tuned because Julia is incubating a product in stealth that will solve this big time.

Over this year, we've received hundreds of messages asking us for a blue-print of our event model. Major companies have reached out to us looking to run bespoke GTM events internally on their product's unique premise or consult them on an Event Reinvention™ (ER™). In this playbook, we share an exclusive blueprint that includes the open-sourced secrets, strategies, and tactics so your success can echo ours. We even believe some of you will be able to do it better than us, so we are here to consult you every step of the way. *(To learn more about our GTM agency, contact us on LinkedIn.)*

This revolutionary book is not just a modern event manual sanctioned by some corporations to sell you the latest SaaS software. (Not that there's any-thing wrong with that.) We intend to help you become wildly successful with your virtual events as we did at any production value and scale you desire, whether it's five people in a mastermind to your next annual conference, sales kickoff, or industry offsite.

Event Reinvention™ (ER™) Customer-Centric Checklist: Ideation, creation, production, execution, and amplification are all problematic aspects to nail.

Ask yourself: Is your idea compelling enough to "pull" a high-quality audience? Are you creating something genuinely innovative that's never been done before? Is the production quality strong? (Good mics, design style, Zoom backgrounds, themes, etc.) How will you execute this in real-time with all the moving parts like coordinating calendars and onboarding in time? What's the pregame and postgame setup? *(See the complete checklist in Appendix II.)*

How can we get all the participants to amplify? Have you made the cus-tomer's use case the heart and soul of the production? You want your audi-ence to come away raving about customer insights rather than what your executives said. We've seen CXOs get on webinars and simply parrot the exact approved product marketing copy on their website. It is off-putting for viewers if they can find the same content on YouTube or your product page. It's almost disappointing, like when you see a stand-up comic, and they make the same jokes or spoil the movie by putting every good scene in the theatri-cal trailer.

In these pages, we will reveal our secret sauce to generating one of the most commercially successful online events in the history of B2B. We garnered criti-cal support from leading analysts and partnered with billion-dollar unicorns as our sponsors (e.g., Outreach, ZoomInfo, Gong, Drift, 6sense, etc.). We featured best-selling authors with millions in book sales and behemoth audiences. Examples include Oren Klaff of *Pitch Anything*, Latané Conant of *No Forms. No Spam. No Cold Calls*, Aaron Ross of *Predictable Revenue*, Sangram Vajre of *ABM is B2B* and *MOVE*, Anita Nielsen of *Beat the Bots*, and Mike Bosworth of *Solution Selling*.

We are reinventing virtual events by putting customers at the center. When you surprise and delight customers, the knock-on effects are explosive registrations, attendance, and revenue.

Nearly every competitor is using the opposite approach consumed by their product slant. Our new category, Customer-Centric Events™ (CCEs™), forms the breakthrough foundation of this book. After Oren Klaff's session, an audience participant exclaimed, "It was so unexpected. I was on the edge of my seat, wondering what would happen next!"

In the old model, sponsors dominated the stage until the bitter end, when there was a controlled audience Q&A. In contrast, our audience can coach sponsors and cross-pollinate their signature skills. Every position in our game democratizes. It keeps the audience on their toes and shows human ability transcends title and tenure. Our advice is to boldly make your customers the center of your events versus the ubiquitous panelists + audience setup. That's why our events are radically different.

A company's sellers and marketers are nearly always misaligned, delineating our ICP at HYPCCCYCL. Instead of holding a sponsored event where whoever puts up the most money talks, we bring VPs of sales and marketing to coach each other and even CEOs to compete. The audience is excited to be there because they eagerly anticipate we might pull them into the action and up on a panel at any time.

Being a sponsor means you'll be coaching someone on a signature drill, like how to optimize an essential workflow in your user interface/user experience (UI/UX). Involving the viewer is exceedingly rare in webinars. Think about it, when was the last time you got to appear *live* in any business webinar you've ever attended?

In this book, we will show you how to:

- Understand customer-centric event models that flip the traditional focus and hierarchy of classic events to create a network effect of customer-led growth.
- Produce a virtual event that goes viral for next to no money or how to produce one shrewdly (and affordably) with an outsourced team.
- Build hybrid gamification into static events that breathes new life into them so your brand stands out.
- Give your network something to talk about so attendees can't wait to come back.
- Create a bespoke event brand that will suck the oxygen out of your industry.

- Amplify your message through raving fans and brand ambassadors.
- Have a total blast doing this so it's fun, active, intriguing, and a smash hit for your community.
- Make an impact by innovating to the level that your event is PR-worthy, newsworthy, and worth it for high-level executives to invest in your ideas.
- Recession-proof your GTM strategy with customer-centric events as the new foundation

Let's get into it.

SECTION 1

Inception: Design, Build, and Execute

Whenever you see a successful business, someone once made a courageous decision.

— Peter Drucker

CHAPTER 1

How to Measure Event Effectiveness: Pipeline Generated versus Marketing Qualified Leads (MQLs)

Measure what is measurable, and make measurable what is not so.

—Galileo Galilei

If you silo every role in a go-to-market (GTM) team and ask "what's the problem in GTM?," 99% of every position will blame marketing. Why? Marketing is not generating revenue, or most marketing activities are not quantifiable. That is why chief marketing officers (CMOs) are white-knuckled to take on a revenue number.

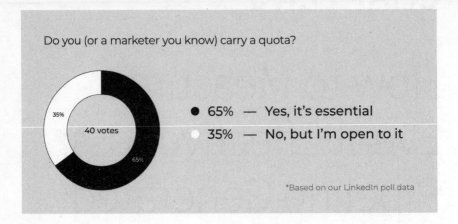

We have this ephemeral "brand awareness" metric that no one knows how to measure other than inferring that an increase in traffic or brand mentions must be positive. We are flustered hiring pricey CMOs who burn millions simply trying to justify their return on investment (ROI). Then they turn and blame the VP of Sales.

Your VP of Sales is quick to make excuses that the nine-month sales cycle impedes hitting the ever-more egregious targets the board sets. At month 10, they catch you holding the bag, but you've already paid out all that cheddar.

Marketing can do nothing, and there's very little chance you could return the ROI on this hire, even within a year when brand awareness takes many consecutive years to build. You can blow through whole funding rounds trying to nail GTM hiring, and that's before you even run your first Super Bowl ad.

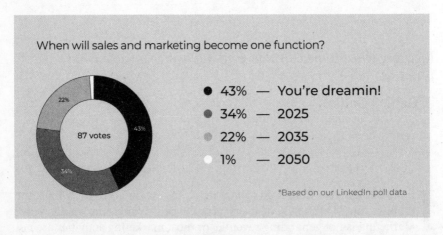

That one time sales and marketing tried to "work together." ☺

Exhibit A: Interchangeable slogans confuse customers so severely that they buy from your competitor, thinking it's you.

Exhibit B: You just signed up for a software as a service (SaaS) and get aggressively retargeted everywhere you go.

Exhibit C: The company's chief revenue officer (CRO) is taking the main stage at Dreamforce to discuss "the future of customer-centric sales," while his sales development reps (SDR) team is stalking you with email tactics from the 1990s—even during the event!

Exhibit D: You receive *engineering* hoodie swag when you work in marketing.

Exhibit E: That $14 million Super Bowl ad with the dancing quick response (QR) code impresses you, but you'd never invest a red cent into crypto.

Let's face it, sales and marketing need to become one function. And before going that far, at the very least, they need to at least talk and collaborate.

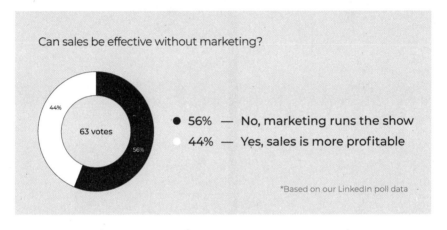

Can sales be effective without marketing?

44%

63 votes

56%

● 56% — No, marketing runs the show
○ 44% — Yes, sales is more profitable

*Based on our LinkedIn poll data

"REV" tech is merging into alpha platforms in the throes of consolidation. The industry is finally shifting to a unified GTM platform approach. Sales and marketing teams come together under the revenue operations (RevOps) umbrella as one function, further blurring the lines. There's a clear and present danger to assigning quotas now—not even a "nice to have" dalliance or futuristic innovation. Management demands that marketers carry a quota as a strategic imperative and generate actual revenue to insulate against stock market vacillation.

We had Seth Marrs from Forrester on the program building a whole drill around getting rid of the MQL model and centralizing the entire organization on pipeline-generated or qualified opportunities.

That's why all webinar effectiveness is traditionally measured wrong because it still hasn't caught up to the new North Star metric: revenue. If you think about your events in terms of pipeline generated and meetings set, you first want to get rid of the crude sign-up form forcing prospects to begrudgingly fill out their email, company name, title, and so on.

In HYPCCCYCL, we use a LinkedIn authentication plug-in to access the content and any event on our platform. We primarily do this to observe real people engaging with our events. We wanted to know this answer, "When they peruse, what pages on our website are they viewing, specifically?" That kind of data helps us generate more insights about our customers than a simple Excel dumpster file.

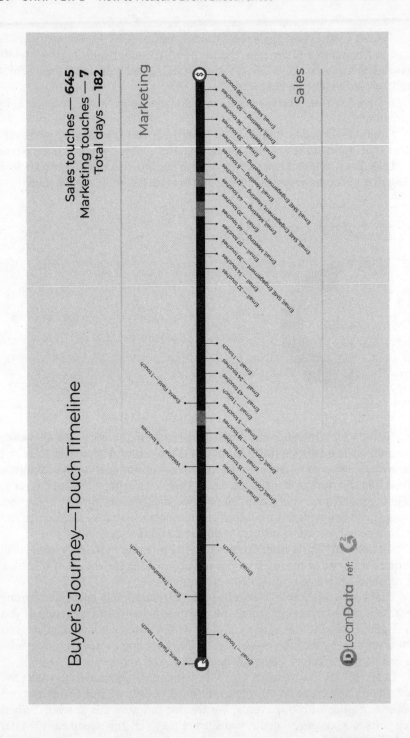

Buyer's Journey—Touch Timeline

Sales touches — **645**
Marketing touches — **7**
Total days — **182**

Marketing

Sales

Event, Field — 1 touch
Event, Tradeshow — 1 touch
Webinar — 4 touches
Event, Field — 1 touch
Event, Tradeshow — 1 touch

Email — 1 touch
Email — 1 touch
Email, Connect — 16 touches
Email, Connect — 15 touches
Email — 19 touches
Email, Connect — 19 touches
Email — 5 touches
Email — 43 touches
Email — 24 touches
Email — 1 touch

Email, SME Engagement
Email — 32 touches
Email — 14 touches
Email, SME Engagement — 39 touches
Email — 57 touches
Email, Meeting — 46 touches
Email — 20 touches
Email, Meeting — 44 touches
Email, SME Engagement
Email, Meeting — 32 touches
Email, Meeting — 32 touches
Email, Meeting — 39 touches
Email, Meeting — 36 touches
Email, Meeting — 50 touches
Email, Meeting — 38 touches

LeanData ref: 2

Rather than measure the MQLs from your events, tie them into retention, renewals, and expansion. Use a tool like LeanData to create an attribution "subway map" of all the customer interaction touch points from first contact to close so you can understand where your interactive events fall in the attribution waterfall. Events can influence big deals even if they don't directly source them.

Our sponsors and partners drove new business during our events and even on the simulated demos. Our contestants pitched real CMOs and got meetings the following week. It was surreal watching these real-time transactions happen. We heard reports of test drives and opportunities generated, even closed-won deals, just from signing up for our lowest tier brand sponsorship, not to mention enriched leads with the higher packages.

The GTM Games became a phenomenal exposure point for up-and-coming SaaS vendors in the marketing and sales technology spheres. In our community, we never placed an embargo on pitching. We implored our sponsors to add value if they were to sell in the community. Give out enablement content, a free trial, an e-book, or anything that is reciprocal—"give to get." Many communities eschew this practice, but our GTM Slack has a "GTM Stack" channel where tool fanatics unite to AB test all the latest REV tech and share war stories. "Buyers buy," we like to say in Yogi Berra parlance.

Measuring effectiveness can come in brand voice lift if you have a social listening platform. Slintel (now 6sense) saw a 30% jump in brand search impressions.

We think the best measure of success is the awareness when you follow up and they remember a particularly spicy moment. We remember how intensely Oren Klaff coached—viewers were raving for weeks about it—or the time Scott Leese gave a seller tough love on his negotiation drill, punching a hole in his business model. He took the feedback like a champion. Your memorable event itself becomes the story. So then the new customer-centric event model can flip every paradigm like this:

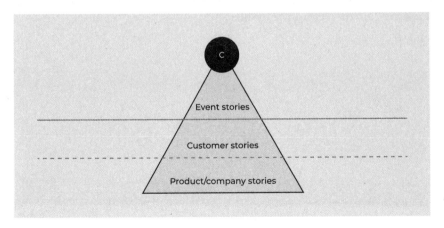

Great minds discuss ideas; average minds discuss events; small minds discuss people.

—Eleanor Roosevelt

Your best and most obvious metric for event success is *booked meetings during or after* the events. Other key performance indicators (KPIs) might include "quality conversations" or account executive (AE)-accepted "opportunities." The major problem with event marketing transitioning to sales is a wonky handoff after the event. Marketing held the event, and now it's the job of sales to close attendees. Sellers and marketers need to cross-train with Customer Success. Reframe this intention to "educating potential buyers." We are helping sellers to be customer-centric and improve their ability to listen and be genuinely curious. For marketers, as per Geoffrey Moore, it's all about owning the market, but in the sense that you're "owning the relationship," the prospect/customer feels that you care, and they're not a marketing "lead" or number for you.

Suppose marketers hand all their leads to sales departments and dump them automatically. If marketing departments would instead call their audience and analyze their pipeline, it would reveal a great degree of insight. As Sean Sheppard instructs, have a conversation with "Ms. Right" to understand who is "Ms. Right Now." When that happens (natural qualification), it's the moment to involve the sales team.

Marketing has to create this smooth transition to give sellers not simply interested people but fully qualified. You have to be willing to say no and walk away versus process every lead who fogs a mirror. If your event was purely educational and they're still wishy-washy about pulling the trigger in the next couple of months, it's okay to leave them alone. Don't hammer and subject them to your carnivorous sales department. Let them come to an epiphany on their own and find the road not taken on their journey back to your door. Then you'll make a customer for life.

CHAPTER 2

Finding Event-Market Fit (EMF)

The best customer service is if the customer doesn't need to call you, doesn't need to talk to you. It just works.

—Jeff Bezos

According to legendary investor Marc Andreessen of A16Z.com, "Product/market fit [PMF] means being in a good market with a product that can satisfy that market." So logically, being in the right market, with a rock-solid event, will be a smash hit, right? Nope, not that simple. It's tough to know what your ideal customer profile (ICP) wants when marketers have become so removed from customer interactions, and even salespeople are spreadsheet jockeys.

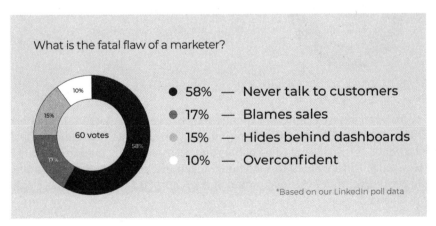

What is the fatal flaw of a marketer?

- 58% — Never talk to customers
- 17% — Blames sales
- 15% — Hides behind dashboards
- 10% — Overconfident

60 votes

*Based on our LinkedIn poll data

It's high time for marketers to expand their skills and talk to customers (fatal flaw?). As insane as it sounds writing it! Instead of sending thousands of emails, think about a new paradigm where the marketing team calls on key accounts to research, assess net promoter scores (NPS) and customer satisfaction (CSAT), and collaborate on roadmap ideas. PMF parallels event-market fit (EMF), but the kicker you'll learn in this book is that EMF could be an adjacent focus area that dovetails back into your product.

The new way to find an EMF is to call people. It's also the new way to do NPS. If you think about it, it's revolutionary. Surveys do not work generally, and it's a paradox because customers are tight-lipped about what they think and often don't even understand their impulses.

We practice what we preach and break the silos in our organization. We merge marketing and sales methods into one workflow with the overarching goal of increasing the productivity/bottom line of our go-to-market (GTM).

Isn't it bonkers that the only proper way to find out PMF is to send the Sean Ellis Test survey: "Can you live without our product?" People only fill it out to redeem the gift card. Every emerging method works until it becomes a best practice in sales and marketing, and prospects' brains stop reacting to it. This question is excellent, but it's not even funny when you receive hundreds of these monthly. But that's a cynical view. Let's ensure we truly intrigue our buyers with provocative questions that matter.

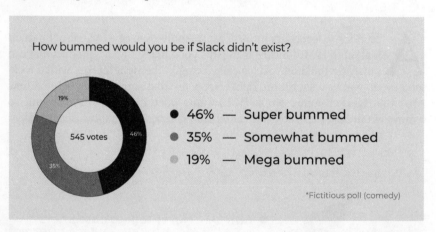

How bummed would you be if Slack didn't exist?

545 votes

● 46% — Super bummed
● 35% — Somewhat bummed
● 19% — Mega bummed

*Fictitious poll (comedy)

You can invest even more money into marketing automation or think differently by working with gifting automation vendors like Sendoso and Reachdesk. Why not send some bubbly and get a genuine conversation going? "Hey, Sally, I just wanted to send you a token of our gratitude for attending the event last Friday. Curious, would you attend again and if so, what would you change?"

Old way. (direct)

"Hey, Sarah, I noticed you attended our event on CRM automation. Are you interested in attending a demo?"

Stop, cease, and desist. It's too focused on you and blatant selling.

New way. (indirect)

"Hey, Sarah, I noticed that you attended the event. Curious about which themes resonated most with you? Which speakers would you like us to invite back again? Or, do you have any ideas for new topics, themes, or thought leaders we should have on?"

The first way is product- or company-centric. Reminiscent of a LinkedIn "connect-and-pitch" or "pitch-slap" where the moment you connect, you hawk your wares. The second talk track is a lateral ask where you sincerely are trying to improve the customer experience and gauge NPS indirectly.

You will know you have reached EMF when promotion stops feeling like pushing on a rope. Your colleagues spread it and your customers, prospects, industry, media, and PR are all moving in concentric circles in a halo effect.

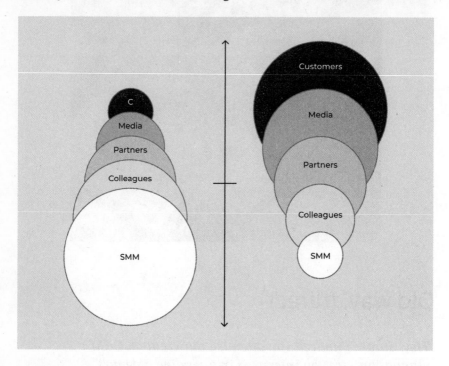

New public relations (PR) starts with customers and radiates out to the media. Even before your colleagues and partners ever get involved. Put them on the stage and let them rave.

Many companies have a PR strategy that constantly press releases the media and sees what sticks. If you can highlight a customer story that gets featured in an event, this has a greater likelihood of being press-worthy.

Per Mike Bosworth on PMF, does it even really exist? EMF exists or simply "potential event-market" problems and pains, opportunities for sellers to solve.

Serial venture capitalist (VC) Sean Sheppard contends, "There's no such thing as disruption. Disruption is created by a market, it's created by adoption."

It all comes down to our WRKSHP™ and focusing on the problem: even problem-market fit. Is your problem a real problem to potential buyers? Suppose you can nail the problem your audience genuinely cares about? In that case, we can discuss PMF and all the metrics and surveys, but it will be evident as acquisition and engagement skyrocket.

The beauty of virtual events is that the cost is so minimal that before building a product or putting up any landing pages, you can test the problem to see if it's real. It's similar to iterative ad testing highlighted in Eric Ries's *The Lean Startup*, where you discover your unique value proposition (UVP) upstream by running ads. We use an event as a proxy to discover the *real* value prop versus creating endless landing pages, not to mention building the feature right away once you see that it's resonated.

An excellent example comes from Sales Engagement software. Imagine you're thinking about adding a custom integration between DocuSign and your product. You'd like to integrate it with intent data by creating a workflow that combines marketing automation and document management. Although there are many incoming requests, you don't want to invest before you understand if it's a real problem and how severe it is.

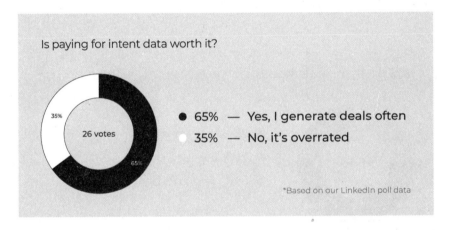

Is paying for intent data worth it?

35%

26 votes

65%

● 65% — Yes, I generate deals often

35% — No, it's overrated

*Based on our LinkedIn poll data

The perfect way to test it is by putting your customer and not your product marketing campaign first. We're engaged in many projects where the client doesn't even have a fully-baked product yet. They're creating a landing page *as if* there's "a new AI-based solution," before it's even developed. They are measuring demand (inbound or outbound); if there's enough, they build it into the roadmap.

A "revenue driving the roadmap" strategy is not a crime, but the best way to do it is to create an event and raise this topic: a workflow that integrates marketing automation, document management, 6sense, and artificial intelligence (AI). Bring your target persona to the event but not as a panelist. Create something more interactive around the use case or theme you're testing. Look at the interaction, talk with your ICP, and gauge the level of interest and response. Turn the event into discovery in real-time—yet another revolutionary idea.

That's how it becomes customer-led and customer-centric instead of analyzing landing pages and registrations. It's much more interesting to bring your potential audience to be part of an interactive event and point the spotlight on them as they share their ideas about this kind of integration problem.

Do not ask them for a solution but inquire "how are you solving this problem now?" Ask about the future and the past to see how profound this problem is. You can AB test the messaging by discussing variations of the proposed new feature. That's how marketing, sales, and product teams can collaborate on campaigns and make them interactive versus just pandering with Starbucks and Amazon gift cards.

New KPIs for Account-Based Marketing and Sales

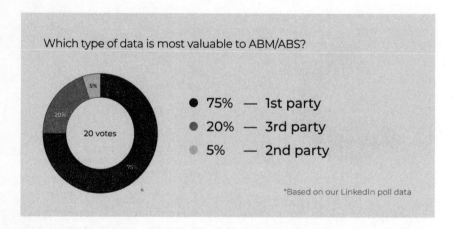

Which type of data is most valuable to ABM/ABS?

20 votes

- 75% — 1st party
- 20% — 3rd party
- 5% — 2nd party

*Based on our LinkedIn poll data

Another big mistake in GTM effectiveness is measuring sales development work on a "meeting set" metric. "Opportunities" generated and approved by AEs is a much better one. Managers can sign off and play referee if disputed, but it's a much stronger filter at the top of the funnel. It's also a fallacy, in our opinion, that sales development reps (SDRs) shouldn't qualify new business. According to The Bridge Group, 40% of the time they roll up to demand gen or marketing, and 60% of the time to sales.

Nearly every quota-carrying rep follows up on in-person dinners, industry trade shows, or online webinars, treating customers as de facto leads just because they attended. To generate an opportunity takes creating desire and active listening. *(See the RRM™ framework in the appendix for tips on this.)* Don't waste a lead list of 100 attendees by cold prospecting them for the two or three amenable to meetings now.

You can point to the late great Chet Holmes for the statistic that "3% of any market is actively looking, and 40% will entertain switching." Thirty-seven of one hundred prospects need to be warmed up through interactivity, probing, and story sharing to move them toward your funnel. It takes real ingenuity and effort to do this consistently. You can't expect it to be as easy as "tag them as an event MQL" and "let's have sales follow up." This is a myopic view but all too common.

One of the greatest secrets to lead generation and event follow-up is ensuring you fly the attendees into LinkedIn Sales Navigator and save them as leads and accounts. Find out who they report to and reach out to colleagues and lateral VPs to multi-thread. You can also keep tabs on job changes and trigger events afterward.

> *"Hey, Jackie, I noticed your VP of Sales attended our webinar on sales enablement, so I just wanted to find out what you're up to in marketing as it pertains to RevOps tech stacks to see if I can add any value by sharing trends and ideas."*

Inbound and outbound teams single thread their approach in account-based marketing and sales campaigns, severely limiting opportunity creation and deal velocity. Build out organizational charts or "account maps" and set a policy on multi-threading; even lock a salesforce field for an additional contact per account to save it.

CHAPTER 3

Targeting: Experimentation, Iteration, and Gamification

It doesn't matter how beautiful your theory is. It doesn't matter how smart you are. If it doesn't agree with experiment, it's wrong.

—Richard P. Feynman

How do you know which audiences to target, much less which event to throw? Ultimately, it's why Julia's cold call battles happened. After surveying her target market, she discovered that her ideal customer profiles (ICPs) were more interested in sales methodologies than an innovative new product. Too often, vendors and teams push their product even if it's five years ahead of the market before adoption is possible. How do you create a link that connects your company's value prop to current market demand? How do you discover what the market needs?

Targeting your ICP has so much to do with understanding your existing product-market fit (PMF). Because we have boldly entered a new era of revenue operations (RevOps), nearly 10,000 vendors targeting go-to-market (GTM) could participate in our opera.

A big part of HYPCCCYCL's GTM agency offering in WRKSHP™ (see Appendix I) is a framework for targeting. Philosophically and strategically, you should target an event at your ICP and your ideal prospect profile (IPP). How can you discover what your particular ICP/IPP finds new and exciting? Linking the most relevant industry trend to the ICP's world is what's groundbreaking about our approach.

First, read all the analyst reports and come up with a set of profound statistics. Forget about your product, forget everything you know, clear your mind, and look objectively at the industry trends. Then ask, where is the industry going, what's happening, what's relevant, what's new, what's problematic, what challenges do potential customers face, and what successes do they share? If you're disciplined and lucky, you'll find an insight. And then, you think about your customers' issues in particular, not only from the vantage point of how your product solves these pain points but moreover, through the prism of researching your specific buyer personas to link industry trends to them. Ask "do you experience a problem with that?" Find out how your customers solve the industry challenges you uncovered in their world, in their own voice.

Creating and getting an event theme off the ground will require experimentation and iteration. We never charged the audience for tickets to attend on principle in our case, but you can experiment with other models. We had the opposite problem: our brand is so sleek that people can't believe it's free.

Outside of emcee announcements, we are ad-free but quality GTM sponsor supported. To create sticky viral feedback loops, we ask everyone to log into our website (hypcccycl.com) with their LinkedIn login (privacy policy intact) so they get access to an exclusive Slack Channel (value-add). If they put Member HYPCCCYCL #1 GTM Community in their LinkedIn work history, we unlock a complete archive of 100+ previous matches for free.

GTM Games Archive

Relive all the pageantry, pomp, and circumstance

Gamification could be anything. We don't mean cheesy "gamer" memes or to cheapen your events with little gimmicks. You need to get extra creative here to design a game worth playing, even if it's simple. What you don't want under any circumstances are static webinars like everyone else, where the audience will constantly multi-task.

Moderated Q&A has been overdone but bird-dogging the right-hand panel of a Zoom and aiming provocative questions at attendees in timed intervals is powerful. Call out the full names of audience members as an emcee, especially ones you recognize from your community to build a lasting bond. At least two team members should always run an event: one to host and the other to moderate the questions in your dark social communities simultaneously (e.g., Slack, Discord, LinkedIn, and WhatsApp). Set it up this way to prevent the itch of multi-tasking. If the panelists seem tuned in to what the audience is discussing, it brings all sides to the table.

Moderation is an art form in and of itself. The formula is always: acknowledge, bridge, and then provoke. Example:

"Great comment, Will. It reminds me of that time Facebook went down. What do you think would happen if there were an electromagnetic pulse that took out the entire internet for a week?" Just making this humorous, but employing this interaction style on all the threads will foster maximal engagement.

We live in an age of distraction. Remember, every audience member, panelist, and participant receives an average of 250 notifications per day. You can't force them to silence their smartphones, but you can deeply engage them via Q&A, feedback loops, snap polls, and opinion sharing. That's why you always want to meter the attention span in blocks of 5 to 10 minutes so you can cue the audience for their views in real time. When they share, they not only retain the information better, it's 1000× more fun and rewarding for participants to play.

We've also done gamified sub-events or "demo slots" after the main Zoom events of GTM Games, sharing AhaSlides (ahaslides.com), where we poll the audience in an interactive quiz from a gifting automation vendor like Reachdesk on pertinent themes like marketing enablement trivia. The winner gets a delicious prize from our partner. We've quizzed them about aspects of outbound email, gifting, and business-to-business (B2B) trivia.

Gamification can be even more subtle, though. We started to keep our contestants on for the sponsor demo and have the sponsor pitch the coach or panelists. It's also never been done before, to our knowledge. It was surreal to see a sponsor's account executive (AE), do a live demo in front of our audience, even try to close the coach, and then turn the camera 180° to get a critique of how that demo went. Obviously grateful to our sponsors for being good sports. One vendor nearly closed a deal in this way, which was thrilling to watch.

Think of it like the old 1980s game show *Hollywood Squares*. You've got 4–5 boxes on the screen. If possible, all the boxes must interact with each other, the host, and every audience member. When you roll back the average webinar, you see one person talking 80% of the time. Why not continuously loop in your audience in the form of a poll, quiz, or random panelist cameo. Interactivity takes viewers heads from buried in their iPhones to back into your event. It's up to your creativity to mitigate all the multi-tasking and perma-scrolling that's made this format so frequently irrelevant. Don't settle for a static Zoom call where dozens of executives blow off steam and ambiently listen in. That's the easiest way to be forgotten. It's the difference between elevator music playing in the background and everyone jamming along playing air guitar to their favorite Queen song.

One way to see which role-plays will work best with your customers is to work up some of them internally on your team calls. You may have some active drills or dry runs percolating in your organization that you didn't even realize happen. For example, before the executive team gives a big board presentation, it's likely key execs rehearse it or even dry run together—quarterly business reviews (QBRs) for the sales team are another golden opportunity to morph that into a customer-facing event.

There's a bunch of drilling happening within the sales team, like mock calls, objection handling, rebuttals, and talk tracks around "battle cards," differentiators, and product knowledge. Sales engineering or solution consulting is the optimal team to tap into for customer-driven scenarios. They are often wolves in sheep's clothing, with technical answers at the ready but always looking to lead prospects and customers to a win-win solution that optimizes customer revenue and company profit.

AB testing themes is critical. We held many matches consistent around themes like cold calling and emailing, storytelling, negotiation, and branding. But then we threw in flavors of the moment like product-led growth (PLG) and RevOps to bring new dimensions to the content story. Diverse speakers resonate more with your ICP and thus pull a vast audience organically. Many speakers are open to appearing several times. Being super famous does not guarantee crowds. A thought leader with innovative ideas is worth featuring to improve your content quality.

Before building our event series, we held calls with potential attendees and did our best to figure out which kinds of drills were most voyeuristic for their counterparts across "the wall." Salespeople are all fascinated by the endless dashboards marketers inhabit. Marketers secretly want to master negotiation skills to unlock their inner Chris Voss.

Many of you are experienced event promoters so we don't want to bore or patronize you to tears with "Events 101." You don't have to make events your full-time job or life's work. But you also needn't present one event in a quarter and forget about it, either. We encourage you to find a happy medium between your company's budget limitations and achieving your grand vision for event supremacy now that you've discovered our blueprint. Quality and cost are no longer mutually exclusive with the growth hacking strategies outlined herein.

Ensure your work here does not harm the whole team's productivity as you experiment with the topics free form. Sometimes you throw an event with the "Most Amazing VC" on a Friday, but it wouldn't pull as much as a "so-so topic" on a Wednesday. The good 'ole "days of the week, times of the day" email marketing knowledge comes into play here. Believe it or not, some of the essential aspects of event promotion can trip you up if you're not careful. But that's for another book.

"Be so good they can't ignore you."

—Steve Martin

You can gamify any event by shifting your mindset from what you want to teach as a vendor (and what you want to sell as a company) to what your customers want to learn. What would make their hour feel like they spent it with value versus 10 minutes multi-tasking, seeing that it's crap, thinking, "you learned your product pitch well," and then bounce?

We know many marketing people in the most famous growth marketing communities where you have to pay thousands per year. The pitch includes "exclusive, selective, amazing." They publicize unique events where visionaries from all the top companies in Silicon Valley teach you stuff. When we ask our marketing and growth hacking, "product people," friends in the same community "why don't you participate in the live cohorts or view the events?," they admit, "I really would love to; I'm looking at it. The topic is amazing, and the speakers are relevant to me. I'd watch it, but there's this football game after work with a cold beer that sounds more seductive."

Your event must be as engaging as that football game. If people prefer to watch sports, eat potato chips, and drink a beer over attending your events, Houston, we have a problem. Make it so compelling they'll shut off the sports and bring the beer your way. During the cold calling matches with the VPs of Sales, the VPs in the audience were curious and engaged to see other VPs cold calling. It was an e-sports-like experience for our industry. Not cheesy, not obvious, but when you see your friend Joe and another VP from XYZ company struggling to cold call, it's fascinating to take in. People took it so seriously and competed hard until it became "B2B football."

That's what we do at HYPCCCYCL. VPs of Sales and Marketing, sales development reps (SDRs), and chief executive officers (CXOs) are competitive and want to win by DNA. Breaking down the corporate hierarchies pushes both sides of the match. Every VP of Sales wants to prove that they are legit and better than SDRs. SDRs want to prove that they're better than their managers; this is their "golden ticket." That happened with Gabrielle "GB" Blackwell of Gong, now Airtable, winning the entire competition against Aaron Ross.

It's unusual that a couple of entrepreneurs live and breathe what we do. If you run an event, you need to prepare for it to become a vocation, even a lifestyle, on top of the full-time job you already have. Julia's teammates used to tell her, "Julia, we can't always be *on* like you." It was tough to overcome this critique and still be successful. The majority of people punch the clock on their jobs. You have to rely on excellent time management skills. With events, one person needs to be available around the clock. You're fortunate if all your speakers and team are in one time zone, but distributed collaboration is the norm. We often see speakers log in from California, Mexico, Australia, Israel, and Switzerland, so managing them is an always-on, 24/7 grind "herding cats."

If you haven't yet, you'll need to hire and train someone *dedicated* to run your event. Everything that can go wrong will go wrong. Speakers and panelists will cancel at the last minute. Your team members will catch Covid, God forbid, all sorts of issues. You need an A-Team in this milieu: someone to act as a marketing ops/project manager (PM) and someone to run comms. One person can rarely combine all of these skills. If you're working in a company, your marketing team often has thousands of campaigns and competing priorities. They will not be running this event for you. Get dedicated resources to coordinate email marketing, social media management (SMM), content and promotions, design, front-end, and comms. Make sure your team's marketing ops lead, or PM plans the work in Asana so it all can happen like a Swiss watch.

How do you communicate with your management if you're doing a customer-centric, interactive virtual event? You can always show your CMO this book or what we are doing at HYPCCCYCL. If you can find a CMO who doesn't love our website (HYPCCCYCL.COM), we'll send them an Amazon gift card (that they don't want). You may need to build a strategy doc just to manage comms to get the buy-in internally to green light this project.

Suppose you want to run a CCE for your company. In that case, you have to treat it almost like a business plan. Show how many registrations you anticipate, what to expect budget-wise, how many hours of the team's time it will require, which team members need to be involved, and how much time they'll need to invest compared to their current task load. What are the customer acquisition costs (CAC) estimated to be? You have to be responsible for delivering all of that vis-a-vis projected return. It's best to draft a "good, better, best" return on investment (ROI) estimate that provides a spectrum from conservative to "aggressive" best-case scenario.

Build failures into the plan. Don't expect to nail it the first time. If you don't succeed at first, dust yourself off and try again. Your management should foster a "fail forward" culture, learning via doing and experimentation. Boldly apply agile development methodology to make your events metamorphic.

Customers don't care about your perfectionism; they are anxious about getting on camera too and often need hand-holding for onboarding calls and more process and structure than you might think. Create a safe space for competency transfer and allow do-overs and mulligans. There's enough pressure to participate in an event where you put them on the spot to talk about potentially sensitive issues like challenges, systems, and internal processes. Get permission to record in advance, if you do that, and give them Cliffs Notes on what their total time on screen will look like. Many will thrive on *not* preparing, but that's a rare breed that typically works in sales, not marketing!

You need to talk about real problems in your industry to gamify events without turning them into a circus act or parlor trick. It all has to serve a potential business problem. Suppose you see that ad costs are rising, and it's becoming a real struggle everywhere for VPs of Marketing to drive leads. Do an event where you set up a customer acquisition challenge, giving growth marketers and CMOs the freedom to develop creative solutions. Rather than provide them with the specifics, foster an environment where participants can innovate together and learn new demand gen tactics from each other.

CHAPTER 4

Shattering the Paradigm of Static

The universe is transformation: life is opinion.

—Marcus Aurelius

C halk it up to fate or drinking our own champagne poured out in this book. HYPCCCYCL was perfectly on-trend with the technology road-map business-to-business software as a service (B2B SaaS) vendors were building toward in 2022 because their target customer base blended in revenue function for the first time. Even sales tools now pull from market-ing budgets. The first venture capitalist (VC) Julia showed the concept to was skeptical about how go-to-market (GTM) Games would scale, but she pressed on undeterred. She went into the market to execute her idea, co-founding her venture with sales superconnector Justin Michael.

HYPCCCYCL

We live in a hybrid world where humans may never work permanently, full-time in offices again. We can't predict the cycle of mutation in pandemics. We could cite countless studies that business people have habituated to flex work. We love working in our pajamas with our intrepid cats and dogs at our side. "Zoom shirt" sales are up at Walmart while slacks are down. We think what you really need is a cape.

Covid changed everything. We saw an explosion of new formats take root, from Zoom calls to webinars and specialized digital events, all trumpeting the "new normal" in uncanny facsimile. We wrote this book because there's a glaring quality gap with virtual events that *nobody* is talking about. Classic movies are still phenomenal to this day because of the caliber of acting, directing, and script. Like foreign films, they don't always rely on production value, explosions, and computer graphics to carry the story. All you needed back then was Marlon Brando. Lest we forget, there are only seven basic movie plots.

The nature of virtual events today is suffering in our always-on Zoom-addled world. Business-as-usual webinars snuff out originality and innovation. We've all grown apathetic toward their poor planning, expected content, and low value devoid of compelling insight.

The user friendliness of staging online events has become a panacea that puts us all to sleep while checking the box on our perfunctory marketing plan recycled from yesteryear. "We have a podcast. Check. We have a webinar. Check." But where's the energy, enthusiasm, excitement, innovation, and above all, results? Are your customers engaged and paying close attention? Could they live without it? Ninety-nine percent of you reading this right now just thought, "Yes."

Static webinars foster low retention, much like popcorn and Netflix experiences forgotten the next day, even the next hour. We've repeatedly proven that hybrid delivery models will surprise and delight your public, help you monetize your dead webinar channel, and attract audiences like the latest Tom Cruise franchise.

Moreover, when you catch lightning in a bottle, it's a blast to put these digital gatherings together and relish the success of buzz, upper-funnel velocity, quality inbound leads, and customer retention. But if you fail with virtual events, the negative word of mouth can sink you, and your successive attempts could turn into a ghost town. Hence the subtitle of this book speaks to "Ghost Webinar" prevention. It is our fondest hope we can save you millions of dollars (not just help you make them) by dodging the proverbial bullet of mediocrity. Some of our Event Reinventions turn into Event Interventions. Founders and startup teams can become stubbornly married to their bad ideas and need to conform. Thus, two wicked slogans for our GTM agency are: "Building algorithms for B2B disruption" and "B2B Vandalism."

HYPCCCYCL

B2B Vandalism

Countless studies show that people remember 10% of what they hear, 20% of what they read, and 80% of what they see. But what about skill-building? Can you gain skills by participating in a Zoom? Our thesis is: only by practicing the skill being shared or taught. Drilling, role-playing, practicing, rehearsing, and receiving constructive coaching are the only ways our brain can learn and retain in such a short period. You have to play it back, "teach it back," coach and teach it yourself.

You are at a crossroads reading this book. Do you want the attendees of your events to come away with faint trivia or powerful new skills and knowledge? Give them a lever to change their worldview, foster new abilities, or sharpen their existing skills. They're desperately searching for innovative ways to be more effective and empowered at solving their most significant business challenges. Lead them toward your solution via education and enablement, patiently walking them up the "ladder of engagement." Talk is cheap—those who *can do* teach in our world. Show me the money, Jerry Maguire.

Even if you produce a running webinar with decent attendance, it's likely edutainment (education + enablement) at best. Like most brands in your industry, this channel has been neglected and is being run into the ground robotically. What if you could create a transformational virtual experience for your customers that left them with fresh perspectives, new skills, and a positive brand association as they benefited by learning long-lasting lessons? Socrates used to hike around Athens in the 5th century BCE with his students and ask "discovery" questions. We think he was on to something!

"How to hold executive events" is a throughline in this book because it's both an art and a science. Our thesis is: that when you facilitate a customer-centric event, the audience is coming to listen to your customers, your guest panelists, and the interplay—not you, the vendor who put it on, or even a distinguished VC emcee. And yet, we see virtual conferences where 5 out of 10 speakers are from the host vendor's team.

While it's a good idea to prepare insightful questions in advance and circulate these with participants in a shared Google Doc workspace to collaborate, you never want it to look scripted or canned. Your role as an event organizer is to help steer the direction of value-laden dialog by co-selecting compelling themes. In concert with moderated audience Q&A, preparation will deepen the relevancy and poignancy of the insights you share. Never, ever stick to the script!

In our matches for the VC Endgame, we often share a Google doc with previous role-play scenario options and ask each VC to tailor a scenario that matches their preferred theme, which could be their investment thesis. It could also reflect a skill or methodology they genuinely believe in as part of the GTM motion of startups they advise: customer-centric sales, Design Thinking, product-led growth (PLG), revenue operations (RevOps), defining ideal customer profiles (ICPs), negotiation, discovery, storytelling, and so on.

Here's a GTM simulation from the ever-brilliant Aaron Ross, author of From Impossible to Inevitable:

Sample Drill—*From Impossible to Inevitable*

You're a GTM leader in a buzzy SaaS startup.
    You need to grow the company from a $0 to $10 million run rate
    You have a limited budget for

– Hiring

– Tech Stacks

– Marketing

Challenge: Based on what I've taught you about GTM Growth, Cold Calling 2.0, Specialization, and so on, what would you do to hit the target?

And Rosalyn Santa Elena, Founder and Chief Revenue Operations Officer, The RevOps Collective:

SaaS company is looking to move up-market

– $70 million run rate

– Need to build out segmentation

– You're starting to look at more of a Targeted Account approach or a hybrid of Named and Territory-based model

– Create marketing awareness and interest through the content you put on your website, social media like LinkedIn and Twitter, and do some events and webinars

– You really don't know what's working and what's not—if it is, where in the Buyer's Journey?

– You have marketing automation (Marketo) and a CRM (Salesforce)

Challenge:

You're the RevOps leader. Management gives you the "green light" to secure technology to set up the organization for success in this new GTM Motion.
What top resources, technologies, or tools would you want to bring in? Which Top 3 are most urgent, critical, or impactful? It can be marketing or sales tech. From my perspective, it's all REV Tech.

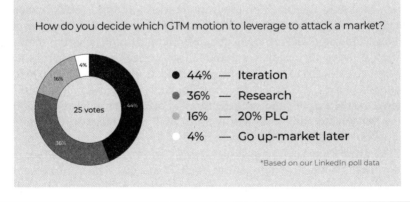

How do you decide which GTM motion to leverage to attack a market?

- 44% — Iteration
- 36% — Research
- 16% — 20% PLG
- 4% — Go up-market later

25 votes

*Based on our LinkedIn poll data

And Seth Marrs, Research Director, Forrester:

RevOps HIIT Challenge

To harness the power of sales and marketing, you need to identify whether the lead, opportunity, account, or contact is the best place to collaborate.

Recommend three tools sales and marketing need to work together and a process that needs to change/improve to align the revenue engine around the buying group.

And Susan Whittemore, Head of Revenue Operations, Teampay:

Your CEO slacks the Executive Team looking for validation of a "bottom-funnel" problem. You (Rev Ops Leader) and the Sales, Marketing, CS, and Channel Leaders are on Slack. You just finished building out a high-level summary of 2021 with targets, results, and the delta between the two.

Based on this data, create the following:

1. *A high-level narrative for 2021:*

   - What does the data tell you?

   - What areas would you like to explore further?

   - What hypothesis would you develop to share with the exec team?

2. *Given the results of 2021 with your narrative, what recommendations would you make to the leadership team to best achieve 2× New Business growth for 2022?*

3. *Based on your recommendations, what role can you (RevOps) play to ensure the best possible outcome against targets?*

We also hold RevOps high-intensity interval trainings (HIITs), where a thought leader builds a scenario more catered explicitly to metrics, key performance indicators (KPIs), and tech stack optimization. The goal is to devise innovative ways to leverage automation and machine learning/artificial intelligence (ML/AI) to solve strategic revenue challenges. With 10,000 SaaS solutions to solve GTM problems (according to Scott Brinker, VP of Platform Ecosystem at HubSpot), choosing the right set of keys for account-based marketing (ABM) and outbound sales is tricky. Will they integrate, do what the vendors say, and generate the desired ROI?

The worst thing you can do is just "wing it" on virtual events and see how it goes. That's not a customer-centric event. That's just "chaos." You want to give your audience the appearance of improvisation while remaining structured in the event design and flow. Design thinking and breaking down your concepts into first principles are handy here. What is the outcome you want from everyone involved in the event? Are you looking for attendees to brainstorm a topic and come away with an epiphany? Seed a content garden that will give rise to the best off-the-cuff ideas. Spirited debates of your sector's intelligentsia are gripping, even newsworthy. One of the reasons Jason Lemkin's SaaStr is such a perennial hit.

Before you hold your event, it's best to do a "dry run" or "onboarding call" where you sync with everyone involved, even for just 5–10 minutes. Hold these calls individually so you can be fully present, and it's not a free-for-all. Go over the permutations of what might occur, discuss questions, take notes in a shared doc, and agree on talk tracks and the nature of the role-play or drill.

What makes our events so unusual is our "zero preparation" environment that creates constructive tension and competitive pressure. However, we still take the time to get to know everyone before hosting each GTM simulation. Any game needs rules; you should write them down in a document, even a few paragraphs or a single page. Everyone needs a contingency plan. What will you do if someone cancels, loses an internet signal, or a panelist falls off? Be prepared. We let contestants play through if they get sick a day or have a work commitment they can't get out of on one of the nine days. Everything that can go wrong will go wrong. Everything you could think of—even air raid sirens— has happened during our events, but nothing could stop us because we were ready.

Pre-event, drop your guests into WhatsApp or a LinkedIn chat pod (multiple people in one LinkedIn message) to stay synchronized on what's happening. The Zoom functionality for private messaging is just not enough, plus it's not that easy to access afterward to review valuable nuggets.

Invest in the webinar package of Zoom as it's worth its weight in gold and is still relatively affordable. It allows you to transcribe, hold break-out sessions in separate rooms, bring panelists on early in a "green room," and do things like restricting the chat. Most importantly, as you plan for success, you want to ensure your event can easily hold over 100 attendees. If a contestant has a lousy microphone and you can barely hear them, turn on the subtitles feature.

It's wise to record your events so busy prospects and customers can get to them after the fact. You could then even gate this content for a membership fee. You can quickly build out clips using a service like Otter.ai, or Zoom now has transcription natively, or YouTube. Leverage iMovie for basic editing and caption videos within 24 hours using a quality captioning provider like Rev.com.

Our thoughts on designing and building out event scenarios: All you need to do is take a pain point or latent pain area, challenge, or opportunity within your current customer journey and freeze the frame. Not to grossly oversimplify, but it is like slowing down an old movie projector. Imagine your SaaS platform solves the problem of recruiting talent more effectively. Freeze the frame. Why not bring on several customers who can speak to the value and use cases you solve? Give them the stage to share their hiring models and best practices for screening candidates, and share the screen to show how they filter out candidates in real time within their user interface. Or, they could screen each other for a hypothetical role that would be fascinating and hysterical for the outtakes.

Imagine your software boosts retention and mitigates churn risk by sending automated reminders and gauging account health by tracking site logins/interactions. You could build a sandbox and bring in panelists to analyze those dashboards with synthetic data and trends in front of a live audience. Many SaaS companies already have "dummy data" in a sandbox—they use it to certify and train their internal teams and can quickly spin up logins the night before. In this hypothetical game, everyone could build a win-back email sequence or create a strategy for preventing churn, with customer judges voting on the best ideas. Build a real-world scenario, make it as realistic as possible, and heed the top point of feedback from our contestants: "Be tougher!"

Everyone wants candid, hard-hitting feedback so they can improve. That's one of the most gratifying silver linings of holding these competitions. Our participants reported gaining new interest areas in their career, getting promoted, and taking the learnings from GTM Games and applying them in the real world in their actual roles within weeks.

Remember to remain in the spirit of a "growth" versus a "fixed" mindset. You can win our games by being coachable, adaptable, and gritty (to echo Mark Roberge's hiring traits). Apply what you learn to win the more important game of life. It's never about who's the best at using software, doing a hard or soft skill, or innately talented at public speaking. Popularity contests be damned! It's more about who actively listens to the coach and then applies what they've learned. Of course, you could build a point system like *American Idol* or figure skating that's less arbitrary, but we don't see any losers or winners. We always joke, "the winner gets the gift of knowledge." Pursue ability, upskilling, and knowledge transfer. Your quest to walk a mile in your customers' shoes is always a "win-win." Understanding fosters empathy, improved communication, and customer-centricity.

Emcees are pretty tone-deaf to what's going on in a typical webinar. In search of making it flow, they never really open up and ask the audience or the attendees how they're doing. Vulnerability, openness, and "dust and scratches" improve the entertainment value. Asking, "Hey Mark, was that question too crazy?" Ask, "Is everyone enjoying this?" Ask, "By a show of hands, who benefited from this drill?" Breaking the fourth wall—when Shakespearean actors would talk to the audience mid-play—and connecting about the event's structure is a bit of a "meta" but will put everyone at ease, and you can pivot.

If someone doesn't feel prepared enough, they might share right away they prefer to pivot to a different kind of presentation. Always ask questions to let your participants clarify what they're role-playing before starting the game. When you do mock drills, let the coach and contestant set the table so they understand the scenario. What position does the prospect hold in the simulation? What stage of the deal are they in, and what's the context of the role play? Introduce the coach to the basics of what the product does so they can intelligently object and give feedback. If you let it get rocky for a second, everything will go smoothly. It's another paradox. Unless you are rehearsing for a play or dry-running the event multiple times, "live" environments are pressure-laden no matter what you do. Humor breaks the mood, making it okay for participants to be real, raw, and unscripted.

Business leaders never think deeply enough about how to make an in-person event "interactive." They are by default, so the art form of translating this online is taken for granted. At a big conference, you may listen to a speech or two, but you also see industry people and get to chit-chat while the speaker is orating. You get breaks to network, laugh, and hit the bar to rub elbows with all the LinkedIn friends you're meeting for the first time.

In contrast to that, virtual events cut out all these extraneous moments. Attendees may not even see who's attending. Speakers may only see a few people on the panel versus in a live event when they can stare into the audience and lock eyes. Webinars devolve into a backyard BBQ for five most rapidly.

To break the monotony and make it more interactive, feature one person emceeing and summoning guests from the audience while another organizer engages them in conversations, calling them out and asking provocative questions during the event. Give your audience possibilities: joining a panel, sharing dissenting opinions, or a snap poll about a polarizing issue.

The best way to do this is just to ask open-ended questions. Our customer-centric event format has competitors working on various challenges during the event. Simultaneously, we encourage our dark social community members to do them in parallel. Moderation is key here, so it's not a free-for-all, but it's a powerful mechanic to bring the broader audience into the game even if they can't log into the live session. When someone provides a great answer, we call them out and make them a panelist, which surprises everyone. Slight moderation prevents mayhem, and filtered curated feedback seamlessly builds virtuous loops from the audience to the social community to the panelists.

To help with that, we always ask our contestants to put their name, company, and title in Zoom so we see which niche they originate from. Similar to discovery, we profile the audience and understand their needs based on gameplay.

CHAPTER 5

Go-to-Market (GTM) Cross-Training Drills—Crowd Favorites

Play the game for more than you can afford to lose . . . only then will you learn the game.

—Winston Churchill

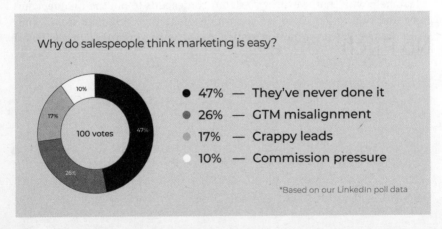

Why do salespeople think marketing is easy?

100 votes

- 47% — They've never done it
- 26% — GTM misalignment
- 17% — Crappy leads
- 10% — Commission pressure

*Based on our LinkedIn poll data

W e've run some compelling snap polls on LinkedIn about which skills sellers and marketers would like to have. One of the big winners is Data Science. When you watch enough sellers and marketers switch roles and lives, you realize that marketing and sales are essentially the same thing.

Marketing is no longer innovating; the ultimate goal of marketing and the core of the function is to find innovation and disruption and tie it to revenue, which is more entrepreneurial. The emergence of the product role has substituted that initial intent. Marketing should do the R&D and try to understand how to disrupt markets, then do it repeatedly vs. just generating leads and copycatting competitors. There's more to performance marketing than just finding the next growth hack.

If marketing gets implemented this way, it becomes the same as sales as you deliver the message 1:many instead of 1:1. The core of the sales function is to find a pathway into the consideration process to convert users. Marketing is sales at scale, how to deliver your pitch to convert customers en masse. Modern marketing is most effective when it embraces many hidden marketing methods, of which the main lever is growth hacking. By AB testing ever-catchier messages, you can find out what's more attractive to *fool* the user. Once they've downloaded the e-book, they realize it's a piece of garbage and feel duped. The core problem is people are not studying to become marketers anymore. Marketing is business acumen personified and entrepreneurial by DNA. It needs to be done transparently.

We thought it would be fun to list some of the most compelling examples of individual Go-to-Market (GTM) Games. These themes highlight our trademark GTM, cross-functional, cross-training framework as inspiration to get your creative juices flowing:

Sales doing Marketing Drills

No Pitch Contest

We invite a top chief marketing officer (CMO) like Latané Conant of 6sense or Sydney Sloan (formerly SalesLoft) and six salespeople to a match where the goal is *not* to "cold pitch" her but instead "edutain." Which means "education meets enablement." The emcee starts a timer, and each contestant gets 3 minutes to pitch. The CMO takes notes, so she *can't* let them in on coaching points to allow them to get better by psychoanalyzing the coach progressively. After the first 18 minutes, she provides candid feedback to all contestants. Then the clock is started again for 2 minutes, and the bottom two contestants go again or all six.

We call this a "teach back." (Hat tip to Kevin Dorsey.) Each contestant drills the skill again, applying the micro-lesson they learned or the area they seek to improve based on granular coaching feedback. Learning to "speak CMO" is best done by facing one. It's challenging for sellers not to show NAS-CAR slides full of logos or feature dump. Most sellers fight the impulse to simply show up and throw up without any discovery questions or interactivity with the CMO whatsoever.

Story Selling

Solution Selling legend Mike Bosworth, now Sales Philosopher at Story Seekers, discovered the power of stories to unlock emotional connection in his influential book *What Great Salespeople Do*. Building trust can bring down the walls of customer resistance to uncover pain and latent pain. That's why we call this drill "story selling" instead of story-*telling*. We've showcased a variety of world-class talent to host it, like Belal Batraway, Megan Bowen (Refine Labs), Shari Levitin, Julie Hansen, Shruti Kapoor (Clari), Dr. Robert Peterson, and Stephen Pacinelli (CMO, BombBomb). Many story frameworks were shared, from The Hero's Journey (Joseph Campbell) to a Pixar-inspired movie plot format. The whole point is to weave in a value narrative focused on the customer versus spewing product knowledge and rattling off "speeds and feeds." This drill is cross-training because it's often alien for sellers to think from a content marketing perspective about narrative arcs, protagonists, dynamics, and elements that a copywriter or screenwriter might inherently understand as tools of the trade.

Personal Branding

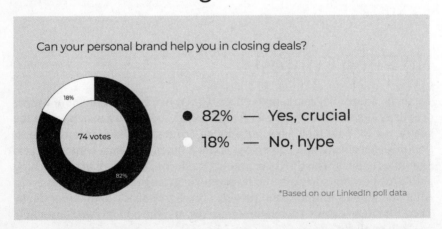

Can your personal brand help you in closing deals?

18%

74 votes

82%

- 82% — Yes, crucial
- 18% — No, hype

*Based on our LinkedIn poll data

Social selling, social media, and personal branding have been overdone and overtrained. We switched it up by featuring leaders such as Viveka von Rosen, Sangram Vajre, Brynne Tillman, and Justin Welsh to provide a challenge around who could best improve their brand while on the call. Coaches tore down profile elements like headline, background image, and positioning/branding live on the call. Contestants switched up their social profiles and then got graded. It's a bold, brave contest to rewrite your LinkedIn headline, "about section," change your background image, and update your profile pic in front of an audience.

The most significant mind shift is taking a static profile that reads like a CV and turning it into a dynamic landing page that converts the best prospects who visit you. But there are all sorts of hidden LinkedIn Easter eggs that Viveka and Brynne uncovered for us. Our audience wrote in that many made real-time changes to their profiles while watching the event. Talk about practical application!

What's the most important part of personal branding?

111 votes

- 55% — Consistency
- 23% — Actual track record
- 14% — Differentiation
- 8% — Confidence/swagger

*Based on our LinkedIn poll data

Metadata RevOps HIIT (High-Intensity Interval Training)

One of the most compelling interactive product drill highlights was seeing sellers learn how to use the Metadata's "MetaMatch" targeting capability to practice building relevant audiences with VP of Marketing Jason Widup. Sellers had to flex their technology quotient (TQ) and become more data-driven to think about segmentation and targeting of ad units—demographics, geographies, and advanced targeting. This marketing knowledge will make them better sales "targeters." Jason set up some challenges on how to slice and dice data that will help sellers sharpen their prospecting sights as they return to the field.

Marketing doing Sales Drills

Cold Calling

Whether it's Alice Heiman, Jake Dunlap, Anthony Iannarino, or Josh Braun, simulating cold call "openers," when marketers attempt "cold calls," it's always a blast to watch. Marketers often cram all week, even drilling with their sales team to be prepared. We notice marketers win the competition more often as they train, whereas salespeople are wont to wing it by their very nature. Many marketers are terrified of this challenge and decide to bow out.

The beauty is they're against other marketers training in a safe space ideal for "competency transfer," as Anthony Iannarino calls it. The whole structure of our event model allows for a mulligan or "do-over" at nearly any time, like an actual coaching session. Alice Heiman's match was particularly intriguing because she shared that as a CEO, she doesn't take cold calls. Her challenge was for contestants to reach her by other creative means: warm intros, direct mail, email personalization, and so on. Nonetheless, the majority cold pitched her *anyway* as a mock call, even after being asked not to. We love breaking the mold at HYPCCCYCL.

Have you ever heard of a cold-calling drill whose purpose is to teach marketers *not to call* a CEO but use any other innovative method?

Email Tear-Downs

Josh Braun led us in an insightful email tear-down drill walking marketers through his signature business-to-business (B2B) outbound email frameworks, line by line and tactic by tactic, in one of our most popular games ever. Approaching B2B top-funnel work linguistically differs from writing traditional marketing copy or copywriting. You need to nail the subject lines, but how long should they be? The opening lines, the bridges, reader psychology, and the calls to action (CTAs) work in unique ways when doing cold email. The goal is to take marketers out of their comfort zone to think like quota-carrying account executives and sales development reps (SDRS) about "jobs to be done." We will share some email tips for following up with your participants later in this book and the appendix.

Negotiation—Not Voss

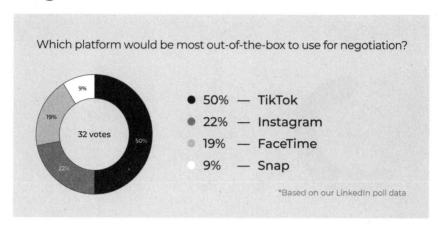

Don't get us wrong—we love Christopher Voss and understand why he's so popular, especially with his heroic work mitigating real-life hostage negotiations. Our goal here was twofold: First, to challenge marketers who typically don't negotiate or bargain with buyers directly and to highlight other negotiation methodologies that might not be as in vogue as Voss's luminous "Never Split the Difference." We featured elite coaches like Carole Mahoney, Mike Bosworth, Ashleigh Early, Scott Leese, and Todd Caponi. They highlighted facets of principled negotiation, disciplined bargaining, buyer psychology, Cialdini persuasion, and ways to keep cool, so you don't easily cave on price. Bosworth shared a remarkable visual about the wet towel squeezed as a metaphor for customers trying to gain concessions. It was particularly eye-opening. Gerry Hill of ConnectAndSell pretended to be a hostage-taker, which was incredibly suspenseful; watch it in the archive! The contestants ALL handled it well and didn't crack under pressure.

Demo-lition

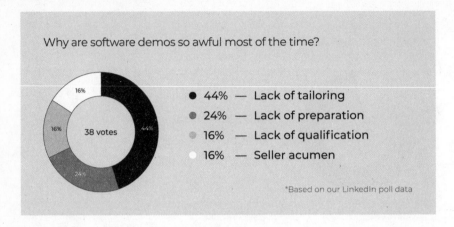

Why are software demos so awful most of the time?

- 44% — Lack of tailoring
- 24% — Lack of preparation
- 16% — Lack of qualification
- 16% — Seller acumen

16%

16%   38 votes   44%

24%

*Based on our LinkedIn poll data

The biggest problem with traditional demoing is it gives salespeople a hall pass to use visuals as a crutch rather than a neuroscience-backed enabler of education, enablement, and retention. Ironically, this ideal visual presentation medium gets abused when visual selling has the greatest potential for cut through. Demos are broken. Salespeople flaunt every last aspect of their product, taking 45 or even 55 minutes of the 60-minute call and asking, "do you have a hard stop?" We call this "demo-boarding." It destroys the goodwill, curiosity, and desire for your best products.

Marketers understand a great deal about product positioning and often can demo well out of the box, even expertly, when they've never demoed to customers before. We had a VP of Marketing who admitted it was the first time she'd ever demoed her product, and it was intense. The GTM Game here focuses them on elements of the discovery done beforehand to tailor the aspects of their platform that they show, customer-centric persuasion techniques, and the various demo methodologies to make this process compelling to modern buyers. Coaches included Kathleen Booth (SVP of Marketing, Tradeswell), David Hoffeld, Kevin Dorsey, and Jake Dunlap.

What makes a great drill? Speakers with charisma and strong social media pull. The non-obvious angle is how practical the drill's problem aligns to our day-to-day lives. Most events that software vendors put on are irrelevant to customer problems. Companies raise money and target their pitch toward investors versus the audience. Fancy slogans abound, and the events are intended to impress analysts, board members, and venture capitalists (VCs).

Companies are constantly copying one another in an ongoing popularity contest. Suppose you take five vendors in a category with the same slogan, different copywriting, and the same message. Everyone is insecure and thinks that the other one knows better. All the marketing department does in place of market research is to look to the competitor and change their headline.

The problems events focus on have to be technical and tactical because every time it's strategic and futuristic, it's not practical and dismissed. "Philosophy" is suitable for analysts and wine events once a year. It's tough to link the event theme to the problem that your product is solving when companies fall back generically, like "let's talk about the future of sales." Every sales role on LinkedIn will watch that event, but you'll get a .5% conversion because organizers have cast too wide a net.

That's why in HYPCCCYCL, Julia listened to Justin's story and realized that even when he was a VP of Sales, he was always asked to prospect. No matter how badass you are in your sales career and how amazing an account executive (AE) you become, you are still responsible for driving your own pipeline. The outbound skill is always essential. That's why many of our simulations are specifically focused on tactical and technical outbound skills for GTMers instead of "the future of revenue intelligence."

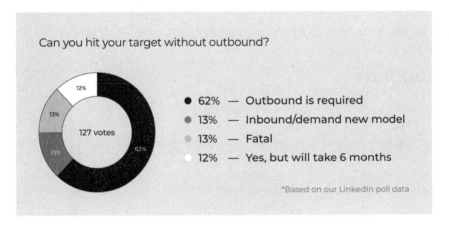

Can you hit your target without outbound?

127 votes

62% — Outbound is required
13% — Inbound/demand new model
13% — Fatal
12% — Yes, but will take 6 months

*Based on our LinkedIn poll data

CHAPTER 6

Creating Hybrid Models That Pull in Audiences

I believe you have to be willing to be misunderstood if you're going to innovate.

—Jeff Bezos

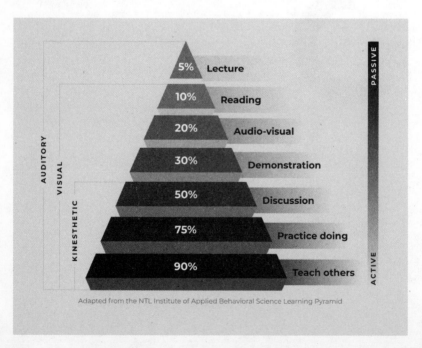

Adapted from the NTL Institute of Applied Behavioral Science Learning Pyramid

The primary model we've discovered to foster retention follows the Learning Pyramid. When participants coach each other and "teachback" elements they've learned from panelists, retention has the potential to shoot up to 90% versus static watching or listening. If you can put participants under the microscope of intellectual pressure in a safe environment, it yields effective competency transfer. Prodding people to go off-script and think on their feet may produce sweat and anxiety, but it also fosters constructive change.

In our model, there's still a tremendous emphasis on discussions, demonstrations, and audio-visual components in the pyramid. In training hundreds of reps, Justin corroborated that aspects he pulled from emceeing Go-to-Market (GTM) Games produce training excellence and reinforce hard skills. The real magic happens when participants coach each other, not just drilled by the coach. Imagine the exponential impact of two customers giving tips and advising each other on ways they can improve a process, system, or skill. Compelling social proof between contestants spurs empathy. Why? We think psychologically, "Wow, that person is just like me. We are both experiencing identical pain. I can get the results my peers are getting and slay the same dragon."

Attendees of your event are seeking value. They want to get better, see their problem from a new viewpoint, be empowered by insight, and come away with utility. You can advise them all day with PowerPoint slides, but behavioral change is unlikely until they play it back to you in their own words. They need to practice, drill, and rehearse it not just with you, the expert, but back and forth with each other to equalize and humanize the mental plane. *This paragraph could summarize the whole book if you take away just one insight.*

HYPCCCYCL

Our first event, GTM Games, was a mash-up between the marketing and sales functions. Nearly every software as a service (SaaS) platform during this time released tools to align marketing and sales more closely through revenue operations (RevOps), so the theme hit the cusp of the coming wave. Alpha-uber platforms like Outreach's comprehensive roadmap include forecasting, deal coaching, conversation intelligence, and guided selling via an artificial intelligence (AI) sales assistant (Kaia).

But these hybrid simulations could be anything.

Julia crafted the T-Shaped GTM grid that follows, which was inspired by T-Shaped Marketing themes.

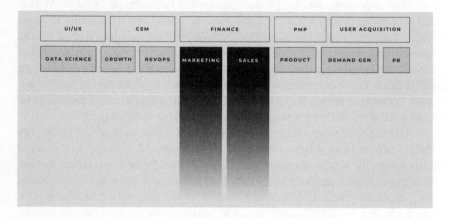

Look closely at the diagram. You could take any two functions and cross-train roles to re-imagine your special event.

Hybridizing event models can mash up business themes like Marketing and Sales, Operations and Product, or Custom Success Management (CSM) and Data Science. We originally had a logo of a fish riding a bicycle because the events made traditional business-to-business (B2B) leaders feel like they were learning to do a proverbial "backflip."

HYPCCCYCL

Julia initially hired Justin to emcee a cold-call competition where CEOs competed at cold calls. Her research shocked the industry in that it revealed that a majority of CEOs not only still loved to make dials but were willing to compete. It also shattered the prevailing myth that VPs of Sales won't make cold calls. Outbound calling is one of the hard skills they used to build their business and move into the corner office. ConnectAndSell (CAS) has been a critical strategic partner in proving this hypothesis based on its data derived from "60MM fully navigated dials per year."

That was the central insight to democratize cold calls where sales leaders at all skill levels would compete for a prize. The boxing theme resonated with our ideal customer profile (ICP). The winner—Gabrielle "GB" Blackwell, a Sales Development Manager at Gong during that time (now Business Development Manager at Airtable)—beat a famous sales trainer and got pink boxing gloves. We even featured Dolph Lundgren of *Rocky* fame and Chuck Liddell of Ultimate Fighting Championship (UFC) notoriety in cameos (cameo.com), urging viewers to "support Julia's event." It was surreal and a great promotional vehicle when we got the actor who played rebel VC Russ Hanneman on HBO's *Silicon Valley* to make a ridiculous cameo video promoting our event.

It was revolutionary that a world-renowned sales leader like Aaron Ross (who wrote *Predictable Revenue*, the "Bible for Silicon Valley Scaling") cold called directly in competition with VPs and CEOs. Even sales development reps (SDRs) faced off against C-level luminaries, leveling the playing field and democratizing the competition. To our knowledge, no one had ever done anything like this before. But correct us if we're wrong because we're always looking for new event inspiration. And you should, too.

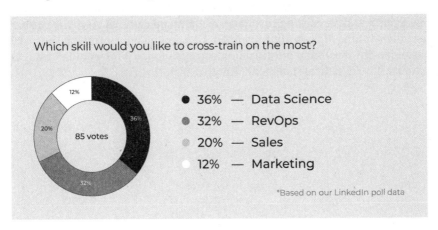

Which skill would you like to cross-train on the most?

85 votes

- 36% — Data Science
- 32% — RevOps
- 20% — Sales
- 12% — Marketing

*Based on our LinkedIn poll data

When we interviewed Doug Landis from Emergence Capital about skills of the future, he cited data science as a top discipline all roles should take a crash course in. If you're reading this and thinking, "we are too narrow, too niche-focused; we can only really throw webinars on our product," take a step back. You'll find many angles to how your product drives value. If you research your ICP about themes they're most interested in, you'll be surprised by what emerges. The secret is dovetailing product knowledge into content-driven events that are customer-centric. Learn via focused research (actually talk to your customers) what compels them and what will add value versus droning on about a product vision that may be disruptive to you but still two to five years ahead. Give them value now. Bonnie Raitt said it best, "Let's give them something to talk about."

Here are four demand types from Steve Richard: make money, save money (improve margin), reduce risk, and satisfy a government regulation. You'll find many customer stories if you dig deeper within your case studies tab or raid product marketing's vault. Get your creative wheels turning. Customer-centric organizations build "customer hero" stories to be evangelized and socialized by frontline reps in the Center of Customer Excellence, versus product marketing supplying feature complexity that can impede sales. It's always exciting to hear Mike Bosworth's thoughts on this topic. (Check out more on *GTMmag*.)

As the godfather of Solution Selling, Mike loves to say—paraphrasing—"peer curiosity leads to peer envy." If your event is about ways your customers have experienced great success with your product, the word will get out in your industry. Attract the butterflies to your garden. Don't promote all the benefits to your customers. You can enable and empower the industry by sharing trends, ideas, and innovation. The key to this book is not to do it flat, static, and predictable.

Why not bring on a customer to share a story about why your solution worked? Turn this into an interview or a talk show. Bring on your product managers and have existing customers recommend features. As a prize, prioritize the winning idea on your roadmap. Can you imagine bringing your best customers into roadmap prioritization conversations? Who wouldn't want to see such a bold, radical statement? Another historic first!

CHAPTER 7

Why Dynamic Environments Foster Learning and Retention

If we knew what we were doing, it would not be called research, would it?

—Albert Einstein

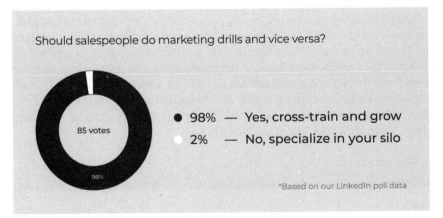

Should salespeople do marketing drills and vice versa?

85 votes

98%

- 98% — Yes, cross-train and grow
- 2% — No, specialize in your silo

*Based on our LinkedIn poll data

Go-to-Market (GTM) Games is our acclaimed GTM cross-training event where sales and marketing leaders do interactive simulations judged by venture capitalists (VCs). The mission is to cut through the hype and break down the silos between revenue functions. It's a monthly two-week challenge where the top business-to-business (B2B) thought leaders on the planet coach and drill GTM executives on skills pushing them out of their comfort zone.

We've talked about the learning pyramid but let's go much deeper into dynamic learning environments. Elsie Boskamp shares, "Companies that use gamification are seven times more profitable than those that do not use gamified elements at work—whether with employees or consumers."

We say *dynamic* because anything can change anytime, like comedic improvisation or full-contact sports. When creating an online event, we believe your audience's primary litmus test for success is *interactivity*. If you do an Event Reinvention right, there shouldn't even be an audience! It will be fully collaborative in the round, with all stakeholders interacting. From Roman gladiators in 105 BCE to the Running of the Bulls at Pamplona in the early 14th century, contests have always held humanity in rapt attention. Not to mention all the hungry squid games and queenly gambits becoming binge-worthy sensations.

Yet, 99% of Zooms seldom feature polls or interactive chats on the right-hand side. Here's a pro tip: shut off the chat functionality in your Zoom. Announce that you're pushing audience interaction to your Slack channel to drive a conversation that will last after the event. Participants who missed it (or will watch the recording) can still react asynchronously to glean insights. Your marketers will gain insight into your best leads based on comment threads on dark social.

The emcee might call for audience participation during our events: "Who wants Jed to look at your email template? Do you want Josh to give you feedback on your cold call?"

Want a simple way to determine if your events are compelling/making progress? Read the room and eyeballs. Are participants multitasking and glazing over buried in their smartphones, cameras off? Your job as the event producer is to make the content, format, and interactive elements so compelling that you get buy-in, high levels of engagement, and chat participation the whole way through. We built our event up until we averaged about 35 minutes of watch time per hour, which is extremely strong. During each match, hundreds of comments cascaded inside various chat platforms, including Slack, Discord, WhatsApp, and LinkedIn.

HYPCCCYCL

B2B Decathlon

HYPCCCYCL

GTM cross-training is Julia's Barkley Marathons, CrossFit, or Olympics of B2B concept, where GTM leaders break out of their silo to switch roles and lives for an entire week. We highlight the core differences between these classic functions that have so much friction. Marketers are accustomed to leveraging data-driven dashboards, whereas sellers spend much more time with customers in board rooms and on calls. What if sellers could become more "data-driven" by cross-training on marketing skills like learning how to target audiences in an ad automation platform like Metadata effectively? How about getting marketers to negotiate their product's commercials, write cold emails, and drill cold-call openers?

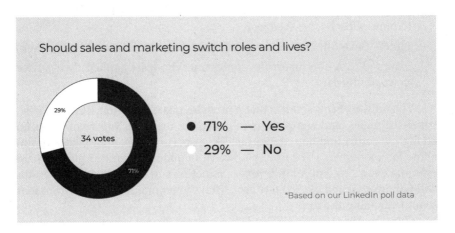

Should sales and marketing switch roles and lives?

29%

34 votes

71%

● 71% — Yes

○ 29% — No

*Based on our LinkedIn poll data

Initially, marketers were "terrified" to work on hard skills like cold calling, even in safety with a top coach. Regardless of empathy levels, it's daunting to backflip into the deep cold water of practical outbound calling skills. We found that marketers would prepare the most, even drilling with their sales team for an entire week. On the other hand, salespeople competing in the marketing drills tended to be overconfident and wing it. When sellers and marketers competed in 2022, we did see the champion profile of the first 12 events primarily skew toward marketing. But we're not sure if that's correlation or causation. I bet you're not too surprised that marketers swept most of the two-week competition over the first dozen games. We will see what happens in Season II, Games 13–24!

Is your event challenging for participants to get outside of their comfort zone and try something new? Could you leverage a novel format to catalyze this electricity? Some creative examples: Make audience members panelists at random times to compete in a game. Break down the walls of presenters and viewers. We turned coaches in our games into contestants. The game could be a quiz, a drill, a simulation, or a role-play—the sky's the limit. The beauty of our events is they require zero preparation on behalf of the participant or the coach. You can create an ad hoc format that becomes almost like a blueprint or formula for each event as follows:

Modular GTM Games Event Framework

5–10 min—Interview the guest/share a short deck

5 min—Introduce a GTM challenge

5 min—Set a timer for 5 min/return to the interview

20 min—Contestants present back/role-play with the judge-coach

10 min—Coach gives feedback

5 min—Bake-off: The bottom two (or all) contestants face off (teach-back)

5 min—Judge eliminates the contestant who least applied their advice (coachability gap)

The beauty of this setup is that it provides guard rails that allow the host, panelists/judges, and competitors to improvise together. You want to set up enough structure and boundaries just like a sports match, but make sure you allow for spontaneity. For example, we've frequently seen our guests share raps and even sing impromptu songs. Sometimes in the events, a contestant will fail the drill and ask to start over. That's what makes a live environment so unpredictable and fun!

Our signature HYPCCCYCL GTM Games™ format is a chess-style elimination challenge where each day, the weakest of the contestants gets voted off the island by a prominent judge, an expert in a specific business skill.

To be eliminated doesn't mean you are the worst. The coach felt you applied the lessons the least and were not as "coachable."

We created a universally accessible format where a complex hard (or soft) skill gets taught in the first 5–10 minutes (e.g., a pitch contest where sellers try *not to* pitch a CMO). Five to six contestants per week battle it out over nine days. They role-play a cross-functional skill in front of a coach, back-to-back (and timed). Then the coach judges all contestants. Finally, there's a dead heat with the bottom two competitors "on the bubble" facing off, or they all go again. Then the coach eliminates the bottom performer. If there's enough time, all the contestants can play the game again. What is remarkable about this format is watching the participants improve their skills in real time.

We create healthy competition and camaraderie as everyone steps out of their comfort zone together. We've put over 200+ participants through this novel format; many went into new career areas and made connections for life. Sellers became suddenly interested in marketing, marketers in selling, contestants launched their own startup companies, and some began to specialize in revenue operations (RevOps) consulting. VCs come in at the end of the nine days to pit the top seller contestant (from week 1) against the winningest marketer (from week 2). A comprehensive GTM simulation is held before a bonafide VC to pressure test everything they've learned throughout the competition.

Suppose you played board games growing up, like Trivial Pursuit, Monopoly, Sorry, Boggle, or Battleship. Imagine how hard it is to be a board game designer and release a classic that stands the test of time. Few make it in a sea of thousands of games released over the decades. In that case, it's relatively easy to build business competitions that echo this type of gamification with trivia, skill-sharing, prizes, and audience participation. The basic rule of thumb is to make people *think*. Make them wonder about something they always look at from a new angle. Examples: Why is sales like marketing? How can machines operate like humans and humans like machines?

Hopefully, this book gets your creative juices flowing to take a risk, step outside of your comfort zone, and create something new in the world of events just like we did!

> *"Talent wins games, but teamwork and intelligence win championships."* —Michael Jordan

In closing this chapter, we can't help but think about teamwork and positive psychology. It is powerful and rewarding to break a customer (or internal) team into groups, empower them to work collaboratively to solve real-world challenges, switch roles, apply new skills, build synergy, and flex teamwork muscle through GTM cross-training.

We've been lucky enough to be commissioned by top software as a service (SaaS) companies to hold internal games for their communities or their company in a workshop format. Getting your team out of its silo and cross-training is fascinating within your company because it provides a different viewpoint about your GTM. How do you solve problems, and what aspects of product differentiation make you unique? Our big suggestion is that even if you do internal workshops and drills, don't forget to include some customers—they'll love it.

CHAPTER 8

Choosing and Preparing Your Speakers

Good teaching is one-fourth preparation and three-fourths pure theatre.

—Gail Godwin

You can have everything in life you want, if you will just help other people get what they want.

—Zig Ziglar

We are consistently building lists of diverse speakers and networking with them. The best way to stay in touch is not to make the direct ask to participate in your events. It's helpful to check out their activity feeds, participate in other webinars *they* are holding, read their books, and comment thoughtfully in other communities where they hang out. This kind of work takes time. Most of us have seen the movie *Pay It Forward* or are familiar with the concept of relationship karma or RoR (return on relationships) from Ted Rubin.

Initially, we advise you to prepare a letter for each one of your featured speakers and take a few minutes to hyper-personalize the outreach as follows with the Justin Michael Method™ (The JMM), Justin's patented email outreach system (in Appendix II).

subject line: sync
Body:

Hey, Jeb, I'm a big fan of your new book on sales efficiency and just watched your recent webinar with Mark Hunter. We're doing an exciting interactive event on sales prospecting tips that could be very relevant to your new book's messaging. Would you be open to a sync to discuss some ideas to collaborate?

This email is nonthreatening, has the WIFM (what's in it for them) component—and constantly adds value. It's hyper-short as a SPEAR (super-short JMM message), and you can utilize it as a Facebook, Instagram, Twitter DM, InMail, WhatsApp, voicemail, and of course, a targeted email. You can take a hyper-short email like that and just tailor it very slightly as follows:

subject line: challenger customer spotlight

"Hey, Brent, Huge fans of your 2nd book, have an opportunity to feature you to our audience of 15,000+ on a VIP email list. I would love to role-play a simulation with you and our GTM audience, high-lighting the gridlock in decision-making committees and how GTM leaders can overcome it. Are you possibly available on any of these dates to make a cameo on our panel? We would love to promote your 2nd book, and congrats on your new role at Ecosystems. Best, Julia"

Once you've got some speakers lined up, you want to offer them a fast sync for onboarding, 10 minutes max. Get to know the speaker, build trust, set them at ease, and even come up with a minute-by-minute ticker of their presentation in the simulation, almost like a board meeting or live show with "marks" for the actors to stand with their lines. That way, there's no ambiguity over what's going to happen. Address all doubts, considerations, and concerns up front, and ensure you know which links and resources to promote to reciprocate to the speaker. Pay it forward if someone graces your stage by highlighting their best work.

Our speakers advise: "don't overprepare and don't overthink it." The best thing you can do is get a good night of sleep. When you appear on a webinar, you need to be fresh, act naturally, and give spontaneous responses rather than be seen like you're reading off a teleprompter or cue cards.

The best way to prepare when you go to an interactive event is to pull up the LinkedIn profile of everyone involved and run a preliminary Google search. Look on Amazon at their books (read the sample), listen to some podcast snippets, and get a good feel for what everyone at the event does. You could put this all in an Evernote file and review it the day before. Plan to prepare. Block out at least 30 minutes before the event to do the research so you're ready to interact intelligently.

We are continuously engaging our ideal customer profile (ICP) on Linked-In and are constantly in discovery mode. The beauty of LinkedIn is that you can see different opinions and an unfiltered stream of consciousness. Lower the veil as a seller or marketer and consider, "what do my prospects think?" You can now do this through social listening. Even if they're not first-degree, it's possible to interact with their content streams through Sales Navigator and get on their radar. Many speakers come from simply commenting on our best content when we have a healthy debate or intriguing conversation. Or we stumble on content that resonates with us and want to expose our audience to it.

Like producing a show, you need exciting ideas with compelling people, even if they're obscure. Often company spokespeople have to hold a party line and share conservatively. From corporate speakers, you get best practices, process-driven talk tracks, and strategic ideas that are proven in the enterprise. We like challenger brands; you can get a contrarian opinion from entrepreneurs or founders. It brings energy and vibrancy to the show to switch it up. And then there are the gurus who built their brand so well that it's a sin not to engage them because they have thousands of raving fans.

CHAPTER 9

G.A.M.E.S.™: A Powerful Formula for Nailing a Customer-Centric Event (CCE)

If you're playing a poker game and look around the table and can't tell who the sucker is, it's you.

—Paul Newman

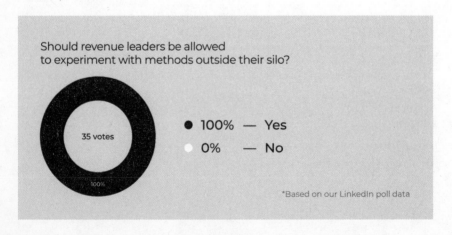

Should revenue leaders be allowed
to experiment with methods outside their silo?

35 votes

● 100% — Yes

○ 0% — No

100%

*Based on our LinkedIn poll data

Wthat makes an event customer-centric? The most obvious answer is putting your customers at the center of the content versus your product, executives, company, or sponsors. But we've developed a proprietary framework to help you break out of your silo and do just that. It's called G.A.M.E.S.™

Why bother holding interactive events? Beyond boosting morale, engagement, happiness, and profitability, "gamification results in 14% higher scores on skill-based assessments," according to the University of Colorado. If you want your attendees to take away actionable learnings and skills they can apply to their roles with your software, then listen up.

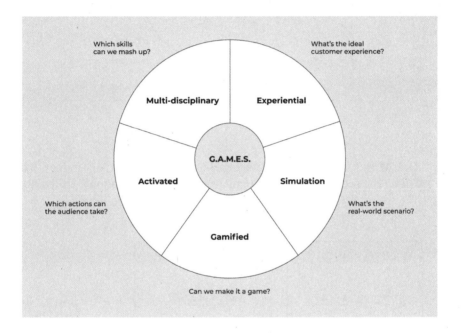

Gamified

Activated

Multi-disciplinary

Experiential

Simulation

Julia invented Go-to-Market (GTM) Games and HYPCCCYCL to bring business-to-business (B2B) and e-sports together in a new category of "customer-centric events (CCEs)." We're not talking about Dungeons and Dragons, a pizza joust, escape the room, Bingo, or Tough Mudder. It's not video games or Metaverse either, although maybe someday it could be. All LinkedIn seems to give us in the way of innovation so far in the

2020s is a shiny new "laughing" blue emoji. The better analogy we cite is a treasure hunt or story framework with a narrative arc as you architect a 45-minute executive interlude, the optimal length based on dwindling attention spans.

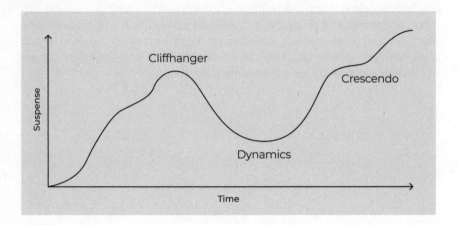

G.A.M.E.S. is our signature Customer-Centric Event™ (CCE) framework for nailing the necessary elements to make an Event Reinvention™ (ER) sing.

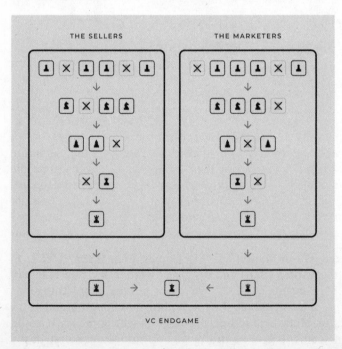

Gamified: The point of this book is *not* to sign you up for a virtual event platform, move you out of Zoom (which is as ubiquitous as smartphones), or make you spend a nickel—although we'll provide higher production value recommendations. At its essence, *gamification* means simply creating a game, even as prosaic as Minesweeper or Tic-Tac-Toe. Our event lasts nine days. Week 1 features sellers doing marketing drills in elimination judged by a top marketing coach. They get removed like *Survivor*, with judges kicking the lowest performer off our digital island. Week 1 progresses with 6, 4, 3, 2, 1 contestants, and Week 2 vice versa: marketers doing sales drills judged by a top sales coach: 6, 4, 3, 2, 1 in elimination by the judges.

We then spike it with revenue operations (RevOps) exercises to bookend Weeks 1 and 2. On the ninth and final day, venture capitalists (VCs) hold a complete GTM simulation highlighting cross-functional strategies and tactics as a mental and practical exercise.

HYPCCCYCL

How do contestants win? As the goal is learning and retention: whoever is the most coachable, adaptable, and shows grit in applying the "signature skill" of each coach takes the "Super Rep" award. We put over 250 people through this revolutionary framework with near-zero preparation. Humans fear change but love spontaneity. In later chapters, we will talk about onboarding participants in your events and getting buy-in for brand disruption.

But anyone can build this. You could create a *Jeopardy*-style game or base it on any quiz show, trivia, or classic game you enjoy. We did a RevOps TQ (Technology Quotient) battle where we asked trivia questions about RevOps featuring the top thought leaders in the world on this new subject. We nicknamed it "beyond thunder dome" to mash up a pop-cultural reference. Julia previously created a TQ Test on Salesborgs.ai that corresponded with Justin's hit book *Tech-Powered Sales* on RevOps, the emerging nexus point of sales and marketing operations.

Game Ideas

Is there a quiz you can build based on the specialized knowledge in your sector? Bring on the most innovative, visible voices and minds in your industry and ask them tough questions live with panelists to judge them and an audience that includes your customers.

Is there a debate you could host (debate team style) about a critical issue impacting your niche? Bring on two or three thought leaders on both sides of the aisle and get a LinkedIn celebrity to moderate it like a presidential campaign/town hall debate.

Activated: We always feel like we're listening to Charlie Brown's teacher when we're on a static webinar. The same banal questions are asked ad nauseam to predictable panels on hackneyed topics. Instead: what is a logical gradient step function that occurs naturally in the event? Think of it as a step ladder. What is the following action the audience might take to jump in and participate? That makes it a CCE. What value can be derived intrinsically and extrinsically—is there a critical takeaway each speaker can impart to a receptive audience?

Talk is cheap. It's all about doing. Can you teach the audience a skill via osmosis? Can they drill it, practice it, and rehearse it live? If you're teaching SEO skills, can they brainstorm keywords? Put them into the action: right down into the weeds of a scenario. Look at the dashboard. Make the cold call. Compose the email or LinkedIn message. Can they open the user interface/user experience (UI/UX) of your software as a service (SaaS) and share their screen for live coaching by actual experts if you're a leading marketing software?

We did this with our partner, Reprise. Sales contestants built product-led growth (PLG) demos on the fly, sharing their screen with a sales engineer, Ben Kipnis. Will the panelists exchange ideas, tactics, strategies, and valuable growth hacks? How can *action* happen in the game and outside in the real world? Make sure participants retain the knowledge from this formative, high-impact experience for weeks, months, and years to come.

Calculate your time-to-value (TTV) for events compared to software products, which is often 14–30 days. Freemium can wildly vary as users define how often they use a tool (habit-forming) and when to share it with colleagues. Users can't experience real value for some products in only a trial period. TTV for an event can happen in the game if you practice, role-play, drill, or in simulation by challenging participants to "do" the skill repeatedly and teach it back. In his "storytelling endgame," Doug Landis gave us a profound insight. "If you get worse, it's okay" because if you become awkward like a wobbly deer in how you present, at least you pushed yourself past your comfort zone, which is where the creation of human ability begins.

Multi-disciplinary: The best way to get creative with your theme is to ask this question: What if we tried to insert _____ out-of-the-box idea? You can use a mash-up of two other event concepts to get out of the box. Go back to our story about how we initially came up with this B2B alien. Like Richard Branson always says, "Screw it. Let's do it!" For example, a boring webinar on hybrid work becomes a quiz show based on trivia questions you design while interviewing industry thought leaders. Now it's a "Hybrid Work Webinar Game Show" where top B2B thought leaders get tested on trends and statistics about the "new normal" work habits and routines in a game with rules, judges, points, audience participation— you name it! How can you take a vanilla idea, mix it up, and generate excitement?

A flat, virtual event on HR Technology trends where experts drone on is now an interactive back and forth between HR leaders and managers. They could role-play and simulate real-world use cases your technology handles, replete with screen shares of the UI/UX. Why not demo your recent product updates on a hybrid CCE webinar with customers and customer success managers (CSMs)? Hybrid synergy is mixing, matching, and mashing up disparate ideas. Our bold event architecture creates novelty that begets "virality." If it's mysterious, the brain pays attention. People will "sneeze" it like Seth Godin's *Ideavirus*, and suddenly it will be the "must-attend" event of the season. Think about it like food truck culture with Epicurean fusions like Asian tacos.

Experiential: "It's just a Zoom call." Dare we say, this is the understatement of the year as it couldn't be farther from the truth. There's a massive difference between sitting and idly watching a talking head drone on for 60 minutes versus *participating as a customer* in a lively interactive event when a brand creates something truly "experiential" for you to enjoy. Imagine a "Choose Your Own Adventure" book where you can turn to a new section at the end of each chapter. Hollywood wanted to implement this in the movie theaters, but it never got off the ground. That made *Black Mirror* so revolutionary as a TV-watching experiment with multiple plot variations and endings. If you only learn one thing from us, it's to repeat this question as your mantra: "What would create interactivity?"

Always foster audience participation in several chat platforms at once. Poll the audience in advance with a Typeform and then pull them randomly onto a panel—quiz the audience from a LinkedIn update or SurveyMonkey. If the audience is involved in your Slack or Discord Channel, hold a vote for whom should receive the prize. Audience judging is something we never see. Panelists can interact in different ways—C-level executives doing activities of frontline employees or vice versa is very *Undercover Boss*. We all love to see hierarchical mash-ups. Switching roles and titles and upending the power structure is always riveting. Everyone would be fascinated to see a chief marketing officer (CMO)/founder make a cold call or a CEO using a marketing dashboard. Behold the wow factor of cross-functional, cross-training, or a hierarchical switcheroo in these two examples.

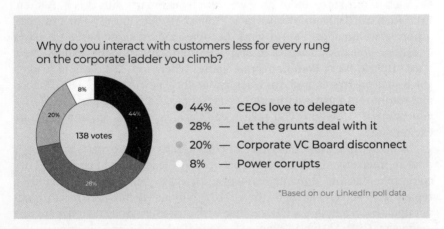

Why do you interact with customers less for every rung on the corporate ladder you climb?

138 votes

- 44% — CEOs love to delegate
- 28% — Let the grunts deal with it
- 20% — Corporate VC Board disconnect
- 8% — Power corrupts

*Based on our LinkedIn poll data

Simulation: Because Julia was the first ever to invent the event concept of GTM Simulations in B2B, we define *simulation* as more than a drill or role-play. Role-play is traditionally limited to repeating a specific skill with light coaching. A simulation is an intellectual exercise that puts the participants and audience into flight simulator mode for their neocortex in 360° 3D.

Example of a VC simulation shared by Lars Nilsson, VP of Global Sales Development at Snowflake, Sales Advisor at True Ventures: Imagine you are in a Series A company that has just raised a $10 million Series B. The leads have dried up inbound, and you need to start going outbound and implement account-based sales development (ABSD) with the optimal tech stack. Which families of technology would you use and why? Which specific vendors would you choose? Do you see how a sales, marketing, or RevOps leader would approach this unique challenge differently depending on their respective lens? That's an accurate GTM simulation, but you could also hold a Marketing Sim, Product Sim, IT Sim, or whatever topic fuels your fancy for the desired audience.

Let's take a traditional static webinar and run it through the G.A.M.E.S. formula as we do when we consult with companies on an Event Reinvention from HYPCCCYCL's GTM Agency.

Before (flat-passive):

Expert Panelists on artificial intelligence/machine learning (AI/ML) for marketing gather to discuss "marketing automation" trends.

After (dynamic-active):

Gamified: 20 questions to guess the top trend in AI/ML for marketing in 2022

Activated: Five panelists will participate in this game, two customers and three industry thought leaders

Multi-disciplinary: The questions will be a mixed bag of sales, marketing, and RevOps trivia. Chief executive officers (CXOs) will get asked tactical frontline questions, and directors/operators will field high-level "strategic questions."

Experiential: Along with guessing the answer, the two players must devise a concrete way to use the industry thought leaders' technology. The audience will judge which contestant comes up with the most creative, innovative use case.

Simulation: The answers to the trivia draw from a more profound framework for marketing strategy in a downturn. Once they guess all the trends, a CMO comes on to judge the finale based on the most creative use cases shared and awards a prize. There could even be a set of CMOs judging from the audience itself.

Do you see how radical this gets fast? It's like adding 5th and 6th dimensions on a four-sided die. As you deconstruct a typical webinar, the critical components are game dynamics, teams, a scoring system, coaches/judges, trivia, problem-solving, scenarios, use cases, and role-plays. The more these dimensions you add, the more complex and robust it will become.

CHAPTER 10

How to Pull Off a Stellar Virtual Event

The whole purpose is to enable people to learn. Your mission is not to transmit information but to transform learners.

—Harold D. Stolovitch and Erica J. Keeps

Perhaps you think you need a couple of quarters to pull off an event as we did, but we assure you it can be done with about 30–45 days of planning if you follow this guidebook. Parkinson's Law states that "work expands to fill the time allotted"; therefore, Horstmann's Corollary is more relevant than ever, "Work contracts to fit the time we give it."

If you're an event marketing team, you may strictly plan your marketing and event calendar so just make sure you create more mini syncs and think "agile." We've found that many speakers have books or active PR campaigns on the podcast-webinar circuit right now with an urgency of "yesterday," and they're bookable 10 business days out. You'd be surprised.

You probably have some form of an active mailing list. The paradox is that if you promote it 90 days out or even three to six months out, executives are a bit fuzzy about what's on their calendar that far on the horizon. By sending out a simple LinkedIn event invite, sharing a Google Calendar, and building out an email campaign of a few touches, you can typically pack an online event faster at the two- to three-week mark.

The best advice for an event is simple: build something you want to watch. Do you admire the work of the coaches, speakers, and panelists? Take the time to buy their books. We can't all be Andy Paul and read every word, but at least skim the chapter headings and read critical parts like the intro. Blinkist is an excellent resource for book summaries and Scribd for longer multimedia formats. If you leave a coach or speaker an online review and send it to them, it's a highly leveraged move, and they'll likely reciprocate by participating.

You need to get into the habit of closing the loop with everyone. Never leave open threads, so make sure you create lists upon lists in Gmail, Evernote, Asana, Monday.com, Trello, or Notepad. Every time a speaker contributes, write them right after via email or LinkedIn. Thank every guest after your event, ask for feedback, and even send an NPS survey.

Think of it as closing open loops. The only way to hurt your brand is to under-communicate. Overprepare, dry run, onboard, drop voice notes, and chat back and forth. The alternative is getting to the event, and it is madness, complete confusion. Consider hopping on Zooms 5–15 minutes early to go over the talking points and interactive structure. Presenters would rather meet on a Sunday evening very briefly to be ready than fly blind.

One key takeaway is that the emcee sets the tone. If you're too fast and loose, casual and laid back, the entire event gets the flavor of a backyard wrestling match or country rodeo. If you take it more seriously, time the challenges, and have a more rigid structure, it will create positive tension, making it much more fun to watch. Think about professional sports like soccer or baseball and how intense the umpires and referees are. Humans are insanely competitive by nature so take what you're doing seriously.

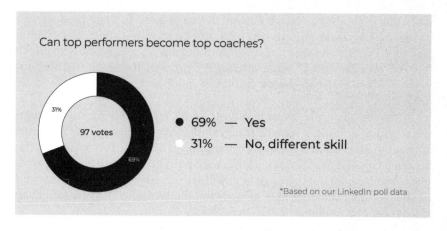

Can top performers become top coaches?

97 votes

● 69% — Yes
○ 31% — No, different skill

*Based on our LinkedIn poll data

The coaches also set the tone. If you're going to feature luminaries judging, get buy-in with the audience and contestants to "coach" on "hard mode." Oren Klaff, Shari Levitin, and Scott Leese provided assertive feedback that the contenders and audience raved about for months. The reality of a simulated business environment is it's rife with emotion, volatility, and chaos. Hence, the expression, "business is war." Running on "easy mode" is unrealistic.

We encourage coaching to focus on "coachability, adaptability, and application." We don't want to see a pass-fail grade, point scoring system, or binary fixed mindset competition. These compare apples to oranges, make people feel bad, and everyone has different learning styles and their own "unique genius," as Aaron Ross loves to say. There are seven types of intelligence as defined by psychologist Howard Gardner, and you need to be able to reward and celebrate each of them in an encouraging environment (Linguistic, Logical-Mathematical, Bodily-kinesthetic, Spatial, Musical, Interpersonal, Intrapersonal).

Now we know this seems to counteract our advice about being "hard on the competitors," but make sure compassion, empathy, and other-oriented selflessness are the hallmark of how you give constructive coaching feedback. Never invalidate, undercut, or criticize your base. We don't want to turn your events into the David Hasselhoff Roast or one of his concerts (sold out in Germany, by the way!).

Sharing the screen is risky business. Presenters must never exceed the 10-minute mark and a maximum of five slides. We can't tell you how often a speaker says they'll present a few slides; it eats 30 minutes into your event. As an emcee or moderator, you want to ensure that you ask participants to stop sharing their screens, so they're not relegated to tiny talking heads. If we're all going to look on a shared Google Sheet or LinkedIn profile and change it up, that's great, but switch back.

It's even better to build a visual template like a Venn diagram on a whiteboard that everyone can collaborate on. If you're going to share product user interfaces (UIs) make sure you do a dry run on an onboarding call or before the event. Pro tip: you may be incredulous but always remind participants to "turn off your cat videos" before sharing their screen. If you see anything out of place when someone shares, call it out immediately, so they close it, fix and reshare.

Attention spans are lower than ever, so it's tough to hold your customer's attention no matter how relevant the problem is to their life. You must constantly pattern-interrupt every 5 minutes to do that. That's where your creativity comes into play. Oren Klaff is the best at this because he's so provocative. Find a moderator or emcee who will say something crazy, make tasteful jokes, or address audience members at random. Basically, "flip the script" all of the time. Pun intended; that's Oren's book.

CHAPTER 11

Innovating Around the Curve

Innovation is the unrelenting drive to break the status quo and develop anew where few have dared to go.

—Steven Jeffes

What's stopping you from embracing radical innovation?

22 votes

- 55% — Leadership lacks buy-in
- 26% — Cost/ROI unknown
- 14% — Risk/fear of change
- 5% — What we have works

*Based on our LinkedIn poll data

Buyers buy into the vision around the corner when marketed to but then close on the product's most essential features when they finally pull out their wallets. A great example is Justin used to sell personalized, in-app notifications and interactive surveys. Still, many buyers wanted to do basic push notifications in their apps when "push" came to shove in buying. Julia marketed a revenue intelligence platform that promised to inform management of the "next best action" at every stage of the sales process. Still, buyers preliminarily adopted sales engagement and CRM (customer relationship management)-to-inbox sync.

Marketers are notorious for seeking out *innovation* in study after study by analysts. At the same time, sellers prioritize *revenue* above all else, not to say that's not also important to marketers. These folks bicker so much because their raison d'être and modus operandi are fundamentally juxtaposed.

We believe you should always play up to the most intelligent members of your audience when you're trying to pull to an event versus dumbing yourself down to broaden the audience. Like a premium product in an industry conveys quality, exclusivity, and thus value, it's okay to be an acquired taste in a sea of "Captain Obvious" Presents.

We think about this like a classic "intelligence close." Play up to the intellectual curiosity in your buying group, primarily if it consists of leaders, because they are most likely to be the innovators and early adopters in their respective companies. They can help you cross the chasm to the larger pool. Geoffrey Moore's timeless wisdom applies to everything, including event marketing. Think the opposite of the content marketing refrain we always hear: "dumb it down," "write it at a 4th-grade level," and "simplify it," even "kill a word!" Why? Because CEOs read 60 books per year when the average person reads one.

Leaders are readers of *The Economist*, *New Yorker*, and *Wired*; they are intellectual by nature and looking for ways to be enabled, empowered, learn, and grow. They give TEDx Talks, sit on conference panels, and pride themselves as trendsetters in their field. You'll attract lower-level decision-makers if you put out content for a 101 audience: 202 content attracts a 303 audience—303 brings 404, and so on. Knowledge is power, so innovative ideas become your garden to attract the proverbial chief executive officer (CXO) butterflies that can transact with your venture.

Creating buzz, media, hype, and PR requires doing something innovative that potentially no one has ever seen. Pull inspiration from other walks of life ported back to business-to-business (B2B), whether music, art, science, economics, or pop culture. We had a blast with Ultimate Fighting Championship (UFC), boxing, and cold calling, which may seem obvious, but with the advent of **Cameo.com**, we got to bring on a lot of kooky celebrities like Carrot Top to announce the matches. Julia documented all cold-calling methods industry leaders used during the events, even custom ones. She came up with the idea that each B2B practitioner has a "unique method" or "signature skill" of their own.

The riches are indeed in the niches. Do you have contrarian views about elements of your industry? Could you transform your idea into a customer-centric event (CCE), putting your customers at the center and making it more interactive? Example: Traditionally, customer success managers (CSMs) don't utilize structured query language (SQL) pulls to query a database. Product leaders can teach CSMs a SQL lesson, and they can build different "SQL pulls" to query for customer data. Let's do a Zoom event where CEOs, customers, and go-to-market (GTM) leaders learn to interpret patterns in data with data science (DS) techniques judged by chief technology officers (CTOs). It's already groundbreaking and bizarrely fascinating.

Q.E.D: Our event is sales and marketing switching roles and doing GTM simulations. To spice it up, we looked around the curve for product-led growth (PLG), Design Thinking for Sales (hat tip to Ashley Welch), and revenue operations (RevOps) emerging themes in our industry of B2B. The event attracted the best thought leaders and sponsors because they wanted to associate themselves with the most cutting-edge content possible.

The No. 1 word in advertising is *new*. In the last chapter of this book, we'll look at disrupting your event ideas when you feel like you have hit a plateau, risk stagnation, or suddenly fall flat.

Watering down your events with familiar themes, mediocre partners, and cliché content is a great way to turn them into "Generic SEO." We're so passionate about standing out that we even satirically made this a drop-down on our site to rank for organic traffic.

SQUARE 1

EVENTS

GTM GAMES ARCHIVE

CCC

PRINCIPLES

AGENCY

ORIGINS

→ **GENERIC SEO CONTENT**

Innovation requires staying ahead of the curve when it comes to industry themes. It's not just about reading *Fast Company* and *Wired*, but studying the megatrends that become grist for the mill fueling these publications. You must steep yourself in analyst research and pull from diverse areas and disciplines.

Justin's solid 20+ year background in B2B sales (including Salesforce and LinkedIn) is the yin to Julia's yang as an accomplished entrepreneur, chief marketing officer (CMO), inventor, and editor. Her Spidey sense as an entrepreneur disrupts markets. GTM acumen coupled with disruptive innovation creates a holistic approach to GTM modeling. Our agency work focuses on helping you to disrupt your market, box out competitors, and revolutionize your given niche. We are unique in combining sales and marketing to unlock your hidden revenue flywheel. Break out of your silo with us!

> *"You never change things by fighting the existing reality. To change something, build a new model that makes the existing model obsolete."*
> —*Buckminster Fuller*

CHAPTER 12

Becoming a Media-Trained Emcee

If you think presentations cannot enchant people, then you have never seen a really good one.

—Guy Kawasaki

Attention follows attention. Whatever you focus on during a live event grows. And if something goes wrong and you fan that spark, it will grow exponentially. So be careful what you wish for and don't panic.

The most potent entertaining factor is self-deprecating wit. Making fun of yourself in a public forum humanizes your brand and endears audiences to you. You need to set the tone for how your customer-centric event (CCE) will go. Humor is paramount, but you want your humor style to be more like Seinfeld than a raunchy late-night comic. Bring all sides to the table and welcome them in.

At Go-to-Market (GTM) Games, we are always a bit serious and don't introduce the contestants (because it wastes time and breaks the intense competition feel). We joke plenty with the judges where appropriate. If you're too informal, the event can turn into a backyard BBQ circus where the golden retrievers jump into the pool to catch a tennis ball. We use this visual metaphor because if you create a role-play, time the simulation, and institute some structured Q&A, the audience will take you seriously and get more out of it. No matter how much fun your audience appears to be having, setting parameters, rules, and boundaries makes the game worth playing, just like "escape-the-room."

Never look up when you're hosting. Make sincere eye contact with your guests and encourage them to do so. Don't smile too much; this is not a cruise ship. Body language must be natural—sit up straight, and the Amy Cuddy TED Talk is an excellent resource to master your "power pose" that brings self-confidence. Great leaders have a "low economy of movement," so gauge how expressive you want to be. Hand gestures and pointing out things are better than dead and flat like you're reading the evening news, but don't overdo it to the point you look like you're on the New York Stock Exchange floor. Pointing at the camera can be considered aggressive.

Do your homework on the panel earlier in the day or the night before. Make sure to research their most recent podcasts, books, and articles. Weave personalization into your interplay if they've been on a webinar or given a presentation at a conference. Think like Joe Rogan and be overprepared. An inch of preparation will give you serious mileage when you go live.

Media training is all about political savvy and diplomacy. It's about knowing what to say, when, and especially, what not to say. If you make a mistake on a live webinar, just own it or move on. Don't pretend it didn't happen if it's severe; acknowledge and say something self-deprecating like, "stuck on stupid over here." If it's a minor mistake, simply keep going. Kenny Loggins said it best, paraphrasing, "If you hit an off-key note, hold it with conviction. Simply go on singing. The audience won't notice unless you do." Easy to say when you're a Grammy winner.

Exerting positive control is what leadership is all about. You need to be the master of ceremonies and ensure guests follow your event format to a tee. If players in the game are stuck, confused, or look like deer in the headlights, you need to nudge them into action gently. A big responsibility is stopping competitors that go long. Play your award show exit music promptly. Be firm but kind. You'll get more respect from the panelists if you're strict on time. If you let everyone walk over your clock, the audience will complain and stop watching.

We didn't want to be the book about posture, dictation, good lighting, a "Blue Yeti" mic, and a state-of-the-art laptop. Good advice here per Jake Dunlap, "Be expressive; use your hands. Make eye contact with the camera, and use their name." But you need to present well. Our big recommendation is to create a custom background for your Zoom calls, even furnishing it to participants while on the game. Here's an example:

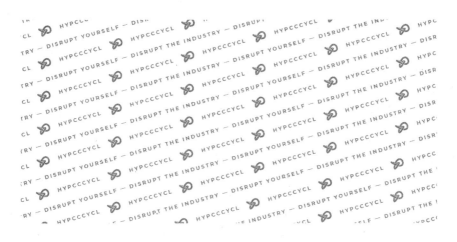

We are intrigued by Oren Klaff's theories on "status cues." In the pandemic, "you can't tell who is powerful." Oren parked his Lamborghini in front of a wall-to-wall flat screen in his sound studio and blew us away visually with it. Tony Robbins has nothing on him now! Talk about a visual metaphor to establish authority and credibility, and no one doubts he's the reigning expert on raising startup capital.

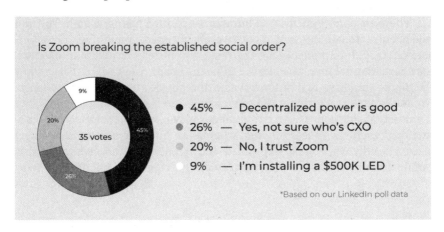

Things go wrong when you're co-hosting, and you need to be able to deftly navigate turbulence and choppy waters. You need to be able to ad-lib. The best thing to do if you get caught flat-footed, stuck, something goes wrong, or speakers freeze is to laugh about it, but not like a hyena to break the professional mood. Instead, immediately ask an insightful question to a contestant. A great one is, "so how has this event experience been for you so far?" Or, "what are your candid opinions about the trends and technology we've been discussing on this webinar?" You've got a jump ball or hot potato on your hands, so don't just look around awkwardly or be silent. You don't want long, uncomfortable silences on LIVE events.

And most importantly, never overreact. Keep your camera focused and stay cool, calm, and collected. Easier said than done we know, but remember the aphorism: attention follows attention.

Customer-centric moderation is about neutralizing your brand. Take your attention off yourself as the emcee, and spotlight the panelists: your audience, customers, and colleagues. We don't even put our images on brochures; the listen-to-talk ratio is easily 90/10. It's not "The Justin and Julia Show." We fade into the background and keep the theme in the foreground. You never need more than one moderator. One collaborator should serve as the director to evaluate how the event is progressing, providing real-time feedback to ensure everything goes smoothly from the viewer's standpoint. Is it engaging enough and interesting, or are people falling asleep?

Remember, you don't have to rely on a script. The best practice is to go with the flow of the event. We always get the feedback that "your events are like binge-watching the best show. It always keeps us on our toes."

There are entrepreneurs and intrapreneurs. Julia has done both. The first rule of entrepreneurship is that you're probably doing something uncomfortable or crazy. Intrapreneurs are the same, but instead of external investors, they have internal investors like the CEO, the board, and CMO. Always show them how you drive real business value and positive organizational change. No one is against earning more money or gaining potential customers, but it's always a compromise. An entrepreneur may have to be scrappier to innovate their events with less funding, whereas an intrapreneur could often get backed heavily while creatively stifled. Intrapreneurs have to comply with a certain amount of rules. If that doesn't work for you, strike out on your own.

CHAPTER 13

Cultivating a Disruptive Mindset—Be Patient; This Could Take a While

First, they ignore you, then they laugh at you, then they fight you, then you win."

—Gandhi

You will not win over hearts and minds or convince your C-level executives rapidly. It will require serious patience and persistence as you seek to secure buy-in for your disruptive ideas inspired by this book. You'll need to launch a mini-campaign and start evangelizing for your customer-centric event (CCE), not to mention winning over your targeted audience. Like Steve Jobs with the iPhone, customers never know what they always wanted. When you present the industry with an out-of-the-box new experience, many people will resist it at first.

You must hold to your vision for trying something new, almost like the Jobsian "reality distortion field." You will get plenty of pushback in the form of, "why don't we just do a webinar?" Drown out the groupthink of sheeple addicted to playing it safe. Now is the time to make your mark, listen to your inner voice, and let your most disruptive event ideas take flight. Fortune favors the bold. Brainstorm with people who support innovation and don't suppress it. The reason it's called a "silo" is it's challenging to break out of it. You need to find a partner for your events, whether a colleague or vendor who is even crazier than you are, to pull these off.

Julia likes to say, "What's the truth/insight?" What's one key takeaway not available anywhere that you can glean from looking at any business system from a new angle, a new lens, a new vantage point? Your personal experience blending learning models and styles is a treasure trove. We all have unique hobbies and meta-skills that define us and make us memorable that we can bring into a business context to transform the dull and mundane. If you want to be inspired by business events, look at history, art, politics, pop culture, music, economics, and science. Disruption will come from outside the system, not just rehashing the same tired formats.

You will face nearly absolute rejection, so like Abraham Maslow and Wayne Dyer stated, we must be "independent of the good opinion" of others. You need to cultivate an anti-fragile mindset like Nassim Taleb. The worse circumstances get, the more demanding and frustrating, the more you learn, and the stronger you get. Khalil Gibran said it best, "Out of suffering have emerged the strongest souls; the most massive characters are seared with scars."

The best way to innovate and break out of your silo? Partner with a colleague who is the yin to your yang on projects. Jim Rohn said it best: "We are the average of the five people we spend the most time with." You should also look to event inspiration not just from the technology industry, business books, analysts, or tech journals. Study autobiographies, leadership, and stories from far outside the business world. As Scott Leese likes to say, "go surfing." Successful disruption comes from daring greatly and taking inspiration from many dimensions of life outside of business.

CHAPTER 14

Low Budget to High Production

Every production of genius must be the production of enthusiasm.

—Benjamin Disraeli

You can build a website for $3,000 or spend $10,000–25,000 monthly on a state-of-the-art, multi-media event experience. If you're throwing an event on a budget, the best leverage point is a simple event page on LinkedIn, your mailing list, and you could create landing pages in HubSpot or a simple WordPress blog.

Which technology could you NOT live without?

74 votes

- 54% — Email
- 28% — CRM
- 14% — Sales Engagement Platform
- 4% — Conversational intelligence

*Based on our LinkedIn poll data.

You can do your registrations in Eventbrite, but always gate it for guest phone numbers so you can cold call the participants and remind them to attend. You can always put up ticket pricing even as a "false gate" with a unique code to lower the price to free. Make it a doorbuster to get people to rush to your event. You can cold call the entire signup list, offering discounts to bring friends, colleagues, and so on. Don't go too far with discounting strategy as you don't want to devalue and commoditize your event.

Running paid advertising for your event can cost anywhere from $30 to $200 per attendee in customer acquisition costs (CAC). Consider putting together an advertising budget of at least $5,000 per month and doing a ton of AB split testing across many platforms, not just Google and Facebook (Instagram).

Look to hire from Fiverr or Upwork, or consider building a distributed global team. Many talented resources will even support your community pro bono to generate leads for their business. If you're budgeting, look for ways to make in-kind trades with vendors who can help you cover the various infrastructure aspects of producing the event. Remember, "there's no free lunch," and you get what you pay for.

Events cost next to nothing relative to other marketing mechanisms. The biggest problem is showing a return on investment (ROI) on your team members' time that you need involved in this project. For that, you need to build a project plan in PowerPoint or build a Miro board.

We will spare you the gory details on building events at much higher production value because then, what would be the value in enlisting us as your agency of record to orchestrate this with you. Shameless plug!

CHAPTER 15

Tech Stack for Modern Virtual Events

Humans have become the tools of their tools.

—Henry David Thoreau

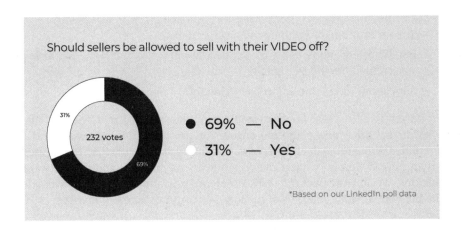

Should sellers be allowed to sell with their VIDEO off?

31%

232 votes

69%

● 69% — No

○ 31% — Yes

*Based on our LinkedIn poll data

We didn't want this to become a "tech stacks for events" book, but after all, Justin wrote *Tech-Powered Sales*, and we get many requests for this info. We were able to build out our whole series on WordPress WP Engine with a Pro Zoom account, but we had professional developers build out all the rest for us to custom specs. Lucky us!

Consider all the players listed below and check out G2 and Capterra for additional solutions. These are just the broad strokes to get you started. We always quote Jill Rowley's cautionary tale for tool junkies, "A fool with a tool is still a fool." There is no bigger, better mousetrap.

You can put your event lobby in the metaverse with Topia, have multiple bobble-head avatars from the wildlife kingdom, stream videos, and even feature interactive games on the screen. If the content is terrible, it's just like satellite TV. Ten thousand channels, nothing on, and you're back on Apple TV+ paying for great content. It's not your tools—"look, a squirrel!" Prevent yourself from falling victim to "shiny object syndrome" even if you leverage a fantastic event platform like Hopin. Build out a process, program, and hybridized theme; then align tech around it to pull it off based on the limitations.

Considerations:

- Number of panelists? Many solutions limit 10!
- Multi-geo, time-zone, pre-recorded?
- Participants over 100, even over 1,000?
- Stream multimedia behind you/special effects?
- Bandwidth of who's using it? Zoom is bomb-proof, but some platforms need a high fidelity 5G signal.
- Simple one: is it "clunky" or user-friendly?

Zoom is the "go-to" because people don't get stranded in a "virtual hallway." If you utilize new platforms, ensure you provide a training session and a simplified onboarding doc. Otherwise, you may squander the first 10 minutes of your event simply herding cats to get everyone in there and the software working. We all remember the early conference software days when downloading the new version robbed us of the first 5–10 minutes of every meeting.

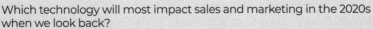

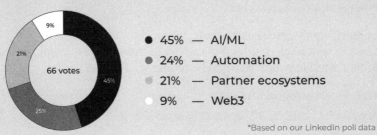

Which technology will most impact sales and marketing in the 2020s when we look back?

66 votes

9%
21%
45%
25%

- 45% — AI/ML
- 24% — Automation
- 21% — Partner ecosystems
- 9% — Web3

*Based on our LinkedIn poll data

The "Essential Event Stack"

– Webinars/Video conferencing (traditional):

Zoom, BlueJeans, Webex, GoToMeeting, Join.Me

– Robust Event management (badging, ticketing, registration)

Cvent/ON24: Analytics, integrations, QR codes—stage, agenda, resources | AI-powered match-making of attendees

Bizzabo: Category leader in blending physical, virtual, and hybrid

Hopin, Airmeet: Multiple tracks, interactive booths, analytics

Goldcast: Custom branding

Eventbrite: They have free and paid packages. As a legacy player, they've kept up with the pace of innovation in this space—syncs with Zoom (provides multiple event modules).

– Multi-platform streaming (live or pre-recorded):

Restream: Stream to Twitch, LinkedIn, YouTube, Twitter, and Facebook simultaneously

Streamyard (Hopin): HD video, easy editing, scheduling, and multiplatform streaming

Melon: Stream *for free* to Facebook, YouTube, LinkedIn, Twitter, and other platforms in five clicks.

– Special effects (virtual cameras):
Use this instead of your built-in camera to show images, words, and presentations alongside your face without sharing your screen.

Prezi Video: Most user-friendly

Mmhmm: Creativity off the Richter scale

Open Broadcaster Software (OBS): *free*

Ecamm: Look better on video!

– Meetings (200 people or less):

OnePgr: webinars, email marketing, chatbot, content library (it goes forever)

Butter.us: Whiteboarding, polls, breakouts, agendas, integrations

– Avatars:

Welo: Spaces that promote interaction; it integrates with most tools

Gather: Minecraftesque and blocky; guests navigate where to go

Remo: Attendees can move from one virtual table to another

Topia: (2D metaverse), highly customizable

– Custom Spaces: Your guests navigate as virtual avatars around customizable maps.

Welo, Topia, Gather, Remo

– Community platforms:

Slack: Amazing for work collaboration, can get unwieldy in chat threads at a massive scale

Discord: Traditionally for gamers. You can boost the server and do all sorts of customizations

Scenes: White-labeled Discordesque community

Mighty Networks: Good for courses and memberships integrated within communities

Circle: Asynchronous: discussions, live streams, chats, events, and memberships

Patreon: Creators love this. You need to be willing to pump out a lot of bespoke content and frequently meet to provide the value of the paid subscription, usually just $10.

Twitch: Traditionally a channel for watching gaming or gaming together in the round, you can do live drills on here, and it's a killer, real-time environment.

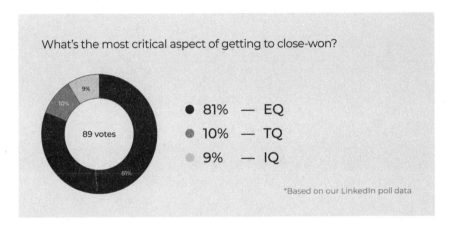

What's the most critical aspect of getting to close-won?

89 votes

● 81% — EQ
● 10% — TQ
● 9% — IQ

*Based on our LinkedIn poll data

So what are your criteria for choosing the preceding platforms? Your audience's technology quotient (TQ) must be a significant factor in selection. Additionally, your company's budget and your team's capacity. Is your target audience used to Zoom? Are they on Google Chrome with software up to date? Does IT restrict specific applications? As listed, audience size and panel size are factors. Are you going to have multiple sessions or break-out rooms?

Are you more presentation-focused or networking? Do you need analytics on participants and to leverage that data later? You might be a small and midsize enterprise (SME) looking for some leads, or you're endeavoring to go Oren Klaff/HYPCCCYCL level and give a masterclass with venture capitalists (VCs).

SECTION 2

Promotion, Amplification, and Monetization

Never doubt that a small group of thoughtful, committed citizens can change the world; indeed, it's the only thing that ever has.

— Margaret Mead

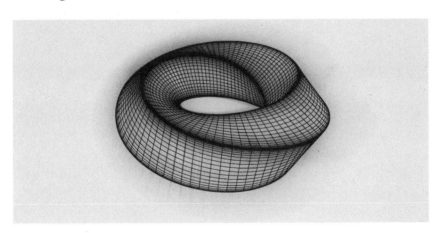

CHAPTER 16

The Art of Branding Events

When people use your brand name as a verb that is remarkable.

—Meg Whitman

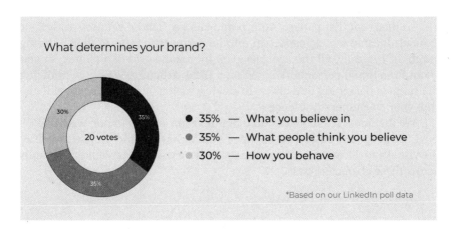

What determines your brand?

20 votes

- 35% — What you believe in
- 35% — What people think you believe
- 30% — How you behave

*Based on our LinkedIn poll data

The 12 Brand Archetypes are from psychologist Carl Jung and represent the collective unconsciousness of all people. These sound like the "Outlaw, Explorer, Ruler, Lover, and so on." Agency work tends to follow these brand profiles rigidly as if it were the gospel. What Julia does at HYPC-CCYCL is help our clients break the mold and thus "break out of their silo" by mashing up contrarian brand features.

Agencies follow a linear progression around these brand voice wheels that jives well with Jungian psychology. The downside is you lose the ability to build an utterly disruptive gestalt because it simply enforces your audience's prevailing, predicted pattern.

Disruptive	Fun Loving	Inspirational
Rebellious	Playful	Daring
Combative	Optimistic	Provocative
Mystical	Friendly	Sassy
Informed	Authentic	Knowlegeable
Reassuring	Caring	Assured
Candid	Warm	Guiding
Brave	Paradoxical	Exciting
Sensual	Commanding	Fearless
Empathetic	Refined	Tough coach

To interrupt that pattern, your brand can be "candid yet provocative" or "knowledgeable yet aggressive" in infinite permutations (as in the preceding graphic). Typically, all the agencies pick four standardized qualities, so you choose the brand personality based on a fixed structure. We are hybridizing the Jungian constructs and others to create a fusion or synthesis that will disrupt your consumer experience.

We include a brand voice and a brand vision section in our WRKSHP™. First, we get you to build a swipe file of brands you like and precisely analyze the visual appeal, and then mark the spot where you believe your brand lands across these characteristics:

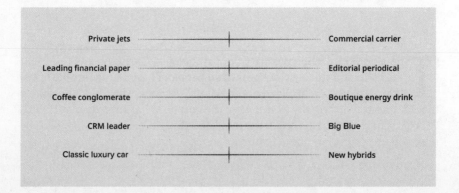

Private jets	Commercial carrier
Leading financial paper	Editorial periodical
Coffee conglomerate	Boutique energy drink
CRM leader	Big Blue
Classic luxury car	New hybrids

"You've got three seconds to impress me, three seconds to connect with me, and make me fall in love."

—*Kevin Roberts,* Lovemarks

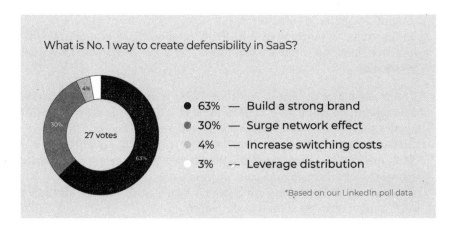

You need to create a brand that communicates your *why*. That communication must happen within 15 seconds before a viewer bounces from your marketing assets. Don't fall into the common trap of copying your competitors. Software as a service (SaaS) is an industry where every category has an identical H1, H2, and H3. It's ludicrous that they immediately copy each other's brand colors, style guides, and value prop within days of making the first move. It's like watching a big school of fish turn in the ocean when another larger fish swims past.

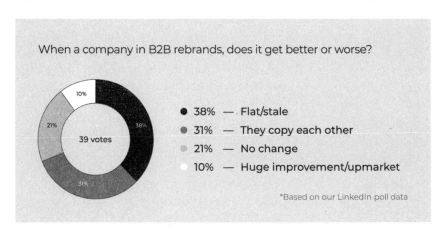

When Julia worked in the revenue intelligence category, she'd wake up to someone announcing a product release or funding round. By the next day, the competitors had also raised and updated their products and branding identically. With events, we faced this too. People try to copy our brand, colors, and concepts, but they're weak marketers because they don't realize the first rule of marketing is to "do the opposite." Furthermore, we had a first-mover advantage of being everywhere overnight and debranded in black and white in stark contrast to a sea of "Blue Calibri." Our journey in SaaS may have only been one year, but many websites and ads we now see riff on the black and white motif design trend Julia started.

To illustrate the outcome of WRKSHP™ and our hard-hitting copywriting approach, here is a summary that reflects how we position Go-to-Market (GTM) Games:

Throw down with the best in real-time. These games reveal how top executives adapt and learn. We put them through a battery of real-world GTM challenges and drills. Wherever you are weak, you will become strong.
Cross-train your GTM skills. What's the best way to make a seller shut up? Make them build a marketing plan. What's the best way to make a marketer humble? Make them do sales calls. Oil and water will mix and float in this revolutionary Battle Royale. No peace on Earth. Scars, stories, and better GTM leaders who "get it." You be the judge!

CHAPTER 17

Build the Buzz Vortex; Become Your Industry Focal Point

Half the money I spend on advertising is wasted; the trouble is I don't know which half.

— John Wanamaker (1838–1922)

Contrarian views stand out, being an iconoclast in a sea of conformity. What do you believe in profoundly that slaughters sacred cows in your industry? What's your "why?" Do you think sales development reps (SDRs) will disappear, replaced by demand gen (peak inbound is already ubiquitous), automation, and artificial intelligence (coming soon)? One of Justin's favorite predictions.

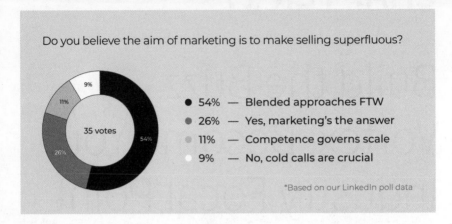

Do you believe the aim of marketing is to make selling superfluous?

35 votes

- 54% — Blended approaches FTW
- 26% — Yes, marketing's the answer
- 11% — Competence governs scale
- 9% — No, cold calls are crucial

*Based on our LinkedIn poll data

We chose to disrupt business-to-business (B2B), although Julia controversially suggested that "marketing and sales" operate like one function (with some caveats; see elsewhere in the book for a deeper explanation). Polarity and innovation magnetically attract and, when done in parallel, become a content marketing supernova or black hole, depending on how you look at it.

Julia invented go-to-market (GTM) cross-training to challenge a siloed industry and take the event format deeper than anyone else had ever done before. While polarization and innovation will pull conversations toward you, it all depends on what you desire your brand voice to be. Controversial content presents a brand risk but often an immediate payoff upside. Is immediacy worth the scorched earth? "All publicity is good publicity" for an entrepreneur, but brands must consider the downstream impacts of everything they do. While you should continuously operate with ethics and integrity, the greater danger is being forgettable. If you pit 31 flavors against vanilla, you better make that the best vanilla bean gelato you've ever tasted in your life.

The legendary Jack Canfield of *Chicken Soup for the Soul* series acclaim once shared with Justin at a charity fundraising dinner when he asked him the secret to pack events something to the effect of, "The whole industry is busy spending trillions building bigger, better, faster nets. Instead, why not build a garden that attracts butterflies." To do this effectively, you must move from a push to a pull mentality and master elements of growth hacking.

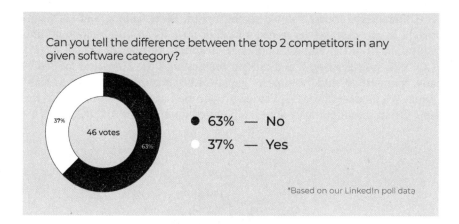

Can you tell the difference between the top 2 competitors in any given software category?

46 votes

37%

63%

● 63% — No

○ 37% — Yes

*Based on our LinkedIn poll data

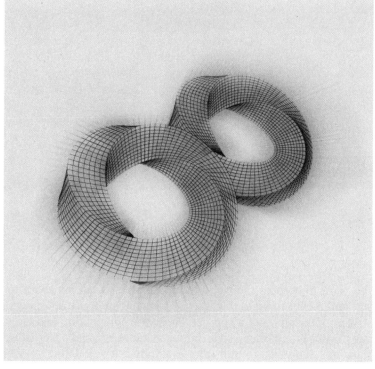

HYPCCCYCL

Differentiate yourself down to the brand, fonts, colors, and GTM approach. In our case, we leveraged a Mobius strip as an infinite loop pulling inspiration from the endless nonlinear customer journey as we see it. HYPCCCYCL satirizes Gen-Z and analyst memes, and the 3Cs stand for "company, competition, and customers." Japanese organizational theorist Kenichi Ohmae is a pioneer of the GTM strategy definition we reference to explain the triple C that serendipitously appears in our company name "HYPCCCYCL."

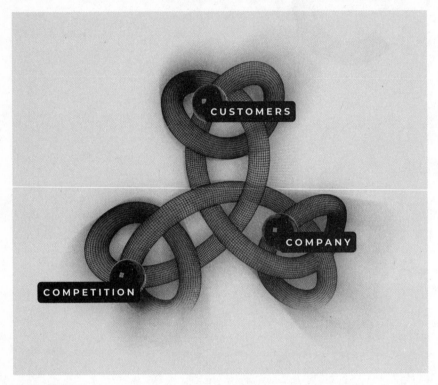

HYPCCCYCL

You want to become the No. 1 thing everyone is talking about in your industry and niche. To build this level of buzz, create a garden of disruptive ideas. Be an innovator, not a copycat. Study the competition and zig where they zag in your brand colors, style, outreach approach, and advertising.

Mash-ups allow you to pull from everyone but still define your brand. Van Gogh said it best, "Good artists borrow; great artists steal." Make your event concept so unusual by mashing up unique ideas that it sparks irresistible curiosity. Could you fuse classic and modern themes? What about functions of business that traditionally live in a silo and don't speak to each other? What about incorporating two or even three random verticals that typically don't mix? You're now a B2B cocktail mixologist, a thematic business sommelier.

The peanut gallery of Event Marketing before we appeared on the scene sounded something like this:

There are two types of events: "built," which means it features a celebrity, or homegrown. A built *event means you feature famous speakers who pull the audience for you. For example, get Beyoncé to headline your venue. It will be pre-packed as a foregone conclusion, and sponsors are already lining up to support her. If you book a local singer/songwriter, you will likely have to ask 3,000–10,000 people just to get 300 to show up by pouring significant funds into advertising and marketing.*

The biggest mistake business people make is assuming mere mortals will pull. In a digital context, if Naval Ravikant or Elon Musk graces your Clubhouse room or podcast, the entire business world beats down a path to your door.

Whatever your expertise is, if you can't afford to pay a celebrity for a "built" experience, you will have to invest serious resources into promoting and packing your event. That takes mostly elbow grease and deft use of social media; we'll get into that in the next chapter.

Of course, there are corner cases like a CEO who is unknown but has a disruptive idea. Another possibility is a famous software as a service (SaaS) company with a respected chief executive officer (CXO) who is obscure compared to Seth Godin but in narrow circles is seen as "credible" for delivering next-level insight as a true expert. There's an art to creating a mix of these archetypes: super famous/celebrities, legit execs, and innovative thinkers.

Here's the New Model That Is "Customer-Led"

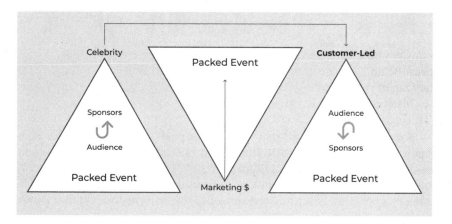

In under one year, we featured the top 100+ thought leaders in the B2B industry in our events. Partly a function of Julia's seven years of work in Salesforce ecosystem companies fostering relationships at the C-level, and Justin's relentless networking to build connections as a best-selling author and thought leader on "technology-driven sales." Our partnership contained a robust network with nodes that could jump into the games early and recommend the experience to other people.

Because we leveraged network adjacencies powerfully, we grew to over 50,000 GTMers in the community. We provided a stage (or platform) for the talent that had intrinsic value to them. Many thought leaders are releasing books, and giving them a new distribution channel and space to freely promote in your community is irresistible. You can also do a giveaway of their latest book with the event as a co-promotion. We're running a promotion with Reprise right now where one lucky demo participant will win a pair of high-end AirPods Max.

Make sure you partner with colleagues and collaborators to create a synergy where the whole is greater than the sum of its parts: $1 + 1 = 11$. When scheduling your special guests, look for a blend of prominent social media followings (too bad Klout scores are gone) and credible insights. It's okay to feature someone with a small following who is a true innovator and will blow your audience away with strategic advice. A core component of our cross-training model is to feature real-world practitioners of each method. A researcher who wrote a book on sales can give one kind of webinar versus a VP of Sales who has carried a bag and sold in the trenches for 20 years versus Mike Bosworth, the Godfather of "Solution Selling."

Mary Shea, PhD	Doug Landis	Oren Klaff	Sydney Sloan	Mike Bosworth	Seth Marrs
Global Innovation Evangelist at Outreach	Growth Partner at Emergence Capital	Managing Director at Intersection Capital	CMO at SalesLoft	Sales Philosopher at Mike Bosworth Leadership	Research Director at Forrester

An excellent analog for this "pull versus push" virtual promotions concept is the success of Expo 2020 Dubai with 188 country pavilions or the Venice Biennale, which includes 213 artists from 58 countries taking over Venice, Italy. The first example is a patch of sand in the middle of a caustic desert, albeit by a beautiful beach and endless source of pearls historically. But Dubai did something so remarkable and unique with technology and innovation that 20 million people visited the expo. Biennale runs from May to November in the floating Italian city. Each year it draws half a million visitors to rediscover the global art world installed in the picturesque palazzos, gardens, and canals.

Consistency, Perceived Exclusivity, Scarcity

Ask yourself, when should you hold your event? Are there any other events conflicting with that date? Is there a geographic location to get to, like Dubai, which also serves as a "moat" or barrier to entry? Making it scarce makes it valuable, just like Chateau Lafite, limited edition Nikes, Panerai watches, red diamonds, or Koons. But don't make everyone schlepp to Fyre Festival.

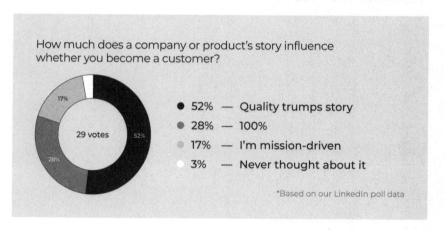

How much does a company or product's story influence whether you become a customer?

29 votes

- 52% — Quality trumps story
- 28% — 100%
- 17% — I'm mission-driven
- 3% — Never thought about it

*Based on our LinkedIn poll data

Consistency—Maintain a quality bar and high standards.

Perceived exclusivity—Think about providing membership to a community as part of the events or an exclusive mailing list. Give to get.

Scarcity—It's a paradox because if something is available, how can it be exclusive? Many top restaurants, concert venues, and sporting box seats are out of reach for mere mortals. You can create barriers to entry by getting "creative" with price, perceived scarcity, and recognition (badges); check out Credly.

Think about these three factors as you build out your events to help them become a resounding success. Many drivers and economies of exchange, in-kind trades, and co-promotions spur amplification.

But the most significant learning is you have to be patient. Rome wasn't built in a day, even though Dubai can seem like it was. The adage, "if you build it, they will come," is a falsehood in a world gone virtual. It will work if you do everything right, then promote it yourself (or with a small ragtag team). But it takes a spark to catch fire, and no one can make a virtual event go viral faster than your customers spreading the gospel. It adds a greater degree of credibility than promoting it oneself. We overestimate what we can accomplish in 90 days but underestimate what we can build in a year. We certainly did, and Marc Benioff inspired this truism as he's the ultimate example.

CHAPTER 18

Dark Social Community Building: Hub-and-Spoke Formula for Public Relations

I don't want to belong to any club that would accept me as one of its members.

— Groucho Marx

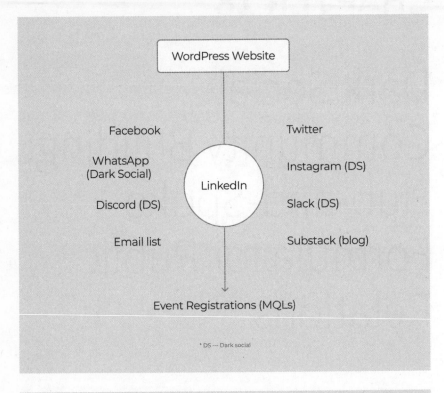

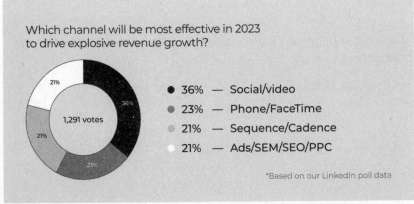

Since the early 2020s, building your community has taken a hub-and-spoke strategy, just like a bicycle wheel. With LinkedIn hitting the 830 million-member milestone and now part of Microsoft, it's the ultimate hub to utilize as the focal point of your online interactive events. However, reach within the platform is limited unless you're willing to "pay for play." You can hit a button for paid advertising to amplify just about anything you do or share on LinkedIn. As an exception, there is a solid, free "LinkedIn Events" feature where you can tag the speakers and drop invites on attendees' calendars.

Leverage this powerful free LinkedIn (LI) feature, as it syncs with Google Calendar and Outlook for convenience. You may be shocked to see the diagram in our "hub-and-spoke" event amplification model and that your website isn't the hub. Why? Network effects and Metcalfe's Law: the value of your network is exponential based on the number of users. Envision an interactive web portal hooked to 61,000 people who follow and comment on what we share versus a website.

Beyond social media prowess, we recommend that you cultivate a juggernaut of vocal brand ambassadors or volunteers to help you amplify your invitations to each event. If you're in a company with a bigger team, encourage your colleagues to help you boost your event but never force them. Virality and word of mouth hinge on it being "their idea." It's wise to build a social media management (SMM) doc with your public relations (PR) and marketing strategy for promoting each event you host down to each tactical step. You should also build a media kit to send to all participants: provide sample LinkedIn shares, tweets, and hashtags along with provocative images to make it a no-brainer to share the event.

Make sure you standardize around hashtags like #GTMG and match up with hashtags that already have a high following on LinkedIn, Twitter, and Instagram. We recommend a blend of highly followed and niche hashtags to feed the hungry algorithms. The riches are in the niches, so you'll get drowned out if you go too wide. If you go too narrow, you might never maximize your visibility. At this writing, #Engineering has 1.9 million followers on LinkedIn, whereas #RevOps has 1,377. Case in point.

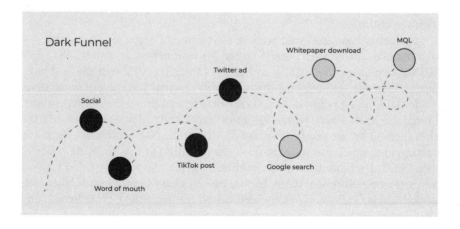

Dark Social and the "Dark Funnel" are relatively new phenomena you need to consider and leverage. It's "dark" because these promotional communities lack attribution or trackability for marketers. You can't measure various touch points along your customer journey or (the inbound funnel) like word of mouth or a private message that tips someone to go to your site, download a whitepaper, and attend your event. Building out a community in Slack, Discord, WhatsApp, and a Substack blog are examples of dark social. You can drop your live event links into these gardens and bloom a rainforest of support.

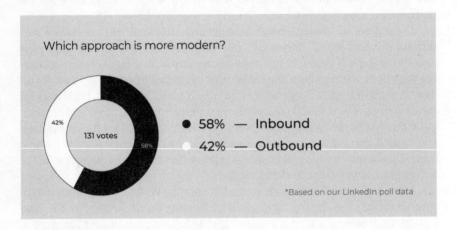

The best way to measure the Dark Funnel is to simply create a new field in your custom relationship management (CRM) called "sourced." Ask customers how they heard about your brand when they complete a standard funnel action. Then take down that lead source to understand where your traffic is coming from when you pull a report later to analyze it over time to find trends to optimize.

No matter how good your website is, you need a bespoke community. Not all audiences prefer Slack. Some prefer Discord; others an email LISTSERV like Modern Sales Pros (MSP), and others LinkedIn. Although the best websites for an event get built on a custom WordPress that you can put up relatively affordable and quickly, it doesn't ensure reach, amplification, or registrants. Even if you SEO (search engine optimization) it and run pay-per-click ads, the ultra-high customer acquisition cost (CAC) can be cost-prohibitive for many startups and small and midsize businesses (SMBs) at this time. Be ready to spend $5,000 per month as a bare minimum to play. Suppose you don't have a designer or development team. In that case, it's easy to build on Mighty Networks, Circle, Patreon (creator-celeb micro-communities), or Substack and Medium (premium blogs), or simply host your event on a wide array of free platforms like Eventbrite.

How do you dominate promotion in dark social communities? Carve out 30 minutes each day to do the work, connect 1:1, and extoll the virtues of what you're doing. It's so simple it's hard. Sorry, no magic bullets here.

Justin has a story about a mobile marketing event he threw on a rooftop in New York City that 700+ attended. People came up the stairs and elevators like rats out of a sinking ship. The head of the mobile marketing consortium asked him, "How did you do it?" He explained that he "cold called 700 people." "Oh, you just did the work," the wise executive replied with a wry smile. There's a cumulative power to chipping away each day building your community. Yeoman's work: "chop wood, carry water." One single tweet or LinkedIn post won't do it, nor can one even hope to invite 1,000 people in a single day anymore.

The social networks will throttle you, even put you in LinkedIn jail, and your Gmail will fail over around 150 sends per day. But think about 30 minutes per day for 30 days to semi-automate 50 personalized emails or make 30 LinkedIn touches (connects, InMails). You can drop into other communities to network with like-minded individuals. Try to interact with 30 strangers daily, which we call the Rule of 900. The cumulative impact of being disciplined here month over month is downright astonishing. Nine hundred new interactions per month should be enough outbound volume (while maintaining quality) to pack attendance if you also call in a few favors.

But you want to be thinking, where are the top two or three platforms my attendees and sponsors hang out on and appear there disproportionly. Spokes around the hub of your LinkedIn presence could include Twitter to broadcast updates, Instagram to share unusual multimedia (photos, short video clips, GIFs), and YouTube (longer-form content) that you can rebroadcast back into LinkedIn. Keep in mind that YouTube is the No. 2 search engine on earth, as Google owns it. So, leverage as many 90-second video clips as you can create so your YouTube channel becomes a robust garden for butterflies. There's that analogy again!

Getting the media to write about you is not easy. Technology journalism typically hinges solely on funding round coverage, but if you innovate a new model, everyone cannot help but talk about you. Doing something curve-jumping is press-worthy. What can your event do that drives value and is a historic first?

- Highlight customer use cases, success stories, challenges, and pain alleviation.

- Celebrate innovative technology breakthroughs that no one is talking about.

- Put the customer at the heart of the conversation, a perspective seldom heard.

- Mash up multiple styles of online events that aren't traditionally blended.

- When you make history, are the first-ever and hands down the most innovative, journalists *must* react and cover you.

B2B Vandalism | No Calibri

It's worth digging into a small discussion here on branding. HYPCC-CYCL is also a go-to-market (GTM) agency, dubbed Nimchinski/Michael at this writing. Our tagline is "No suits, No blue, No Calibri" as we do experiments into "Business-to-Business (B2B) Disruption." If the industry is blue, go magenta. If everyone uses safe fonts, do something bold and angular with serifs. Seth Godin's *Purple Cow* is a huge inspiration for creating visual ideation that genuinely stands out from the herd. That's why we "debranded" to solely black and white minimalistic and contrastive in an industry saturated with color for the first year. Almost every competitor and dozens of B2B vendors copied.

Your brand is not just your logo and the name. Your brand becomes an amalgam of what you curate and share. We have spent unlimited hours curating, synthesizing, and pulling insight out of the global GTM arena to make our feeds compelling. Hence, the singular data we extracted from the LinkedIn snap polls featured throughout the book. Julia is a self-subscribed "design freak" in this area, so we throw WRKSHPS™ to help startups, scale-ups, and established enterprises nail rebrand transformations.

There are nearly unlimited books and resources on building effective content strategy (hat tip to Ann Handley), but Julia's simple rule is: does your campaign content contain "an insight"? Consider leading analysts' viewpoints so that you can become an authority in your space by defending your positions with hard data. Don't be just another talking head spewing hot air. Will you be an editorial column or a scientifically backed journal? Maybe there's a happy medium. Justin's approach to content is to push the bleeding edge of provocation with metaphors galore. He's the only sales consultant ever to 100% open source his methods. Pick a style and stick to it.

When we launched HYPCCCYCL, we immediately saw a tie-in to event monetization, agency work, and consulting companies with our GTM agency to help the world's leading brands build and scale disruptive, bespoke events. (Ask about our unique GTM WRKSHP™ that will help you identify, clarify, refine, and scale your GTM strategy, including events.) Possible avenues to monetize events include sponsorship, influencer marketing, and native posts. The list is nearly endless. Fodder for another book, and we do apologize as that's proprietary for clients.

We use a bespoke Venn-diagram–driven process to unite sales and marketing as a branding exercise to disrupt your brand and thus your industry that is worth sharing here.

CHAPTER 19

WRKSHP™ Framework: Define the Big Problem That You Solve

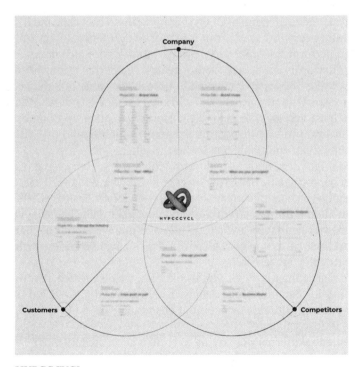

HYPCCCYCL

As a go-to-market (GTM) agency, companies come to us seeking an Event Reinvention™ (ER), and we do it through strategic analysis. Essentially, they want us to consult them on disrupting their brand and "reinventing their virtual events."

Our proprietary WRKSHP™ pulls the *CCC* from HYP**CCC**YCL into a deep-dive exercise to disrupt your industry as a challenger brand. The *C*s stand for *Customers*, *Company*, and *Competition*, assessing your GTM strategy through the prism of these three lenses as you move clockwise around the Venn (see preceding graphic). We aim to unite your genuine customer need with your company's solution to make you stand out inexorably from the competition. We help you win any market by thoroughly disrupting it. At the core:

Instead of starting with your product or solution and building your whole brand and GTM around that (the old way), we are reverse-engineering the process into customer-centric insights.

We are trying to understand what prevalent trends resonate with your customers the most. Forget about your solution or what you're selling. Instead, think about the niche that you're playing in. You can hire a user experience (UX) designer/analyst or try to fill those shoes yourself. You'll need to think objectively about what's happening in your industry and what most resonates with your customers. Example: CEOs secretly want to cold call, and it's a sport for them. But you won't read about it in any analyst journal. You will figure it out if you perform the "discovery" by talking with your customers.

Overcoming "discovery resistance" is the greatest secret that our favorite sales philosopher Mike Bosworth uncovered to unlock the value of Solution Selling. The main issue with new sellers and marketers is they do not take the time to build the trust necessary to get their customers to open up to them. They dive straight into invasive lines of questioning, which freak out prospects who haven't built an emotional bond with the seller.

Your solution might have nothing to do with "cold calling," but even if it's revenue intelligence, you can tie back your answer to analyzing cold-call data. Out of all the insights you generate in the workshop, you must consider where your solution can align with industry trends and customer data. The goal is to understand whether your software can tie into any uncovered trends that correspond to customer pains you can solve. If it doesn't, just be honest with yourself and go on with your research.

In the classic marketing playbook, you think, "Oh, we discovered a problem. We are solving it." No one thinks deeply in this day and age, "What is *actually* troubling your customers or potential customers" vis-a-vis "What's happening in the industry today?"

Sales engagement platforms were trying to build a new category in 2011–2015 but reached the cusp of peak adoption in 2020. In 2011, they started with a problem, and they began to market and hammer away at it even before the customers were ready to adopt a solution. Perhaps they could have found a trend or problem that was very down-to-earth, not obvious, but *real* for their ideal customer profile (ICP). They could have generated 10 similar issues or pains to gauge if their solution would naturally gravitate to one and honed in on it as their positioning.

While we could expand WRKSHP™ into an entire reference work on its own, here are some themes and principles to extract to get you thinking about "brand disruption."

- How can you disrupt yourself to disrupt the industry? Easier said than done.
- What big problem is plaguing your industry? What is your selling point? We help our clients conduct objective, high-quality discovery to understand what their target audience *really* cares about. We challenge them to widen the aperture in their GTM analysis to put their customers first vs. relying on their rusty product pitch deck.
- Mike Bosworth's writings are an excellent resource for a "Discovery 3.0" framework he calls "Intelligent Discovery." Dig deeper here!
- You can hire a user interface/user experience (UI/UX) designer (or us) to make an unbiased, objective discovery of your industry. Definitely check out the superb book *The Mom Test* by Rob Fitzpatrick.
- While you can read analyst research, based on our brainstorming sessions, we collectively pinpoint the biggest objective problems in your industry to focus on your brand/event transformation.
- You now have to think about who your ideal ICP is *actually* and what their biggest pains are.
- In the first exercise, we looked at industry problems, not individual ones. So one is macro, and the other is micro. We are linking your product to the ICPs and trends. Ask, "How can we refine our trend analysis to customers with a universal pain now, and can we solve it?"
- You need to find your "*why.*" Like Simon Sinek says, "People don't buy what you do; they buy *why* you do it. And what you do simply proves what you believe."
- Now discover your brand voice. Unlike every marketing agency with 12 strict brand voice models we find limiting, we've unbundled all possible variations into spectrums so you can be "edgy and inspired" or "disruptive and warm." You don't have to fall into the mold strictly.
- We then touch on the brand vision and visuals—another series of sliders, from Big Coffee to Energy Drinks. (See the illustration in the Branding chapter.)

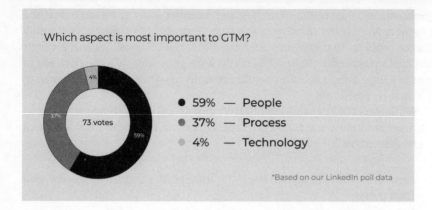

Which aspect is most important to GTM?

73 votes

- 59% — People
- 37% — Process
- 4% — Technology

*Based on our LinkedIn poll data

- What are your principles? Usually, people talk about "mission, vision, values, and so on." Principles build brands. Tenets govern behavior and set the tone for your "culture," which radiates into everything you do across your GTM: people, process, and technology.

PRINCIPLES

He who lives by the crystal ball will eat shattered glass.
— Ray Dalio

- If we're breathing — we're learning. Therefore learning is infinite.
- Learning is in the doing.
- Cross-functional cross-training is not just for sports.
- High Intensity Interval Training (HIIT) applies to e-learning.
- Every executive generalist started as a specialist.
- Everything in life is a spiral. It's your choice if you're going up or down.
- To disrupt the industry you must disrupt yourself.

Tenets

HYPCCCYCL is designed as a meritocracy where GTM Leaders from all walks of life compete and exchange innovative ideas to cross-train hard skills.

Our motives are egalitarian and purely B2B focused.

We elevate all stakeholders in the revenue supply chain to carry the industry forward with explosive and electric GTM experiences.

Our views are our own and do not represent the views of any company sponsor, participant, or coach.

We operate by one criterion: common sense.

Competitive analysis is paramount in assessing markets and where you seek to dominate. You need to do more than just understand your position in a nouveau grid. We've all seen umpteen four-box graphs, grids, quadrants, and matrices. These are fun exercises for MBAs. Per Al Ries, the most powerful thing you can do is to create a category and lead that category. Out-innovating the competitors has more to do with originality and disruption than a set of features to flank them.

More Bosworth, paraphrasing: When a vendor loses a request for proposal (RFP), Procurement tells them, "You were our favorite, but the competitor had these features we liked." Then Product Marketing returns to the product team and demands the missing features. The result is the creation of Franken-stacks with 73 features because they mistakenly believe the bells and whistles lost the deal when the seller simply got "out-sold." How did it happen? They lacked the appropriate levels of discovery to build sufficient rapport to get the customer to open up to them. They didn't take the time to co-create a compelling, achievable business case with the chief financial officer (CFO) and get to know the C-level executives. But the competitor did! Product Marketing is training the new sellers on product knowledge to be consultative, but what is needed is "intelligent discovery" not more "speeds and feeds."

In the last phase of WRKSHP™, we even explore your business model, including new monetization channels. What are the blades on your razor you can either add or sharpen? Have you looked into broader ecosystems and channel partners and understood the nuances of your potential revenue streams? Are you building out pricing models where the unit economics make sense?

We were recently surprised to view a consultant's proposal where the revenue operations (RevOps) work outlay was 100+ hours, inadvertently devaluing them to $10/hr. Are you adding value or fully commoditizing yourself? Have you leveraged software to AB test software as a service (SaaS) subscription tiers? What about various GTM motions like product-led growth (PLG), sales-led growth (SLG), and customer-led growth (CLG)? We map these out together.

(DM us if you need our help customizing the principles and techniques in this book.)

CHAPTER 20

Marketing in a Sales Way/Selling in a Marketing Way

As marketing converges with customer service and sales, marketing today is more about helping and less about hyping.

— Joel Book

Who handles pressure better?

75 votes

11%

89%

● 89% — Sellers
○ 11% — Marketers

*Based on our LinkedIn poll data

The $64-million question is: how do you go from marketing qualified lead (MQL) to sales qualified lead (SQL) effectively? But we believe it's a trick question discussed in the first chapter. If you apply our work accurately, you'll eliminate the MQL, switching to an opportunity model or North Star key performance indicator (KPI) of "revenue." On a pure event level, the new metric could even be "event registrations to opportunities." Converting audiences to ultimately pay for software after an event is always an erratic puzzle. Usually, marketing teams see 1 in 1,000 people convert to paying customers.

From the marketing perspective, this problem stems from the saturation of crappy ads with ultra-low click-through rates (CTR). Clicks are dismal, descending toward .25% on banner ads. Your analytics dashboard is overflowing with fraud, spam, and bots, whether you'll admit it or not. In reality, most of what's perusing your content, site, apps, and ads is not even human!

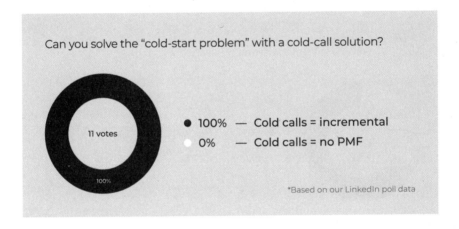

Can you solve the "cold-start problem" with a cold-call solution?

11 votes

100%

● 100% — Cold calls = incremental

○ 0% — Cold calls = no PMF

*Based on our LinkedIn poll data

From the lens of sales, there's a heavy debate that the role of sales development rep (SDR) should be sunsetted. Bad actors blast automated sequences from a cannon. SDR teams are wantonly sending tens of thousands of messages per week with reckless abandon. SDRs often lack training and come across to prospects as displaying low buyer acumen. Using the same cliché personalization templates to manipulate prospects to click is no different than SPAM. SDRs are expensive to train and churn out at an average of every 14 months per The Bridge Group. If they're good at their job, they seek promotion to account executive (AE) rapidly because the compensation is better.

Modern buyers are assaulted by SDRs when they download anything on the internet or enter a marketing funnel. The software keeps getting architected to contact buyers faster and studies bolster "speed-to-lead" as a best practice. Although we do not deny compressed timeliness can be effective, you risk burning out your best prospects unless you do it elegantly. The other big problem is the KPIs we incentivize SDRs on, like "meetings booked," are not a leading indicator of new business when SDRs aren't allowed to qualify or perform proper discovery. The quality of an opportunity, or ultimately revenue creation, is what we're seeking as a byproduct of solid go-to-market (GTM) motions like an event. Since the commission is only about volume, activity, and pre-funnel KPIs, we incentivize the wrong behaviors and get a dog-eat-dog, *Lord of the Flies* culture.

The predominant flow post-event breaks down in the existing sales and marketing model. Why? We have the reps least familiar with how the product drives value for customers, following up aggressively to qualify and steal time. Did they even participate in the event? In contrast, imagine if customers who attended your events talked to other existing or prospective customers about why the content and experience were so valuable to them? One step away from this is a savvy product rep being present to help brainstorm and solve painful problems consultatively right from the first call.

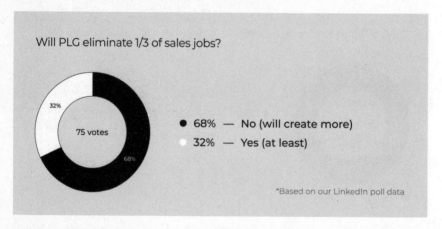

Will PLG eliminate 1/3 of sales jobs?

32%

75 votes

68%

● 68% — No (will create more)
○ 32% — Yes (at least)

*Based on our LinkedIn poll data

One of the significant reasons product-led growth (PLG) even exists is how badly SDRs messed it up for the others. A chain is only as strong as its weakest link—paraphrasing VC Doug Landis of Emergence Capital on one element that may explain the explosion of PLG toward 2025.

Sales need to learn to be process-oriented, data-driven, and more precise in tailoring from marketing. Both need to learn to be customer-centric. Marketing needs to know how to be more customer-centric by talking with customers, but here's a more extensive list. As the adage goes: nothing happens until somebody sells something.

What can Marketing learn from Sales (x-function/x-train)
- Intelligent discovery
- Tying your activity to revenue generated
- Negotiation
- Reading customers

- Presentation
- AB testing in real time by handling objections and rejections
- Qualification

What can Sales learn from Marketing (x-function/x-train)

- Defining more precise ideal customer profiles (ICPs)
- Better organization and time management
- Active listening skills and research
- How to build a strong brand
- Positioning to the C-level executives
- Product marketing and design thinking
- Ad targeting to influence sales targeting (e.g., Metadata's audience-building drill)

In the next chapter, we will look at myriad ways to do this outreach right with "humans in the loop" for customer-centric outbound selling and innovative event follow-up strategy and tactics. But first, let's hear from a GTM legend.

On Intelligent Discovery to Align Sales and Marketing

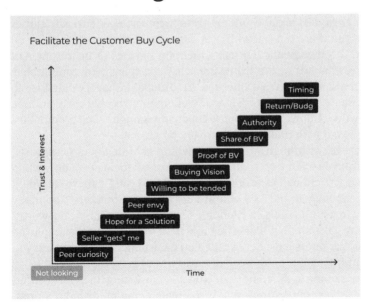

Mike Bosworth Leadership 2017

According to Mike Bosworth, the vast majority of salespeople have not figured out how to overcome the natural discovery resistance most buyers have toward salespeople. We interviewed the sage creator of Solution Selling and Story Seekers on why some sellers he trained struggled to implement "Solution Selling" and what causes the rift between sales and marketing. The "secret sauce" of Solution Selling was intelligent discovery questions authored by situational experts, but questions like these cannot be asked before the buyer is ready to answer them.

"Discovery resistance is the biggest problem with solution selling. Sellers must emotionally connect to build trust. The top 20% will keep their discovery questions in their pocket until they have emotionally connected and built some trust. The bottom 80% do not know how to connect intuitively and started asking their discovery questions too soon for the comfort level of their buyers. The bottom 80% need to study how to connect emotionally and build trust before they attempt intelligent discovery. The first step in selling is to overcome discovery resistance."

We invite you to read Mike's LinkedIn posts and white papers to figure out how to do that.

Marketers need to strive for customer experience marketing. "Peer curiosity evolves to peer envy." You'd interview five customers on how they use the product, develop "customer hero stories," and circulate that out to the field. Ask: "How does your product *help* your potential buyer make money, save money, achieve goals or solve problems?" Case studies can't be stiff. They need to be conversational. In order to stimulate peer curiosity, you need to make their peer and your customer the hero, and there must be emotion.

We talk a great deal about thinking like a therapist. Peer curiosity stories work, and you can even cold call with peer curiosity. "Tell me what's going on in your world." It's therapeutic. Focusing them on the area of the business or their world that whatever we are selling impacts yet keeping them comfortable.

Intelligent discovery is what's needed. Traditional discovery didn't teach people to eliminate "discovery resistance." Sellers interrogated early and the buyer went "whoa, I don't know you or trust you enough." The bottom 80% are just going to fail with traditional discovery processes.

Mike's new breakthrough in Solution Selling is "Intelligent Discovery," which stems from an axiom: you can "elevate a suspect to prospect only when the buyer trusts you enough to admit their problem to you." Otherwise, you'll sell a lot of technology to the 13% of a pre-chasm target market. "Too many companies are inventing 'solutions' looking for a problem." Classic Bosworth!

While we respect product marketing and it's a tough discipline to master, "most product marketers have never called on a customer." They can tell you all about their product but not how their customer uses their product.

Tactical marketing is different than strategic marketing: too vastly different skill sets. Tactical marketing's role is to create demand for today's products today.

CHAPTER 21

Booking Post-Event Meetings with Strategic Unconventionality

The chief enemy of creativity is 'good' sense.

— Pablo Picasso

If everyone else is zigging, zag. Look out across the messaging templates in business-to-business (B2B) endorsed for cold calls and emails. Notice a pattern? A great deal of it looks the same. When you receive an event follow-up email, it typically comes across as identical from each vendor in the category. In a best-case scenario, you'll get a gated white paper on the event's theme. Perhaps a sales development rep (SDR) will call you with little research (didn't even glance at your LinkedIn profile), treating you as a lead assumptively mistakenly believing just because you attended, you're qualified. Ironically, when Julia worked in revenue intelligence, almost every competitor tried to sell her when she downloaded content on its website.

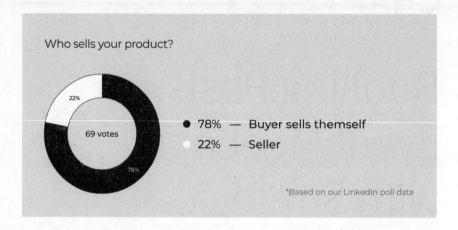

When you connect, a more customer-centric approach is to foster a conversation around the event's themes. Spark up convos with prospective customers, share insights and trends, and give them time to "make it their idea" with the freedom of saying "no" to using your technology versus pitch slapping on LinkedIn or treating them like a warm lead, marketing qualified lead (MQL), or another number. Think of this as Ms. Right Now versus Ms. Right. Customer-centric approaches require better analytics: for example, what actions have they taken after the event: revisited your website, read content, asked about the recordings, and so on

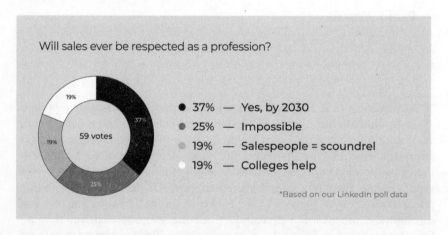

Get creative about sending swag. Maybe send them a jersey of their favorite team's MVP athlete with their last name and the number 23. Donate to a local charity where they sit on the board or do some clever social engineering to find a secret hobby so you can mail them a gift certificate to the

running store. You can always succumb to Japanese whisky or Venmo, but have a sense of humor.

We all see most of this "generic SEO" level content: vanilla. Blasé. Run-of-the-mill—par for the course. Try the same military strategies in a war over and over, and you'll lose. Again and again.

So how can you differentiate yourself and stand out in the follow-up? Using a combination of first principles thinking and tried-and-true pattern interrupts, we've honed over 20,000 hours of calling and sending millions of emails. Throwing hundreds of events, we've learned what cuts through the clutter—and separates the signal from the noise. Welcome to unconventional communication.

If you feel uncomfortable reading these approaches at any point, it's working.

First Principles Thinking

To stand out from a sea of vendors, you need to break complicated problems into essential elements and reassemble them from the ground up. This concept is called "first principles thinking." Elon Musk inspires us all to think more deeply about this practice. He looks at a rocket ship and thinks along simplified lines. The model breaks down. Instead of waiting years to get approval from a government agency to build one, he thinks, "What if I deconstruct it to its simplest elements and start rebuilding these from scratch like steel and beryllium?" Then came electric cars and solar panels.

So how do we break down event outreach to convert attendees into buyers? Furthermore, the complexity of our products and value proposition needs to be distilled down into its purest, most potent form so it will resonate with attendees of our events. Will they understand our value intrinsically and want to eventually enter our funnel to buy of their own volition?

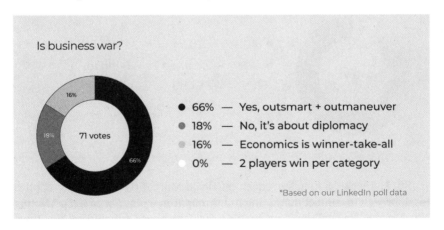

Is business war?

71 votes

● 66% — Yes, outsmart + outmaneuver
● 18% — No, it's about diplomacy
○ 16% — Economics is winner-take-all
○ 0% — 2 players win per category

*Based on our LinkedIn poll data

In its simplest form, sales is akin to warfare, tactically speaking. Like a castle under siege, we're trying to break through to the right person. If sales is war, how do we view our prospecting through that lens? Looking at the most effective strategies, we see metaphors arising from guerilla and asymmetric warfare.

Classically, these methods of waging war are inherently disruptive. Hit-and-run, attacking from different fronts, angles, and through varying methodologies have allowed conquerors throughout history to win. How do we develop disruptive messaging and win the accounts we seek?

But this view is primitive and soon made obselete by a customer-centric approach: collaboration. So we can dispense with warlike metaphors. Through a method hunt analysis akin to a "product hunt," Julia found dozens of sales methods and, get this, dozens of hidden marketing methods. As a prime example, check out Sangram Vajre's superb *MOVE: The 4-Question Go-to-Market Framework*.

Pattern Interrupts

The Purple Cow by marketing guru Seth Godin is a simple application of the neuro-linguistic programming technique we call "'pattern interrupt." Write something so bizarre that most are unlikely to forget. This idea influences every word of our messaging approach, the concepts in branding our event, the sales approach for garnering attendees and, ultimately, customers from your effort.

What's the craziest way you've ever gotten a meeting?

- 46% — Stunt
- 40% — Waited in parking lot
- 7% — Bribe
- 7% — Sent a brick

15 votes

*Based on our LinkedIn poll data

Stu Heinecke, a fantastic coach on Go-to-Market (GTM) Games, applies this approach to contact marketing in his magnum opus *How to Get a Meeting with Anyone*. He explains how he got a 100% response rate and set meetings with "impossible to reach" executives by sending original cartoons on large poster boards via courier.

If everyone is zigging, zag. If all the brands are blue, go red.

Application: Outbound Emails + Cold Calls

Studying the most common email templates in widespread circulation unveils a sea of sameness in templates even gated at hundreds or thousands of dollars. Try even just a simple thought experiment scaling the proposed three-paragraph "personalize, value prop, social proof, personalize, call to action (CTA)" format to the point where everyone leverages the concept. It makes you wonder why anyone thought it was a good idea. Same with the popular phone scripts du jour.

The follow-up sequence techniques we recommend prove effective because short-form messaging is processed in 3 seconds, whereas three-paragraph emails take 11 seconds. (See Appendix II.) It's just armchair neuroscience to us. We process images 60,000 times faster visually than in text. As a kicker, it's also out of the ordinary to open a Venn diagram or explainer GIF (use CloudApp or make a Loom video) as a reply bump to the three-sentence sales email that cuts like a hot knife through butter. Anything other than self-worshipping product marketing language would make you double-take.

Shawn Sease puts four blue dot emojis 🔵 🔵 🔵 🔵 in his subject lines and pointed out that Best Buy started using the technique. Did Best Buy catch the wave from Shawn? As Homo sapiens , our complex language skills allow for a wide range of pattern interrupts, so here are some specific and fun examples we use because we've seen them convert empirically.

Examples: Time-Tested Tactics

1. Remove pleasantry—no need to say "hope you're doing well" or "in these uncertain times"—we need a 10-year moratorium on these phrases.
2. Lack of formality—"Hey, Jane," versus "Hi" or "Dear Sir or Madame"—generally speaking, colloquial speech works better.

3. Drop expected formatting—No first name, no CTA, no formatting, no capitalization (Aaron Ross classic!), no salutation, no sign-off.

4. Grammar funk—Don't even write in complete sentences. Make it look choppy like business poetry—humanize and desterilize your language.

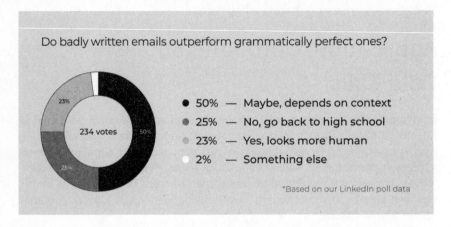

Do badly written emails outperform grammatically perfect ones?

234 votes

- 50% — Maybe, depends on context
- 25% — No, go back to high school
- 23% — Yes, looks more human
- 2% — Something else

*Based on our LinkedIn poll data

5. Just a picture with "thoughts?"—also a pattern interrupt because it's a one-word reply email. (Venn diagrams with competitors on the outside, you in the middle work great.)

6. Hyperbole—"Would it be a crime against humanity if I asked you to spend 7 minutes with me?" Voss-like negative labeling coupled with the fact you're asking for 7 instead of 15 minutes. Justin asked for 13 minutes, and the prospect sarcastically responded, "I'll give you 12!"

7. Humor—"Before I start checking milk cartons, think we could hop on a Zoom?" Take a risk to be funny; it converts. You can never make everyone happy, but you should also avoid self-limiting beliefs.

8. GIFs—Embedding a GIF into an email in a world where everyone else is hyperlinking. SpongeBob converts.

9. Facetime drop—Can you imagine jumping in via this most personal and typically stranger-free medium?

10. Hyper-personalization—This is the kind where you synthesize multiple insights combining both deep industry insight and references customized for the individual. Examples: quoting and timestamping a value nugget from a recent podcast they were on, their quote from an article, and tying it together with relevancy. Avoid hacky and forced personalization like, "I noticed you went to BU. Go Terriers! BTW you want to buy something?"

A picture is worth a thousand words. Sending a Venn is advisable, even if it's a back of a napkin sketch (they convert!), or sit down with your marketing team to build a polished version. Precisely why you should send one: it's disruptive. We usually send them as the third part of our sequences, so they get past the spam filters and keep them under 200 kilobytes. The core idea is to show your product as an all-in-one solution relative to various companies offering single, disparate features.

Your company is the definitive solution for your target's problems. Here's how to make a super-strong Venn diagram, the quintessential instrument of "visual prospecting":

1. Open Google Sheets > Insert > Drawing.

2. In the Drawing sandbox, click the Shapes button and add 3–6 circles in a concentric pattern. You can adjust the circle transparency by clicking "Custom" on the color picker.

3. Place a title next to each circle representing a feature that your solution offers—for example, Business Analytics, Legacy, Point Solution. And then place the logos of companies providing just that feature/category in your space.

4. Use custom Google Image searches to find HD PNG company logos to place in those feature circles. Include the word "png" in your search and click "Tools," and then select "Large" to get a hi-res logo. Click on Image > Tools > Color > Transparent to find a version with an empty background to make it easy to superimpose. You can also pull quick templates from Lucid and overlay the logos (no need to draw the circles).

Here's the first Venn Justin ever created in all its glory:

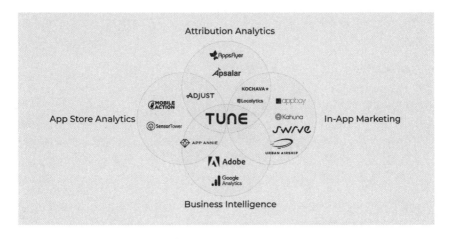

Meetings, Meetings, Meetings

On the first attempt, Justin set a meeting with the chief digital officer (CDO) of a major quick service restaurant (QSR) chain. On the first send, the VP of Mobile at a Fortune 100 called back his cell phone number in his email signature and demanded, "Pitch me!" Unconventional messaging works if you work it. Implement this Venntastic pattern interrupt, and your metrics will improve drastically for event follow-ups.

CHAPTER 22

Customer-Centric Outbound (Oops, Sales Time!)

Change before you have to.

— Jack Welch

T here's a gaping chasm between educational content that your audience wants and the selling point or value prop of your product or service.

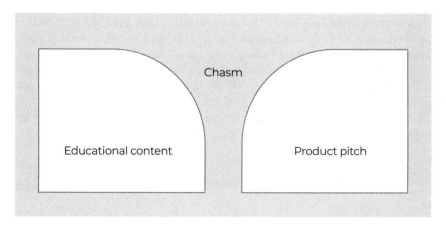

Building a bridge between the positioning of products and the use cases they solve through the lens of the customer is the challenge of a modern go-to-market (GTM) content team that's aligning sales and marketing. Product marketing coughs up product diagrams and one-pagers with bullet points on the customer's external factors, like key performance indicators (KPIs), outcomes, and quantitative return on investment (ROI) claims that look eerily similar to your competitors. If you can switch out your most significant competitor's logo with yours in your outreach, you may need to listen closely to the advice in this chapter.

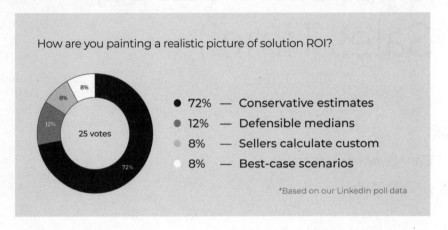

How are you painting a realistic picture of solution ROI?

25 votes

- 72% — Conservative estimates
- 12% — Defensible medians
- 8% — Sellers calculate custom
- 8% — Best-case scenarios

*Based on our LinkedIn poll data

We're talking about a move toward storytelling from an emotional and human-centered perspective that can resonate with buyers versus marketing brochures. Welcome to a new paradigm for most outbound teams, even from famous unicorn companies that you'd expect would already embrace an elevated GTM motion.

You can't convince anyone of anything in sales. You need to do the discovery to uncover whether your product fits before pitching. The first step of any sales process is creating desire in the buyer. Only they hold the key. As Guy Kawasaki calls it, "the art of beguiling." If you need to sell a revenue intelligence platform after a cold-calling event, you'd need to link it back to your product value prop. You could send them a guide on cold-calling tactics—utility-based content, or "youtility," as Jay Baer calls it. You must include one more step of adding value to earn a conversation. Make credits, not debits, in their knowledge bank. That middle interaction builds a bridge and is very effective for event follow-up.

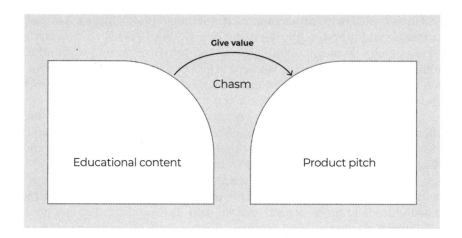

We benefited from cross-training on this internally with each other, which is why we are cross-training GTMers as a new best practice for up-skilling. We encourage you to think of GTM holistically instead of marketing in a silo using newsletters or letting your sellers hammer prospects with manipulative tactics until they submit or mark you on their spam blacklist.

Sequence DESIGN—How to Build and Architect Conversions

At a high level, for sequences to be effective, they should resemble text messages, not expository marketing essays. Please don't put this book down. We're serious. There's no greater gift than giving a senior-level decision-maker back precious time in their busy day.

We extoll a hyper-concise email sequencing framework called The Justin Michael Method™ (JMM™) that looks like text messages or ad units. It is highly visual on the email front, coupled with a "pitch later" cold call framework that seeks referrals using discovery up front, and flips polarity on the first call. (See Appendix II/reach out to us for the complete system.)

"Sales development reps (SDRs) doing discovery? That's ridiculous. We need to specialize the sales process for *Moneyball* with distinct openers and closers." How customer-centric is that baton handoff where your prospect gets interrogated twice with a game of 20 questions? It's exhausting. Anthony Iannarino said it best, "Opening is the new closing." Therefore, we believe all sales cycles should start with probing and pain investigation up front, so you're not pushing on a rope. We need to give our event attendees more reason to meet with us and preview our software than just the allure of another mundane product pitch or soporific demo.

Open questions that dive into customer issues are advisable before and after holding customer-centric events (CCEs). You also want to do this kind of research to pick the themes; they're seldom the ones you think you should showcase. That's what our WRKSHP™ uncovers.

We advocate for training your team on classical strategic selling frameworks, even from the front end of the outbound sales cycle or with warm inbound leads to probe deeper into the pain. Peeling the onion is a powerful driver of urgency. Most business-to-business (B2B) prospects are only aware of symptoms on a surface level versus actual problems lurking below. We take on the countenance of a doctor, detective, or therapist to perform a real-time "root cause analysis" fueled by sheer curiosity about the rest of the iceberg we can't see under the waterline. We want to solve the real problem a mile deep.

One of the most outrageous pieces of this sequencing method is the "thoughts" bump. On day two of any initial email campaign, you simply send the word *thoughts*, all lowercase, nothing else. It cuts like a laser to set meetings and wake up old threads with prospects that ghosted you.

A *sequence* is what your emails say, while a *cadence* is how often you fire messages from sales engagement platforms like Outreach and SalesLoft. Marketers need to think like sellers to build hard-hitting sequences that garner responses. Sellers need to be more data-driven like marketers. We've had phenomenal drills on this from leading minds like Josh Braun. *(Check out the appendix for a sample event follow-up sequence.)*

Personalization at scale is not enough. Relevance at scale is now not enough. We will get into the multi-faceted nature of "hyper-personalization," something only you, not a computer, can do *for now*. A machine or algorithm would unlikely be able to simulate a proper understanding of a customer in this decade, even if vendors claim it's possible. We call it **personalization stacking**.

You'll notice these emails are concise. Julia attempted some JMM-style one-liners hitting up the media and was amazed to see a 90% response rate. It takes the average reader 11 seconds to read a three-paragraph expository email but only 3.3 seconds to scan a SPEAR™ in our method. And the beauty is you don't trigger the fight-or-flight response in the amygdala or croc brain. By now, you'll all be familiar with the F-Tracking eye diagrams Hotjar-style for sales emails read by executives. Why waste an executive's time, eyes darting in

F-curves, when you can be blunt (under 25 words), strike at the heart of the matter, to garner an immediate response?

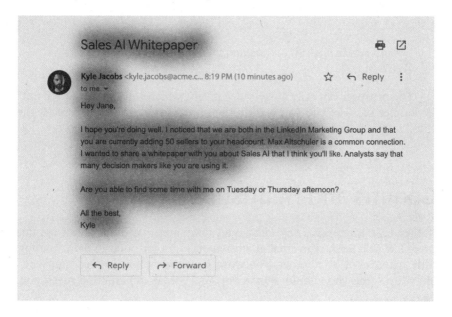

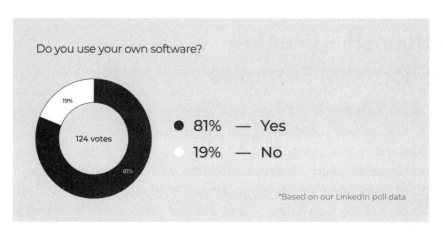

No matter what you're doing with events before or after, you'll vastly increase response rates by making the communication "straight to the point" under three sentences. Even remove the pleasantries as crazy busy decision-makers don't have time for this. They're getting an onslaught of emails and 250 mobile alerts per day. Make it simple to give you a one- or two-word response.

Another fun way to build the email is to get your prospect to answer "No" instead of Yes.

> *"Would you be opposed to coaching an interactive event about HR Tech trends?"*

The prospect can only answer negatively, which is a "pattern interrupt" to decades of, "Hey, do you want to be on our webinar?" which seeks the "Yes" response.

Comms and Heuristics

Rather than share an array of canned templates, we think about comms more like Bob Ross, who created frameworks and formulas to paint "happy, little trees" as if by number. The word *heuristic* simply means "shortcut." Here are some you should always consider when constructing messaging of any kind.

Heuristics (Mental Shortcuts) Examples:

1. simplicity-brevity—50 words, even under 25
2. social proof—ROI of similar customer that's relevant
3. specificity—exact numbers 4.57% versus 5%
4. fear/pain—emotional resonance "challenged by, stressed out about, etc."
5. BS alarm—does it make you think, "that's BS!"
6. soft call to actions (CTAs)—up for a convo? Versus can we meet Tues or Thurs for 15 min? (80s lock-downs)
7. visuals—Venns, GIFs
8. funky grammar—no spaces or dashes, incomplete sentences, spelling errors
9. storytelling—right brain, left brain

Hyper-Personalization Theory

Most outbound prospectors stop at personalization as "Hey, {{First_Name}}, I notice that your team grew by X over Y period." "I noticed you just secured funding." "I notice we both know Kyle Coleman." "I noticed we're both in the marketing space." We refer to this as Personalization 1.0 or "Vanilla Personalization." The problem is that it's so widespread it's entirely expected by your prospect base.

Jeremey Donovan, EVP of Sales & Customer Success at Insight Partners, points to a specific moment in a podcast as a flavor of "customization." To us, hyper-personalization is doing a Google search for one particular data point, referencing the skill tags on location intelligence (LI), and job requisitions on their career page, which includes hints on what tech stacks they are using. Use this as competitive intel in lieu of buying technographics (HG Insights), but that's also a good idea. You could customize your messaging based on a recommendation they received, peruse their recent activity feed, and tie a relevant data point they were passionately sharing/debating back to your product.

"Hey, Jeremey—I downloaded the PDF your venture firm put out, and on page 13, your insights about sales and marketing alignment increasing shareholder value stuck out to me. I also noticed you have a Six Sigma green belt and are obsessed with process optimization. Would it be a bad idea to hop on a call and share some technology that surfaces imputed growth signals on key SaaS players? Thanks, Kylie P.S. Nice cats!"

You can also stack various elements of personalization, aka Personalization Stacking. Example:

Subject : Altschuler + ad targeting

Body: "Hey, Alice—Noticed you just switched roles; our marketing automation tech was installed at scale where you worked last. We both know Max Altschuler. Noticed you just attended Collision Conference in Toronto—how did you like it? Open to looking at our AI assistant for ad targeting that created a 31.6% increase in margin for {{your.competitor}}? Talk soon—Patrice"

Cold-Calling Mastery

One of the biggest requests we get from GTM leaders, and probably our most popular *x-function, x-train* drill, is centered around cold calls. The most crucial heuristic to master on a cold call is "pitching later." You want to delay the instant gratification of immediately vomiting up your elevator pitch, no matter how compelling you think it will be to a prospect. When humans are interrupted, they are emotional. They buy on emotion and close on logic and reason.

First, remember the most valuable thing you can do in any system, be it marketing or sales, is to isolate the 20% of the efforts that drive 80% of results. You would never work a lead list of 100 people and think they are all weighted equal depending on where they are in the buying process: awareness, consideration, in-window, and so on. You want to start obsessing about the 20% of your possible actions that can move the needle on revenue growth. If you have a list of potential prospects, parse the list by triggers and intent. If you are working an 8-hour day, figure out how to complete it in 1.6 hours by prioritizing essential components and laser focusing.

Cold calling is the most highly leveraged 80/20 activity possible. Want to see the power law work like magic? Human-to-human (H2H). Leaving your genuine voicemail (VM) with a tailored value prop catches executives off guard. It triggers them into a buying cycle because they see themselves in your effort and can't help but reciprocate. The tenth employee at Marketo, now a chief executive officer (CXO), says he gets so few calls, that if a rep even attempts one or leaves a VM, he just takes the meeting!

Never look at a customer list, attendee list, or group of opportunities symmetrically again, not even in a bell curve. Think about the power law, the Pareto Principle, and the long-tail distribution of everything. As the legendary Richard Koch preaches in his work, "less is more, more with less."

Most sellers leverage permission-based openers (PBOs), but we feel that lowers your status frame, a concept popularized by Oren Klaff. You don't want to immediately call attention to the fact that you're interrupting or soliciting in the first 3–7 seconds of your call. Don't point out that you're selling, interrupting, or being a nuisance or intrusion. Never make prospects feel guilty, either! Instead, confidently identify yourself, your full name, and your company. Ask the prospect to help you with a straightforward question. (See the complete Route-Ruin-Multiply [RRM] formula in Appendix II.)

ROUTE. "Who's in charge of your __X function__ strategy?" Instead of asking to sell the product or trying to close for a time, you're closing the ROUTE. There are now 6–10 decision-makers in the buying committee. If you call up a marketing division to assess fit on personalization technology after your event, your best bet is to figure out which VP handles that problem. A third of the time, the data is terrible, so they'll just refer you, and you can prove the referral with a screenshot. A third of the time, someone else has replaced that decision-maker, and a third of the time, you go to VM.

Listening is a gift. It's like making deposits in their bank. It's a "give" that reduces friction and lowers prospect resistance. When you leverage RRM techniques efficiently, it's a breakthrough in 100 years of outbound calling because your listen-to-talk ratio of 80/20 disarms the prospect. It becomes their idea to bring their colleagues to the next meeting to see the software. They often remark, "Wow, you don't seem like most salespeople I talk with."

This call style can run very long, but that's okay—so consider cutting bait at 10 minutes. You're waiting for the polarity to shift. Let's say the prospect suddenly reveals an issue. Keep peeling the pain onion, uncovering even more with probing questions. In that case, they will eventually experience an epiphany, becoming interested as if waking from a coma or fever dream. Essentially, it's their idea to learn more about what you do. "Wait, who are you? What do you do again?" That's the power of actively listening and a pitch-later framework. Marketing leaders become proficient with this fast and conduct their own discovery for product-market fit (PMF) and post-event real-time Net Promoter Score/Customer Satisfaction Score (NPS/CSAT).

Handling Objections

You're going to get a ton of objections, so it's critical to realize that the first pushback of "all set," "not interested," is simply a brush-off or recoil. It may even be a comment. You need to get a minimum of two to three "no's" per prospect to know where you stand. Our framework for objections is acknowledge–peel, "ack-peel." You acknowledge the objection, buy time, and then peel the onion. You can defuse the situation humorously or challenge customers to earn their respect. *(Reach out to us for a guide with over 50 top objections.)*

Tailored Voicemails and Video Drops

Leave tailored voicemails after events and "voice drops" on LinkedIn. Send personalized Vidyards and Loom video outreach, and even send them through WhatsApp. It may sound invasive, but if highly relevant, it converts extraordinarily well. You should be utilizing all 50 InMails per month you get with LinkedIn Sales Navigator (Nav) for teams. (For every message rejected, you get back a credit.) Over time, these outperform email when fully utilized.

Interactive Video Prospecting

Reaching out over video is powerful if you can pull up the prospect's LinkedIn profile as you narrate it, double-clicking on relevant personalization factors that show you're not a bot. You can also show your product in a super-brief demo and simulate it actively working on their site. This is a show stopper if you sell chatbot software because you can mock up exactly how it would look in their native environment with a chatbot emulator.

Show aspects of the user experience/user interface (UX/UI) that are most relevant to solving their pain. To make it more entertaining, utilize iMovie, Final Cut Pro, or other video editing tools to cut between different scenes and your software. People mistake sharing the same static, beige background video and sending it nearly identically to everyone, just changing the first name, as "personalized." Without hyper-tailored elements to make it stand out and resonate with prospects, it's a wasted effort. Video is extremely unlikely to convert the way 99% of GTMers use it, so apply these techniques to think outside the box.

Visual Prospecting—Venns

Another compelling element you'll see in all our work is the utilization of a classic MBA device most Big Four consultants have known about for decades: Venn diagrams. Visuals unlock in the brain at 60,000× the speed of words, and 90% of the information the brain stores is visual. Therefore, a picture is worth a thousand words, and you can break the speed limit on sending 5–12 touches over multiple weeks in a *single image send*. Product marketing understands this, which is why nearly every website features powerful visuals and diagrams to help your pay-per-click campaigns convert from the ZMOT (zero moments of truth) coming off a Google search query.

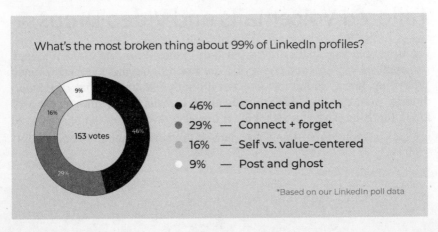

What's the most broken thing about 99% of LinkedIn profiles?

153 votes

- 46% — Connect and pitch
- 29% — Connect + forget
- 16% — Self vs. value-centered
- 9% — Post and ghost

*Based on our LinkedIn poll data

For this book, what's most relevant is that your marketing and sales team can cross-train to make your event promotions even more impactful. When product marketing invests in arming the sales development teams with powerful diagrams, videos, testimonials, and sizzle reels, you can quantum leap attendance and post-event conversion versus blasting text-based spam that gets you blocked. Ignore neuroscience at your peril.

Contact Marketing

Many out-of-the-box ways to "contact" event attendees hinge on sending customized swag in direct mail. The Stu Heinecke–level "contact marketing" classic follow-up contains a cartoon on a poster board. We highly endorse his superb work *How to Get a Meeting with Anyone*. After an interactive event, your overarching goal is to stand out with branded swag. One #contactmarketing idea is to share books like Stu's with all attendees. Even better if your CXO or product leader wrote a book extolling the virtues of the value of solving the problem that your solution addresses. Stephen Pacinelli, CMO of BombBomb, graciously sent his book, *Human-Centered Communication*, to our combined audience. Be careful not to give basic swag like socks with your logo. A better idea: give socks with their logo on them!

Political Selling

Running a sales campaign requires political selling. Very few people compare selling to politics, but everything inside a target organization is politics. The industry tends to focus on features, functions, benefits, or competitive differentiation. Making the customer a hero in the eyes of their boss is the best way to sell a product post-event. The attendee is the champion to drive the commercial conversation forward and help you multi-thread their org chart.

If you sell to VPs of Marketing, find an attendee who was blown away by your interactive event as they will likely make intros to their CMO, CFO, CEO, CRO, and so on. Buyers seek internal approval or public recognition, which is a priceless intangible return on investment (ROI) that they typically won't admit but you can leverage. Sellers are disproportionately over-indexing on the product, the benefits, the features, and the ROI business case and seldom take time to understand the politics moving in the account.

You can't rely on advertising alone. Public relations (PR) drives advertising, as per Al Ries. There's been a lot of banter about the Sales Development Rep-Account Executive (SDR-AE) model going away to be replaced by pure-play inbound marketing and demand gen. By running our event, we can tell you conclusively that you must be willing to become your own SDR.

When reaching out to an audience, don't hesitate to reach out directly to CEOs and get delegated to team leaders. But if you get a warm referral, ensure that you let the referring exec know that you'll get back to them. Build out sequences for various personas in your ideal customer profile (ICP), from C-level executives to managing directors and frontline leaders.

When you follow up with attendees, leverage simple NPS scoring and CSAT survey tools to give attendees a safe place to provide candid feedback. Make sure you reward constructive criticism, even negative feedback, by giving them a quick ring. It will make everything you're doing stronger.

Qualification Frameworks

Qualification frameworks abound, but we use a signature framework called "The Anchor" (hat tip Tony Hughes). Rather than BANT (Budget, Authority, Need, and Timeline) or new popular frames like GPCT (Goals, Plans, Challenges, Timeline) or MEDDIC (Metrics, Economic Buyer, Decision criteria, Decision process, Identify pain, and Champion).

The Anchor ⚓

Budget

Timeline

Compelling Event (Compelling Reason)

Success Criteria

Organizational chart

The essential part of any deal is the "compelling event" or "compelling reason." It typically comes in the form of a trigger event. Per Craig Elias of SHiFT Selling, the most potent trigger events are "job-relationship" changes, even though "bad supplier" and "awareness" are so widespread in marketing. You see tons of "personalization at scale" marketing spam to congratulate executives on a promotion or funding round. Look for a prospect whose account manager/seller turned over = relationship change. Look for a prospective customer with a new C-level in the seat. In the first 90 days, incoming CXOs typically deploy seven figures in capital.

The Law of Principled Disinterest works like magnetics. If you are clingy, servile, and bow down to the prospect, they will lose respect for you. You want to meet the prospect always as an equal. You are the CEO of the Problem you solve.

Study the organizational chart because you are also selling to the CEO of the Problem. At any moment, lower-level stakeholders can become very powerful, which re-organizes "the situational power base," per Jim Holden. You need to identify who has political clout and social capital. That could be the CEO's niece, a whiz at IT systems and coding. You never know! You will need to understand the lay of the land with all relevant stakeholders in your prospective and existing accounts. Map this out on a whiteboard or flowchart it in Miro.

Watch out for blockers or frenemies that could sink you in new or existing accounts. Keep meeting and developing new contacts by bringing them into your event, which will help prevent churn. To land, expand, retain, and renew major deals, you must always be multi-threading accounts as a cornerstone of your sales process, even GTM strategy. Being single-threaded is the kiss of death.

Higher-Risk Outreach Methods

Have you ever thought about sending a Loom Video through your WhatsApp or over a text message? Extreme high conversion, 99% open rate, 90%+

response rate. What about connecting with C-levels in a cold FaceTime drop? Get their number on LeadIQ and drop them into WhatsApp or FaceTime. While it seems incredibly invasive, if you're relevant enough, you might get away with it and set a meeting/book a demo.

Customers are all ordinary people like us. The formal world of pressed business suits is gone. In the 2020s, it's all going down in the DMs. A big part of throwing a momentous event should be bringing everyone into a text thread, WhatsApp Group, Slack Channel, or Discord to keep the conversations going. It's a mistake only to target your customers on business-to-business (B2B) platforms when you could put up a viral page on Facebook, get active on Twitter, and be creative visually on Instagram, Pinterest, TikTok, and Snap.

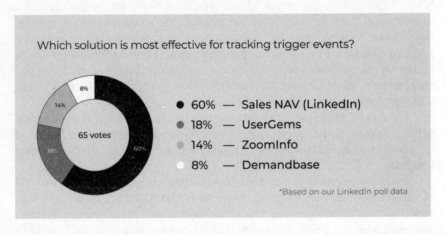

Which solution is most effective for tracking trigger events?

65 votes

- 60% — Sales NAV (LinkedIn)
- 18% — UserGems
- 14% — ZoomInfo
- 8% — Demandbase

*Based on our LinkedIn poll data

CHAPTER 23

Methods for Sophisticated Outreach

We have two ears and one mouth so that we can listen twice as much as we speak.

— Epictetus

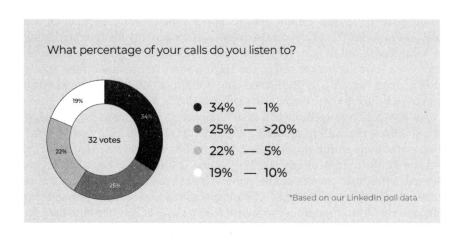

W e can't think of anything more customer-centric than recording and listening back to all your calls. Use technology like Gong/Chorus (ZoomInfo) to analyze keywords like competitors mentioned. Ensure you are gauging listen/talk ratio and keep track of open questions. There are all sorts of analytics bells and whistles that you can run on calls (first gaining permission to record them depending on which geo you are in). Radically, our snap poll showed under 1% do it. It's similar to manually entering data into your customer relationship management (CRM) versus auto-capture. By implementing these best practices and technologies, sales leaders have a golden opportunity to improve visibility into forecasting and guided selling to unlock the full return on investment (ROI) of CRMs and sales engagement platforms (SEPs). (Thank you, Seth Marrs!)

The psychology of the phone has been vastly oversimplified. The majority of outbound phone techniques are fatally flawed. The spotlight is on the rep, while it must be on the prospect to gain influence and positively impact the sales process. Read the Route-Route-Multiply (RRM) and Route-Ruin-Rip (RRR) frameworks in the appendix if you haven't explored this topic/fully road-tested it yet.

Marketers are often terrified of "cold calls," but ironically, sellers are too. Remember, an event follow-up or even a quick call to invite a prospective customer in your ideal customer profile (ICP) to attend your event is not actually "cold." Maybe another attendee made a warm intro based on who else they thought you should invite, so that's a great segue into calling up a stranger. "Hey, Russ, Jacqueline thought you'd be a big fan of this event."

If they look and smell like your best customers, they are *warm* by our modernized definition. Phone calls are still a superpower, and many of the best go-to-market (GTM) leaders at every level are making them in marketing or sales. Break out of your silo! That's why we've placed great emphasis on marketers learning to cold call in the GTM Games competition. Julia boldly took it upon herself to dial partners and attendees and leave tailored voice messages utilizing these techniques with promising results.

When a phone technique transfers power to the prospect (Alpha), it marginalizes the seller (rendering them Beta). We call this "swipe left." There are many mindsets, skill sets, and methods to reverse this polarity, but the Route-Ruin-Multiply (RRM) method is one of the best. Much gets missed in the basic phone openers popularized in the LinkedIn feed. They're about as effective as a coin toss. The most comical part is many phone techniques come from thought leaders who haven't cold called in over a decade. We're serious!

The nuances matter because it's all about human psychology, persuasion, and new customer-centric models that require active listening and skillful questioning. Advanced phone techniques; deeper, philosophical meaning; and intent can unlock 20-minute conversations that close on the first call. Understanding how to use these frameworks will help you convert attendees into loyal customers after a customer-centric event (CCE)—gold springs from these pages. If this isn't relevant, hand this section to the sales development reps (SDRs) or quota-carrying reps that report to you to feed your pipeline daily. This applies to you if you're on the Events Team and work closely with SDRs to do lead follow-up on webinars.

Inherent Power Dynamics

Decision-makers are high alpha operators. They are used to being courted. We knew a prospect that once received a Fender electric guitar and has been frequently offered an all-expenses-paid ski vacation to the Swiss Alps. Why are event coordinators and teams so apprehensive about calling on their VIPs? "Oh, there's no need to follow up by phone. Our prospects are strategic. They prefer an email; we polled them, and they told us." We call B.S.

Beware this pervasive fallacy; even if you interview your customer base and dig this up, customers are in denial, once-bitten twice shy by errant SDRs. They say they prefer digital as an outreach channel to protect their self-respect. We cannot understate the benefit of insisting on phones, Zooms, and getting back in front of everyone participating in your event. It will dramatically improve engagement and conversion. They'll open up and get to know you.

We need a whole new calculus to take someone's desire and flip the polarity to make them want us or our solution. People don't buy products. "They buy you" (hat tip to Jeb Blount). They become convinced (emotionally) for reasons only they understand based on the experience with the seller and justify it with logic.

What's the most vital thing you can do with the powerful? Not bow down, appease, or supplicate. Point out a flaw and admit vulnerability. Words like *love* show far too much enthusiasm and can repel. You need to maintain calm. We call this an Air Traffic Control or the counter of the Department of Motor Vehicles (DMV) approach. It means you are the prime mover unmoved regardless of clout, status, or title and take an egalitarian approach to every prospect. Practice "the subtle art of not giving an F" when you're in sales, and it's all upside.

When you call up influential people, you need to remain calm, not pitch and maintain a beam of curiosity. Otherwise, they can smell your commission breath coming from a mile away. A customer-centric event (CCE) requires a "customer-centric call" as a follow-up. What was the most exciting topic or moment? What's the value they derived? What would improve the experience for them? What didn't they like? Honestly. . . . How can you involve them in future events? Be ready for open, honest, and transparent feedback, even if it's hostile. Then implement what they recommend, so they have skin in the game because if you're doing this right, they do.

Sophisticated Call Anatomy

All prospects are disinterested and "all set." They use a competitor and are just fine with the status quo. That competitor is usually "do nothing," per Tony J. Hughes. The Justin Michael Method™ (JMM™), in every incarnation, is designed as an art form that meets science. Nearly every massive deal opened or closed by quota-carrying reps on five continents started with "not interested" or rejection. Stop looking for low-hanging fruit when you could create demand rather than service it. Trigger your own sales cycles. Don't wait for 3% of the market that may be inside the buying window now. Create events, follow-up content, and messaging so compelling that you tip your best customers into your funnel.

Alphas and Betas

You're not calling in high enough if you're talking to "nice" prospects. Decision-makers are elusive, salty, and play "hard to get." Based on their DISC (Dominance, Influence, Steadiness, and Conscientiousness) profile assessment, these folks are a unique breed of *D* for *Dominance*. They control the profit and loss (P&L), and can put you on "burn notice" in the account.

Do you think the most "human" sellers and marketers are the ones who will be most successful now?

72 votes

- ● 72% — Yes, empathy/creativity rule
- ● 13% — No, PLG replaces
- ● 8% — Self check-out
- ○ 7% — GPT-3 communicates better

*Based on our LinkedIn poll data

Nearly every prospecting system would have you believe that if you interrupt them and are logical enough and persuasive enough, they will submit, stay on the line, and book a demo. It's not how it works at all—positively controlling a decisive executive on the phone before or after an event is an exercise in applying active listening versus an exercise in futility if you simply pitch, akin to riding a bucking bronco.

You must deftly place open-ended questions upfront and move into onion peeling, diagnostic motions from the outset of the call. If two alphas meet, you suddenly have a game of chicken magnetically. Locked horns!

Polarity can't match. Two positive magnets repel. What's the solution? You control Alpha energy by feigning Beta. Play possum like an animal pretending to be dead. Fall on your sword of Damocles. Introverts can be incredibly soft-spoken on your calls because, in this new method, the tone is not how you're controlling the call. Prospects don't care about you or the product. You're guiding them to talk about themselves (only!) and to go higher, Alpha, but then you're the puppeteer.

Powershifting—Social Aikido/ Social Tai-chi

A sale can only occur when "the pain of the same is greater than the pain of change," to paraphrase Brent Adamson. Nearly every phone framework is a) interrupt, b) persuade, and c) handle objections and rebuttals. "The reason for my call is. . .." "I don't care," thinks every prospect viscerally.

It can't work because you're causing a reflexive recoil. You're triggering the amygdala to "fight or flight." You're calling their baby ugly; all they can do is get defensive. The prospect had to accept their stack in the job description when they took the role. They are vested in protecting the incumbent's solution already in place.

You can't come in fists swinging because they'll just defend and justify digging their heels further in the corner of the ring, even if your solution is superior. We realized early on that calling influential people and listening to them about "why" they're so powerful or intelligent is the most disarming thing we can do. Letting them talk is a gift, a deposit in their bank, and they'll reciprocate with their desire to see your demo/hear your value prop.

They don't want to talk to a seller/vendor and don't want to talk about you. WIFM (what's in it for them)? Validate their status quo. It dismantles them. Oh, how the mighty fall! "You don't seem like a salesperson. You seem like a friend," CEOs bemusedly remark. "I wasn't going to keep talking with you initially, but I think I'll recommend your [events/product/service] to my friend Jane at Beta Corp."

The line Justin always hears verbatim is, "Honestly, I never take calls like this, but I like you." Nobody listens to them in this life, not their boss, spouse, or kids—trust us! Their locus of control is minimal, and their sphere of influence is not to exceed a desk cubicle. It's probably just that one P&L they control, so encourage them to flex their power. Then you can judo roll them.

Mastering Political Factors

Believe it: prospects don't buy because the product is excellent (FFAB—features, function, and benefits). They don't buy because you differentiated against the competitor (compete selling). They buy optics. They want to look like a hero in the eyes of their boss, so they get promoted. The peak selling stage after this level is a trusted advisor. Hunters always search for elusive insights to become the vaunted "trusted advisor" and spend excessive time on needless research to impress when it's pretty simple. Help your prospect get promoted. (We love Jim Holden's thoughts here, read all his work.)

Ask questions about their career advancement goals in the top script of the call after the RUIN step of Route-Ruin-Multiply. "Where do you see yourself in two to five years?" Customers buy products and services to "look like a hero" so they'll get promoted in their company. Politics is the ultimate driver. When they receive the return on investment (ROI) of your solution and create a far better state, they have the leverage to get promoted.

Symptoms versus Problems

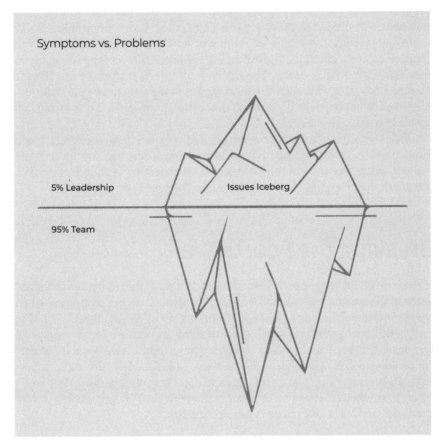

Symptoms vs. Problems

5% Leadership

Issues Iceberg

95% Team

Every prospect is like an iceberg. You can try to identify pain, but you'll generally hit a symptom, not a genuine problem. We talk a great deal about peeling the onion. Issues happen in chains. Getting to the bottom of a real problem takes some rigorous detective-doctor work. For example, our sales development rep (SDR) team *can't* set meetings. "Okay, why?" "Oh, the CFO cut funding, so we use a team that doesn't even make cold calls and relies on email only." "But why?" "We hired a phone team, and they failed in '02." See our point? You see, nobody buys anything. Prospects typically get moved to change based on "latent pain." Let's define it to eliminate any misunderstanding:

Latent is an adjective to describe something capable of becoming active or at hand, though it is not currently so. The adjective *latent* is tricky to define because it refers to something there but not there.

As we'll dive deeper into the "customer-centricity" chapters later, prospects "never knew what they always wanted." It's a pure Steve Jobs iPhone moment applied to go-to-market (GTM). Steve Ballmer was sure Apple's new phone would fail. Next thing you know, they were tenting in lines like a sci-fi premiere. A phenomenal seller can lead the prospect to understand themselves like a gifted therapist. Peeling the onion allows the prospect to at least articulate what's wrong. The truth about selling disruptive solutions is it's rare a prospect wakes up one morning knowing they need your solution. Examples: What happens if you don't make this change? What is the financial upside if you fix it?

When you make calls after events to sell your solution, seek latent pain instead and go in with an open mind to see how deeply you can understand your customer's world. Put the intention to set a meeting in your back pocket. Start with the preceding; focus on the quality of your open questions.

Breaking the Fourth Wall

In the days of Shakespeare, "breaking the fourth wall" meant the actors turned to the audience and opined on the scene. We always use this technique when we get shut down during a cold call. "Not interested. We're all set." "Oh, I'm sorry, I was trying too hard to sell you this thing and came off all wrong—can we please hit pause on our conversation. How could I have done it better?" People love to give opinions, so the best way to keep a disinterested prospect engaged is to say, "Hey, just out of courtesy, can I get your opinion? How could I have positioned this product or event better with you?" Break the fourth wall if you get wedged. Leverage an "opinion heuristic."

Mindset

You need to transition from an insecure, weak mindset of waiting, wishing, and hoping for a sale to knowing you'll set a meeting. You must become the most venomous snake in the Australian outback. A fully causal mentality means, "if this prospect picks up, I will get the referral, sale, and even close." We joke about this, but a prospect can only make one primary mistake when facing you, "answering the phone." That's how confident you'll become in your phone skills if you utilize pitch-later frameworks with an 80/20 listen-to-talk ratio and supercharge your active listening skills. You'll gain the self-confidence and certainty that you will prevail if prospective customers talk with you. You need to be the apex predator, the peak of the food chain. Imagine a great white shark breaching sea level to clinch a sea lion in its jaws in grizzly suspended animation. Sharks have incredibly thick skin and never give up. They even swim in their sleep. Which animal are you?

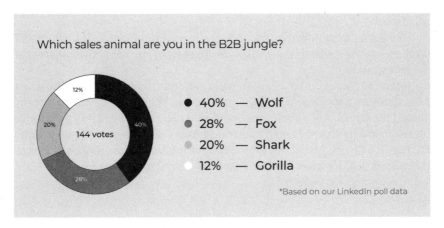

Which sales animal are you in the B2B jungle?

144 votes

- 40% — Wolf
- 28% — Fox
- 20% — Shark
- 12% — Gorilla

*Based on our LinkedIn poll data

You can't approach calls subserviently. Your entire goal is to get the prospect talking and keep them talking with open-ended questions for 2–15 minutes. Listen-to-talk ratio should be 95/5. Gong has probably never even analyzed a ratio like this because Route-Ruin-Multiply is revolutionary as a "pitch-later" framework, the first-ever since 2002, when software as a service (SaaS) companies hit $100 million run rates.

Advanced Phone Strategies

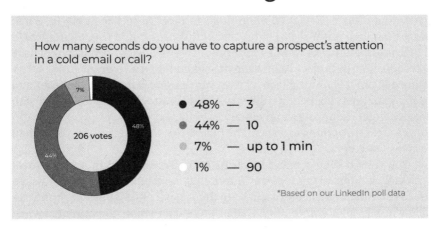

How many seconds do you have to capture a prospect's attention in a cold email or call?

206 votes

- 48% — 3
- 44% — 10
- 7% — up to 1 min
- 1% — 90

*Based on our LinkedIn poll data

You should try all sorts of pattern interrupts when you're on a cold call before or after an event. The main meta-philosophy of pattern interrupt mastery is, "whatever a prospect does or is expecting, do the opposite." If a prospect throws a curveball at you, flip it back.

"I'm not interested." "How do you know? I haven't even told you why I called yet."

"Send me more information." "Honestly, I would, but the last 50 times I did that, I never spoke to that person for the rest of my life.... So is that what you're insinuating?"

Get off the script, off the beaten path, and improvise fearlessly. The worst thing that can happen is you'll get hung up on. With events, you've already greased the wheels with a relevant invite, and people are relatively gregarious toward spending time learning something useful with their peers on a webinar. Fortune favors the bold in prospecting stunts when reaching chief executive officers (CXOs) from FedEx envelopes to FaceTime drops.

Voicemails

A voicemail (VM) should be left on every call and in one breath. Why? Because it spikes open rates on emails and InMails. Practice deep breathing like a pearl diver and leave the entire thing in one fell swoop. Make sure your voice goes down at the end (down tone). Never ask for a callback. We personally never do VM drops, which are fully automated pre-recorded voicemails often sent out of a sales engagement platform.

Justin likes to leave the slightest bit of personalization but makes it relevant. Don't bow down and fawn over all their awards and accomplishments. Mention a quote in a publication (it was legendary getting the chief marketing officer [CMO] of a top hotel to meet from her quote in *Wired Magazine*), call out a skill tag on their LinkedIn profile (Six Sigma Green Belt), or something relevant to your product—tie it back. "I notice you have a certification in project management that could be a relevant fit for leveraging our process mining tech." Leave your phone number at the front and back. Again, never ask for a callback. Always close with, "I'll follow up with a quick note." Your follow-up email should always be, "Per my voicemail," to weave these motions together. The purpose of the VM is to get your email response rate up.

You should keep a note file during and after an event in a spreadsheet with collaborators to mark down "interesting moments" in the event you can use later strategically in outreach. Keep track of who asked questions, and catalog who's in your community. Gather more data points to customize when you follow up with attendees, so your approach is highly personalized.

Generic Is the Enemy of Effective Event Follow-Up

Whom to Call

Here's the harsh reality. The real economic buyers are hard to get to. If you are aiming at directors and VPs, it's too low. Go Senior VP, general manager (GM), CXO, board members, and venture capitalists (VCs). You'll get "delegated down to who you sound like" per Tony Hughes, so reach for the stars, and you just might hit a mountain.

The top two mistakes in phone teams are a) not calling in high enough and b) assuming that friendly, easy-to-talk-to people can buy. We love salty prospects, ones that dodge us and hang up. Big money is in the deep water with the fewest fish. You need to target super senior prospects in the company and get used to live fire with them. That little pang of fear in the pit of your stomach right before you make the call is the best indicator of successful targeting.

Justin was calling up some super evil mega corp but couldn't get through. So he messaged a board member on Sales Navigator with an InMail. The prospect pinged back in minutes providing his cell phone. That first call steeped in active listening set the tone to be invited in to a full board room meeting on-site the next week with his entire C-Suite. One InMail at the board level of a Fortune 2,000 company can move heaven and earth. Another time, a single InMail booked a meeting with the chief product officer (CPO) of the biggest news conglomerate in the world using the methods in this book. No guts, no glory. Wingsuit base jumping only.

If you are too shy or terrified to use a fully outbound approach, take the time to build personalized Loom videos and send them out one at a time hyper-personalized via email, WhatsApp, or LinkedIn. Your tailoring is highly appreciated and will get you noticed in a sea of generic "personalized by template" spam.

Trade Secrets

Whether it's 20,000 hours on phones, studying relationship dynamics, or the power of "persuasion" with Dr. Robert Cialdini, game theory, social engineering, cracking the top funnel by calling and emailing is one of the hardest things to do. We have sat inside many a CEO's LinkedIn inbox and seen recurring patterns. Justin called the same phone number 50 days in a row and left a VM every time. To analyze our phone approaches for all your pre- and post-event follow-ups, here are some random pointers to focus on:

Tonality: Be completely calm, cool, collected, and matter of fact (detached).

Humor: Never take yourself seriously—cracking-wise, the entire call de-stresses it.

Finesse: Don't ever give the prospect the satisfaction of knowing it's a script if you use one. Inherently easy if you just follow Route-Ruin-Multiply.

Pattern Interrupts: Start any phone script with an open question versus convincing or pitching. Validate the competitors. Ask career-oriented questions to build trust. Be genuinely curious. If you land the technical demo after an event, ask prospects to sign an MNDA (first commit) before they talk with you, so they are comfortable being as forthcoming as possible with insider baseball. What a solid qualification mechanism. (If they won't sign a mutual nondisclosure agreement [MNDA], how serious are they?) Once you build trust, you can ask questions, but bluntness too early in the sales process will sink you.

Buy Cell Phone Data: Test every possible source be it ZoomInfo, Cognism, Lusha, or LeadIQ (varies widely by geo and vertical, so experiment). You will need direct dials (cell phones!), so spare no expense. It unlocks the entire technique.

Multi-threading: Reps are nowhere near assertive enough about this. You need to be directly calling three to five stakeholders in an account. Analysts say the buying group has ballooned to 11. Get to know them, bug them, and discover their unique perspectives and motivations.

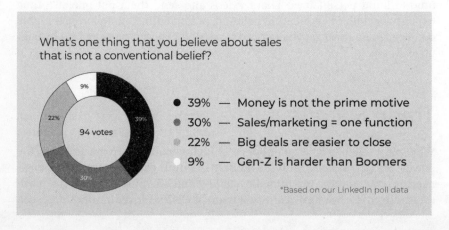

What's one thing that you believe about sales that is not a conventional belief?

94 votes

- 39% — Money is not the prime motive
- 30% — Sales/marketing = one function
- 22% — Big deals are easier to close
- 9% — Gen-Z is harder than Boomers

*Based on our LinkedIn poll data

Massive action: Make 10× the dials you want. Follow up 10× as much. Every lever needs to be "turned up to 11." Reps simply don't take enough action. Outreach's data shows it takes 27 touches to unlock an account now.

80/20 Rule: What 10× and fanatical prospecting methods missed is the Power Law. 20% of your actions are driving 80% effectiveness. Apply Pareto as an overlay to everything in go-to-market (GTM). Like gravity, it never fails by physics law.

Calling on signals: Set Outreach to "Ruleset 3" so you get a task auto-dropped in your reminders from the home dashboard for any message opened over three times.

If someone views your LinkedIn, TRIPLE them (call, VM, and email under 90 seconds). If they reply, triple them. If they open your email over 3×, triple them. Make direct dials to cell phones the tentpole of your outreach. Don't get stuck in Zoom gridlock. (Hat tip to COMBO Prospecting)

Use PADs: You need to be on a calling system that makes 4–10 dials per second, aka a Parallel Assisted Dialer (PAD) like ConnectAndSell (CAS). Manually dialing a phone in 2022 is a primitive move: Dark Ages. If you're lucky, you need to invest in tech that enables you to make 1,000 dials a day, yielding 20 conversations versus 5 per day with executive assistants on 100 attempts with older tech.

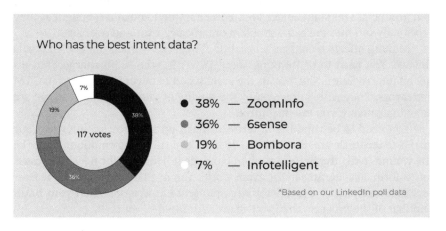

Who has the best intent data?

117 votes

- 38% — ZoomInfo
- 36% — 6sense
- 19% — Bombora
- 7% — Infotelligent

*Based on our LinkedIn poll data

Psychographic data is the next frontier: Intent data like Bombora and 6sense are all the rage now, crossing the chasm from early adopters and innovators to the latent majority. Psychographic data is even rarer. It doesn't just figure out which accounts click on keywords but which granular persona you should target. It leverages artificial intelligence (AI) and many ingestion points (via application programming interfaces [APIs]) across social to do this flawlessly.

Self-Actualized Prospects

In a customer-centric model, no one can buy anything or be convinced to attend anything. Let us dig deeper into this. Our job as sales developers is to awaken the flame of desire in the prospect. We must build experiences that intrigue and pull our prospective customers toward us from the optimal ideal customer profiles (ICPs).

As long as you're persuading, cajoling, and convincing—you will fail. You are, in essence, pushing on a rope. We learned from doing large, full-cycle deals that there is a magic moment when the polarity shifts and the customer drives the sale.

Suddenly, we noticed traction in the back tires in the muddy bog of ambivalence. Justin watched all bizarre things happen with sales cycles as he sold in the same industry for 15+ years, Mobile AdTech-MarTech.

He'd kick off a deal at one vendor point solution in New York City and close it three years later in Seattle for another vendor. Why did this happen? They bought into "him," his expertise and brand. He established the trust over time and eventually created enough desire to transcend buyer resistance and organization gridlock. Many times that stakeholder was on an upward career trajectory where they gained more clout in the power base to decide where the budget would go on tools. He owned the relationship with the end customer outside the bounds of software as a service (SaaS) companies, brands, and products. This stakeholder became a champion and at last bought as they repeatedly ran into the same problem organically, over and over again.

Making effective cold calls is subtle. There is so much more than meets the eye. You need to be thinking about POWER, who is "in charge," but it's not an interrogation. Curiosity is the great secret to never burning out in GTM endeavors. They will "know you by the quality of your questions." If you are listening actively, you are in control.

You need to be thinking in terms of push-pull interest/disinterest. Your goal is to create desire. How do you do this? You stimulate emotion. You poke the wound, twist the knife, and then bandage it. Hunting for new business is an art form, as is comms in the event world. You need to aim high and be fearless. Neuroscience is deceptively easy, but you know more about your brain and that of the prospect than you've ever admitted to yourself.

SECTION 3

Customer-Led Everything

A satisfied customer is the best business strategy of all.

— Michael LeBoeuf

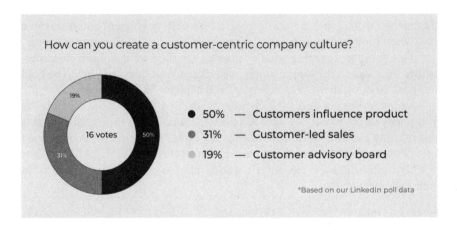

How can you create a customer-centric company culture?

16 votes

- 50% — Customers influence product
- 31% — Customer-led sales
- 19% — Customer advisory board

*Based on our LinkedIn poll data

Market research and product development are bassackwards. It's what Steve Jobs implied—paraphrasing, "customers never know what they always wanted." Apple released iPhone, and Steve Ballmer at Microsoft was certain users wouldn't want touchscreens as they preferred the physical button keys of Crackberry. Why wouldn't you ask your customers what they want and give it to them? You thought this was a section on "customer-centricity. His advice is confusing. Customers respond to product teams with the tech they want, but when the companies build for that, it doesn't sell. Look at phablets, glassholes, and self-driving cars.

Customers understand their pains and needs, but can't consistently articulate the solutions that translate into products. They don't know the outcome they want from your answer, but it's up to you to create a new paradigm to get them there. It's been the same way with our event. If you asked Justin his favorite theme for a drill two years ago, it would have been a "cold-calling battle." But now that we've done 100 events on go-to-market (GTM) cross-training, all the ideas are about GTM themes. Why? It's taught him how powerful it is to break out of the sales silo and align with cross-functional revenue teams like marketing, product, customer success management (CSM), and operations to drive revenue holistically as one unified revenue team.

So don't necessarily ask your customers for solutions or event ideas. They have gaps in the innovation process and are often reactionary/ruled by emotions. Your research and development (R&D) group, user interface/user experience (UI/UX) research, and empirical observations can be more consequential. Survey data is often flawed for this reason unless anonymized to get the real answers, not what your customers say for "optics." What's the goal of using the product or service? What's the pain or latent pain to alleviate? Maybe they like the convergence of their iPod, phone, music, movies, and so on, all in one device. Perhaps they want to be able to consume far less fossil fuel but don't mind driving the car versus the endless techie urge toward "driverless." Maybe they won't lament a small screen if it's battery efficient and lasts three days when they go glamping. Do the research. Do the "intelligent discovery."

It's a paradox. Ignoring what customers say they want is more customer-centric. Just like in the sales chapter, we talked about being willing to be bold and push back on them to earn respect and achieve "status" parity.

Almost everyone gets their customers' desires wrong. Now with all the technology in the world, we have too many data points. A thousand channels and nothing on. A million streams but no signal in the noise. People don't know how to provoke their customers and read through all these data points to truly understand the customer's world, what is enticing them, and what their real problem is.

HYPCCCYCL Discovered an Insight That No One Else Could See

Julia realized that secretly all of the sellers are curious about marketing even though they hate on the function outwardly, and there's this constant debate. They are still secretly voyeuristic about data science, new analytics systems, and MarTech platforms.

The same goes for marketers: they are secretly curious about selling as much as they dismiss salespeople as dumb, primitive creatures who waste their best leads. Marketing wants sellers' confidence to go out there and demo their product, do the cold calls, spend time uncovering problems, scoping solutions, and talk to real customers. At the core of all of this, there's insane fear, insecurity, and doubt.

That's why when we marketed our event, despite how sellers rejected it, "I'd never do that," the hidden core insight resonated with our potential audience, and our combined networks flooded in. That's how you become customer-centric in B2B. You have to uncover real insight about your target audience that is not necessarily in the analyst reports.

Typical companies will never surface this kind of insight because they solely sell marketing or sales solutions. Companies sporadically target market-ers and sellers, so most of the content produced and sponsored by these tech-nologies does not show real insight. You read the siloed white papers about sales, marketing, and revenue operations (RevOps) tech, and are nonplussed. To uncover the secret desires of your audience objectively, you need to talk with them and hang with them. They need to let you into the "circle of trust."

How do you provoke people to share something intimate like that? What everyone is thinking, but no one quite has the courage or maybe the conscious awareness to speak their mind. How do you notice an insight like that? How do you arouse curiosity? You need to walk a mile in their shoes. You need to sit down on the same side of the table and reduce friction in the relationship (pros-pect resistance) to the level where they open up to you. Uncovering latent pain is not easy. We've all seen the executive iceberg diagram from Sidney Yoshida where ±74% of the problems remain hidden from upper-level management. Empathy is a powerful force to unlock the real issues. In sales and marketing, we are moving away from the bold people pleaser and lone wolf archetypes into the era of the doctor, detective, and therapist (hat tip to Jeff Thull). Seeing the world from your customer's eyes is at the heart of an effective GTM.

Which Go-to-Market strategy is most effective?

103 votes

- 73% — Outbound + Inbound
- 17% — Outbound
- 7% — Demand Gen/No outbound
- 3% — Inbound

*Based on our LinkedIn poll data

The new paradigm shift to customer-centricity is about placing customers at the center of a journey to unlock and resolve pain points at scale. When you lessen pain, you open new revenue. Customers reverberate from the center of your GTM as a starting point versus being the end-all, be-all of traditional linear GTM campaigns.

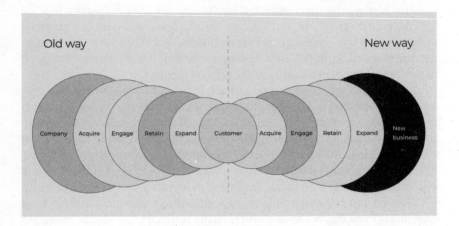

We live in the age of the customer' Marc Benioff has proclaimed. The customers are more intelligent than they used to be, with too many options on the market and harsh competition among vendors. Customers are picky because they're ready to substitute you with your competitor haphazardly.

And you could fill a Library of Congress with the number of marketing books hitting the *New York Times* bestseller list that glamorize this concept. But how do you apply it to events to transform your webinars? Since conferencing technology hit its stride in the 90s with WebEx and GoToMeeting, Zoom finally allowed us to jump the hurdle of getting everyone on to the call without 3–5 minutes of download and set up. The barrier to entry is gone; the fidelity is always high on 5G and even holds up at slower dial-up speeds. At last, in the 2020s, all the participants can even show up! As comical as this sounds. *Cue the hilarious YouTube videos on the awkward first 5 minutes of online meetings.*

Let's zoom out before we zoom in and look at who's attending these virtual snoozefests. Millennials.

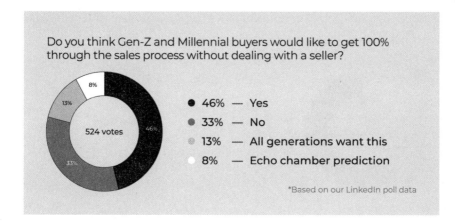

Do you think Gen-Z and Millennial buyers would like to get 100% through the sales process without dealing with a seller?

524 votes

- 46% — Yes
- 33% — No
- 13% — All generations want this
- 8% — Echo chamber prediction

*Based on our LinkedIn poll data

Millennials already comprised 50% of the workforce by 2020. So the old way of thinking doesn't jive with digital-first, always-on smartphone natives. Millennials are mobile-first, self-aware, mission-driven, distrusting of false ROI claims, and they put their faith in peer reviews versus your company. Aka customer-centric, generationally. They'll multi-task you, turn their camera off, and listen in the background if you're not careful.

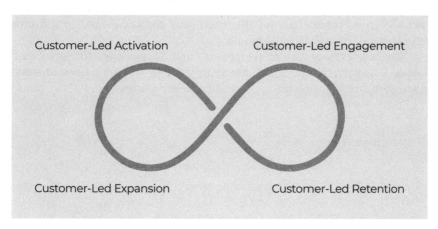

Customer-Led Activation

Customer-Led Engagement

Customer-Led Expansion

Customer-Led Retention

The old marketing funnel was always Acquire Engage Retain Expand linearly or cyclically. In our CCE (customer-centric event) model, customers lead the charge to acquire more similar customers in an infinite loop or Mobius strip—the shape of the HYPCCCYCL brand logo. M.C. Escher fanatics eat your heart out.

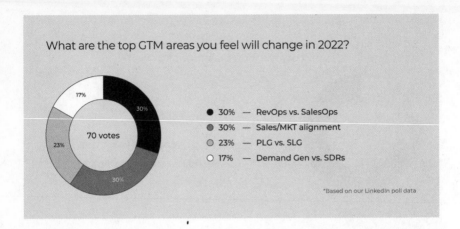

That's customer-led growth. And so naturally, we introduce customer-led events where the customers help decide the theme, flip the script, and sit on the panels. Your customers share and promote the event. Your customers enjoy the recognition of success, culture creation, and community building by participating in your broader community that creates a halo effect around your brand and digital gatherings.

Customers deepen their engagement with the audience. Raving customers (NPS [Net Promoter Score] 10) retain your audience/clientele and thus can expand it through word of mouth.

You can leverage hybrid themes to build an audience for any event, deepen engagement, and foster retention through various outbound sales, inbound marketing, advertising, and demand-gen tactics.

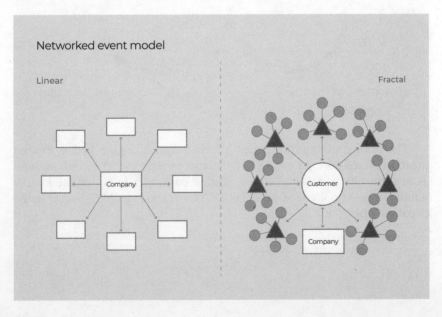

From a marketing perspective, it comes down to network effects. If you can make your customer truly happy, you can facilitate fractal growth of your networks even without the site mechanics of Clubhouse limiting invites or stratifying VIPs. If your customers love it, they will bring their network to your network, which becomes a network of networks. Start working like a CSM, and instead of new user acquisition, start feeding the existing users you already attracted with unexpected value. They can boost customer acquisition collaboratively with you.

The 2020s GTM megatrend is that the SaaS technology industry is collectively seeking a single source of truth for marketing and sales to coalesce. RevOps platforms that bring sales and marketing data under one roof are constantly combining, innovating, and getting acquired. We can forever argue how to align sales and marketing, but centralizing the data they're exposed to with agreed upon key performance indicators (KPIs) must come first. Seth Marrs, Research Director at Forrester, describes a bold vision that marketing and sales people will look into the same customer relationship management (CRM) view daily to share the pipeline. This will smoothly streamline and align all their "account-based everything" activities around North Star metrics. We need not only a single dashboard view but new KPIs. Companies like ZoomInfo, Outreach, 6sense, and Gong are feverishly building toward this disruptive future.

CHAPTER 24

Customer-Led Acquisition/ Activation

I think the purpose of a piece of music is significant when it actually lives in somebody else. A composer puts down a code, and a performer can activate the code in somebody else. Once it lives in somebody else, it can live in others as well.

— Yo-Yo Ma

To activate your base, you need to be willing to sell 1:1:many, not just market. So here are counterintuitive tips on selling. They require customer-led growth (CLG). Your customers become your raving fans, and they co-promote your event. When you drive value to an audience, the value will organically grow by word of mouth.

You can win in the arena by design, branding, and marketing. Still, ultimately, you will have to roll up your sleeves and sell this creation whether you're a solopreneur, intrapreneur, or part of a startup event marketing team. So what are some concrete tactics?

Customer-Led Growth and Selling

Rather than a full-frontal assault, the better way into critical accounts is to have one of your raving customers sell the deal for you. Positive word of mouth from ardent fans is also the best way to garner event attendees. In the past, you'd hold on to your essential customer referrals for a rainy day and only let them talk to a prospect at the end of the sales cycle if you got to the "put the deal in writing" phase. That's myopic because the front end of the deal is where your customers can do the heaviest lifting. Just like last-click attribution is a fallacy when we all know the first click drove the purchase intent in the attribution waterfall.

Build content around customer success stories. Your prospects will see themselves in these stories and drop into your funnel. Part of this is fear of missing out (FOMO), innovation, and social proof: "Well, if it worked for them, it could work for me."

The fastest way to become customer-led is to place a video camera into your next event or during a major conference where many of your customers are. Capture footage of each customer in 90-second clips as they explain to the camera why they are successful with your product. Load those all up to YouTube with minimal production, then link it from your website "Case Studies" tab, Twitter, Facebook, and LinkedIn. Are your sales and marketing teams armed with this information? Go to market client video first. Put "customer hero" video case studies and testimonials front and center to create a snowball effect of positive word of mouth as these videos will pull in more user-generated content (UGC) video testimonials. Nobody can sell your product better than your satisfied customers.

You should also consider hosting a weekly or biweekly podcast on the industry's main themes and challenges your solution addresses. Per Edison Research, "41% of the U.S. population listens to podcasts every month, while 45% of podcast listeners are more likely to have a household income of at least $250,000." Why not pull highly qualified leads in your target ideal customer profile (ICP) toward you by a new podcast gaining registration of serial listeners. Plug your events frequently on the pod and drop links. Interview your best customers on the blog, and turn them into Zoom video clips posted on YouTube and indexable from Google. Push all this stuff to your company pages on Facebook, LinkedIn, and Twitter.

You need to enable your website to set off network effects. Create referral mechanic functionality. When customers register on your site, engineer a flow to a) recommend a friend, and b) simply copy an affiliate link and get paid a certain percentage for bringing new people and include this in newsletters and all your web properties. Remember, for every action users take on your website, they should intuitively be aware of this networked-enabled functionality that pushes them to spread the word. The most obvious winners here are Superhuman (email reimagined) and Clubhouse. You can limit invitations, unlock them for power users, or dole them out in return for social/email promotion.

CHAPTER 25

Customer-Led Engagement

Good listeners have a huge advantage. For one, when they engage in conversation, they make people "feel" heard. They "feel" that someone really understands their wants, needs and desires. And for good reason; a good listener does care to understand.

— Simon Sinek

People get event marketing all wrong. They think, "if you build it, they will come." Julia likes to say, "Okay, we nailed the concept. Now we have to promote it." "Okay, we wrote this great book. Now we have to market it." You can't rely on luck or overthink your content until you have a masterpiece. Without network effects, brand building, creating buzz, seeding word of mouth, and leveraging employee and customer networks to amplify, you'll have a dead magnum opus with five people attending just collecting dust. It's just like a fantastic value prop; even product-market fit (PMF) is only one piece. Competitors will eat your lunch without executing a rock-solid go-to-market (GTM) strategy, even if you have product superiority.

You need to use this book to create a playbook for growth hacking, AB testing, and modernizing context so you engage your audience even better. We AB tested everything to build out HYPCCCYCL GTM games, including our website copy, H1 tags, email subject lines, ads, white paper content, and themes.

Customer-centric marketing is about putting your customer testimonials into advertising. It's about a sophisticated YouTube strategy with highlight reels of your event that add value every time they are aligned with a disruptive theme. It's worth taking the time to transcribe and combine the best moments from your events with some light editing; even grab iMovie yourself to build out some clips with captions.

We made sure to bring credible sales, marketing, and ops leaders to the competition. We then democratized it so our audience would see themselves inside each match. GTM Games keeps every gathering fresh with consistent brand themes, repeat guests, and new challenges based on mash-ups inspired by our T-Shaped GTM grid.

All you have to do to get customer-led engagement for an event is invite your customers and ideal customer profile (ICP) to participate in the panels or the judging. Customers will love the exposure and enjoy this golden opportunity to compete, collaborate, and upskill. Experiment with single contestants and teams. Contributing to an old-school webinar panel is dull, and you wait your turn. In a customer-centric event (CCE), anything can happen. Customers become panelists on a whim. It's much more exciting to participate in and watch. Let them share their success stories with your brand, even competitors. The key is to share how they overcame the challenges you solve. Try not to control the narrative too much. It will go a lot better for everyone.

Measuring how much time your audience spends at your event is essential. Your goal should be to convert most to stay for over half the event. When you analyze this, look at root causes and leading indicators. We average 35 minutes out of 60. Your onboarding funnel should include registration, calendaring, reminders, and pre-event promotions. All of these factors impact the retention of the event because of how you frame it up. Ensure participants clear their calendar to be there. One school of thought says to throw events after hours to accommodate work, but we've found it's just as effective to schedule during work hours if it's highly relevant content. Pick some time zones or build specifically for a region. Remember, APAC (Asia-Pacific) and India cannot attend West Coast events.

There are so many creative ways to foster customer engagement during a live event. Call out customers out of the blue. Make sure the audience is not bored and does unexpected things during the event. Always ensure one person is watching and directing while another hosts. You can ask an audience member a question, randomly make them a panelist, or incorporate a slack thread back into a live event. Every 10 minutes, try to do something completely unexpected. Allow a coach to take a contrarian stance on a drill similar to how Alice Heiman did a cold-calling drill on *not* cold calling her but utilizing any other creative means necessary. One of our favorite pattern interrupts is to flip the camera and get the coach to do the drill. So if Josh Braun is teaching you cold call openers, now we flip it and watch Josh Braun open the call.

CHAPTER 26

Customer-Led Retention/Expansion

The test of a first-rate intelligence is the ability to hold two opposed ideas in mind at the same time and still retain the ability to function.

— F. Scott Fitzgerald

Al Ries is the godfather of Fortune 500 branding, and we've found some lessons in throwing our events that are worth sharing here that coincide with his thinking. How you design every last detail of your event dictates the power of your marketing, and it all starts with the brand. Design thinking is a process of creative problem-solving from the customer's lens. Design thinking has a human-centered core. It encourages organizations to focus on the people they're creating for, which leads to better products, services, and internal processes. You put the human at the center and do proper user interface/user experience (UI/UX) research.

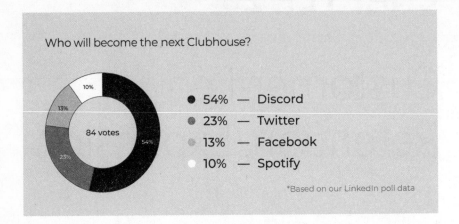

Who will become the next Clubhouse?

84 votes

- 54% — Discord
- 23% — Twitter
- 13% — Facebook
- 10% — Spotify

*Based on our LinkedIn poll data

Will you build your community in Dark Social on a lesser-used business-to-business (B2B) platform like Discord, which initially gained traction with gaming? How can you meet your customers in the gardens where they spend most of their time learning, sharing, or blowing off steam?

Julia's keen eye for design led her to craft our brand devoid of color, debranded, desaturated, and in stark black and white. We even released our YouTube video highlight reel channels in this desaturated mode, which stood out and caught wildfire visually in the industry. Everything we did had a high production, sleek, premium feel, which only impeded us because audiences felt there might be a high admission fee. We needed to shout from the mountaintops that our event tickets were free. All you need is just a LinkedIn login at **hypcccycl.com**. We researched the ideal customer profile (ICP), and noticed that they got bored with B2B "blue Calibri," so we put the customer first, and that's why our design is so different.

Customer-Led Growth (CLG): This is a relatively new go-to-market (GTM) motion where the customers essentially help evangelize your mission with you. In essence, your best customers birth more customers without the heavy hand of the company controlling the narrative. It's like organically amplifying word of mouth or "mouse." Making your customers the stars of your virtual events creates a CLG or customer-led event (CLE) motion.

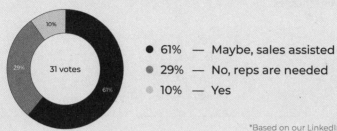

Do you think a pure-play PLG strategy can work up-market?

31 votes

- 61% — Maybe, sales assisted
- 29% — No, reps are needed
- 10% — Yes

*Based on our LinkedIn poll data

Product-Led Growth (PLG): As you highlight customers interacting with your products as the theme of your virtual event, you've now created product-led events. PLG is a venture capital (VC) business model darling that takes over where freemium left off but is distinctly different. You offer a tier or level where prospects can sign up to become customers, even fully demo the product with a solution like Reprise, Demostack, Pocus, or Walnut on their own from the front of your website. Then you can upgrade your customers later via new "sales assisted" motions. By putting your documentation up on GitLab, engineers can reflect on the open-source code. You can release demo videos and digital onboarding (WYSIWYG [what you see is what you get] site wizards) so prospects never have to deal with a salesperson.

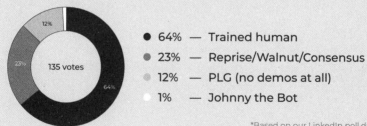

Who is better at demoing products—a human or a machine?

135 votes

- 64% — Trained human
- 23% — Reprise/Walnut/Consensus
- 12% — PLG (no demos at all)
- 1% — Johnny the Bot

*Based on our LinkedIn poll data

Ecosystem-Led Growth (ELG): The next level above in our "customer-led everything" pyramid is ELG, where channel partners or affiliated companies are involved in co-branding, co-sponsoring, co-hosting, co-selling, or integrated event themes.

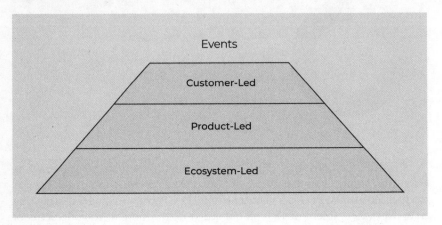

SECTION 4

Lessons from 100 GTM Events x 100 GTM Leaders

Give me a lever long enough and a fulcrum on which to place it, and I shall move the world.

— Archimedes

After throwing 100 interactive go-to-market (GTM) battles, we earned a Ph.D. in go-to-market strategy from some of the top thought leaders in business-to-business (B2B). We will highlight some unique challenges, including designed simulations, and then pull out an insight you can use for your events GTM as a mirror.

We've hosted a variety of go-to-market cross-training challenges and had august speakers from the B2B sector host a scenario around the skill or competency of their choosing. We thought it would be fun and instructive to highlight some of the GTM Games theme elements here and talk about why they matter to your event GTM approach. Venture capitalists (VCs) set up illuminating simulations from a sales, marketing & revenue operations (RevOps) perspective. Think about our G.A.M.E.S. event architecture/execution framework and be inspired and challenged by these stories. You can catch the sizzle reels if you go to YouTube and search HYPCCCYCL.

You can access all these games free of charge in the archives by logging into hypcccycl.com and badging your LinkedIn profile history as follows:

Member

HYPCCCYCL is an invite-only, professional community where top B2B revenue leaders cross-train their GTM skills with venture capitalists (VCs).

Let's get to the GTM challenges, the heart, and soul of this book!

CHAPTER 27

Revenue Operations (RevOps) Consolidation— Outreach

Which company is most likely to become the next Salesforce?

232 votes

- 46% — Outreach
- 24% — ZoomInfo
- 23% — Gong
- 7% — 6sense

*Based on our LinkedIn poll data

Mary Shea, Global Innovation Evangelist at Outreach, walks sellers through the critical facets of tech stack consolidation for revenue operations (RevOps) excellence. You shouldn't pay for redundant solutions that don't talk and integrate. There's been an overreliance on customer relationship management (CRM) as the one ring to rule them all. New Alpha-Uber platforms like Outreach are ascending to the status of sales engagement clouds.

Pressure points

- Competitors have more funding.
- Company strategy plans to become cash-flow positive in 18 months.
- CFO has asked for tech consolidation—move from $3,000/rep/mo to ~$1,500/rep/mo.
- Reps are pressuring RevOps to have top-tier enablement tools.

Contrarian view: Is a CRM even needed?

Scenario:

You run RevOps for the following company and have been tasked with consolidating the go-to-market (GTM) tech stack from a collection of disparate marketing and sales point solutions. Focus on maximizing your purchasing power, increasing your organization's predictable, efficient growth, and delivering buyer-centric experiences. To disrupt legacy and more highly capitalized competitors, you will have to be very savvy and creative in making the right bets such as, which tech categories to prioritize and why (you can't buy everything!); which vendors make the most sense for the size and sophistication of your organization; which vendors will provide the deepest functionality across the revenue cycle; and which vendors have a vision that you can get behind regarding the future of buying and selling in the business world.

Details:

Revenue Innovators, Inc.

B2B SaaS Company, 100 employees

Series C fundraise earlier this year.

5 SDRs

10 AEs

4 CSMs

1 RevOps

50/50 outbound and inbound

ACV: $25,000 annual recurring revenue (ARR)

Average Deal Cycle: 90 days

- Velocity: Enterprise approach, mid velocity, personalized outreach 30 prospects per day

Challenge:

Explain how you'll consolidate your current tech stacks across

CRM

- Sales Intelligence (i.e., ZoomInfo, Dun & Bradstreet)

- Intent (i.e., 6Sense, Bombora)
- Account-based marketing (ABM) (Terminus, Demandbase)
- LinkedIn Navigator
- Sales Content (i.e., Seismic, Highspot, Mediafly)
- Sales Engagement (i.e., Outreach, SalesLoft, Groove)
- Conversation Intelligence (i.e., Gong, Outreach Kaia, Chorus)
- Sales Readiness (i.e., Lessonly, Allego, Mindtickle)
- Sales Social Engagement (i.e., EveryoneSocial, Hootsuite)
- Revenue Ops/Intelligence (i.e., Clari, Aviso, Outreach Commit)

GTM Lessons

This drill is near and dear to our hearts as it's very much the subject of Justin's first book *Tech-Powered Sales*. When planning and staging an event, you need to analyze the overlap in your inbound and outbound solutions. We encourage you to invest in a sales engagement platform like Outreach that does much more than just automate your outbound touches: forecasting, Artificial intelligence (AI)-driven sales assistance, guided selling, revenue intelligence, and so on. Disclosure: they've been a fantastic sponsor and supporter of our GTM community.

Key Quotes

"We must have 360-degree visibility into our prospects and customers' actions across all channels they want to interact with. We must stop forecasting in a way that leans into the art rather than the science because we now have the science."

— Mary Shea

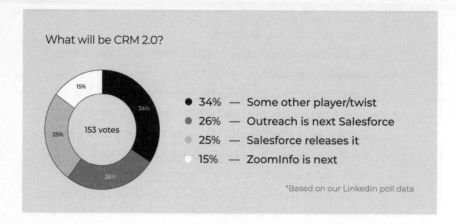

What will be CRM 2.0?

153 votes

- 34% — Some other player/twist
- 26% — Outreach is next Salesforce
- 25% — Salesforce releases it
- 15% — ZoomInfo is next

*Based on our LinkedIn poll data

"CRM is dead. . .is something that I have a contrarian opinion on. I don't think CRM is dead. I think it has a really important role, but that it's in the process of moving from front to back of the office, and part of that reason is that it was never designed for sellers. It was designed to accelerate invoicing."

"I just started to think about this Revenue Innovators concept: a leader who puts buyers at the center of all their strategies, who over-indexes on data rather than intuition to make business decisions, and who values sales and marketing technology. They arm their organizations with the most innovative technologies to continue that circle of engaging in a buyer-centric manner."

CHAPTER 28

Product-Led Growth (PLG) Game— Formative Ventures

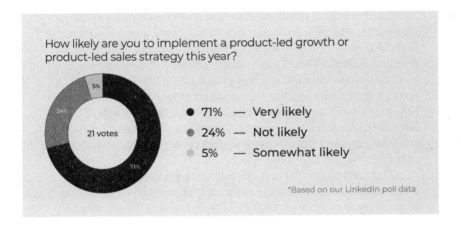

How likely are you to implement a product-led growth or product-led sales strategy this year?

21 votes

- 71% — Very likely
- 24% — Not likely
- 5% — Somewhat likely

*Based on our LinkedIn poll data

David Boyce is an investor and CEO at Formative Ventures having led strategy at XANT. In this "endgame," he shared a revenue structure for product-led growth (PLG) with various forecasts and funnel charts. Based on how the top seller from week one and leading marketer from week two gained an understanding of PLG forecasting and revenue motions, only one winner could prevail. Dave went super deep into what run rate you want to be at to implement a PLG motion, the various revenue curves, and crucial inflection points to make from hiring to product innovation to marketing motions depending on each scenario.

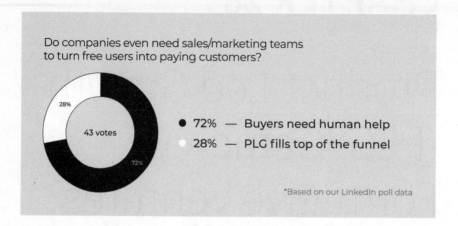

Do companies even need sales/marketing teams to turn free users into paying customers?

28%

43 votes

72%

● 72% — Buyers need human help

○ 28% — PLG fills top of the funnel

*Based on our LinkedIn poll data

This challenge was instructive in understanding which types of business models are more effective for scaling by mitigating mistakes as Dave sagely lays out how to refine go-to-market (GTM) in a downturn:

"Product-led growth is software's version of an industrial revolution. Capitalists of the first Industrial Revolution found they could move faster and more efficiently by hiring machines instead of humans to do repetitive tasks. The PLG revolution is doing the same thing.

In an economic climate where growth needs to fund itself, software companies are looking to sustainable growth models. No longer can we or should we pay humans to do what software can do. PLG hires the product to acquire, activate, monetize, and expand customers. Humans are thereby freed up to work on higher-order things with customers, like strategy and impact.

There is a pattern for building unicorn software companies. Understanding the sequence of what matters when is crucial for any team trying to go from $0–$100 million and beyond. First and most elusive is achieving product-market fit (PMF). Product-market fit for a PLG company can be defined as X% of new customers achieving Y in timeframe Z without human assistance. Only after product-market fit (PMF) do you work on go-to-market fit (GTMF). GTMF is getting the unit economics right (LTV:CAC > 3). After GTMF you can work on scaling. Each time you hit $10 million in recurring revenue you can consider launching a new GTM motion.

Take these out of order (e.g., work on scaling before PMF), and you will waste a lot of money and time and ultimately fail. Follow this pattern and you will have a far greater chance of success than the current 1:1,000 chance of a funded startup becoming a breakout success."

GTM Lessons

Applying Dave's advice to event models stems from letting go of your obsession with endless marketing promotion for net new leads and fostering sustainability out of your current customer base. Implement customer-centric events (CCEs) with your existing customers as a beacon to attract others and improve customer happiness and net revenue retention (NRR).

Dave adds, "We built all our marketing and sales machinery around the 'win' to count closed-won deals and dollars. If we want to stack revenue to the sky, the most stackable GTM motion is PLG. I call it stackable revenue."

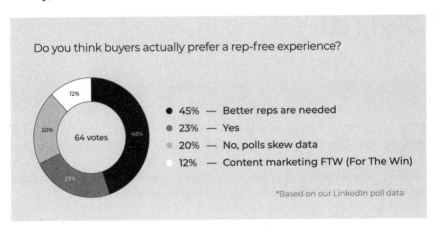

Do you think buyers actually prefer a rep-free experience?

64 votes

- 45% — Better reps are needed
- 23% — Yes
- 20% — No, polls skew data
- 12% — Content marketing FTW (For The Win)

*Based on our LinkedIn poll data

CHAPTER 29

Tech Stack Optimization Game— Sonar

B rad Smith, Co-Founder and CEO of Sonar Software, runs the "Wizard of Ops" Slack community and is brilliant in operationalizing revenue operations (RevOps); his unique perspective brings Engineering elements into the workflow. Scenario: A company reaches a $10-million run rate and needs to invest in the top five pieces of software to keep growing.

GTM Lessons

Brad teaches us that "something's got to give" with RevOps. Ultimately, you can't buy every tool as it's cost-prohibitive, especially now that we are in the budget freeze, cost-cutting, and tool-cutting consolidation phase of "death by tech stacks." Management will question the role of RevOps again, but downsizing there is shortsighted. There's an impulse to trust every alpha/uber platform that bundles together "generalist" tools versus compiling a tech stack of "specialists." The truth is, you need to do both. Consolidate as many solutions as possible and then choose best-of-breed point solutions where it's essential to achieve your GTM goals. Hire for internal/external RevOps muscle to glue it all together so it "talks." *(Check out our whitepaper: TECH STACK SECRETS REVEALED to look under the hood of 30+ top GTM leaders: https://hypcccycl. com/gtm-tech-stack/)*

The lessons from this event are about tech stack consolidation and specialization. It's the same reasoning as you invest in events. How much time, energy, and effort will you put into the event relative to return on investment

Submarine, Inc.

B2B SaaS Company, 50 employees

Series A fundraise earlier this year

10 SDRs

12 AEs

4 CSMs

1 RevOps

50/50 outbound and inbound

ACV: $20,000 annual recurring revenue (ARR)

Average Deal Cycle: 30 days

Velocity: high velocity (high call volume, high email volume)

Challenge:

Please select the top seven GTM software solutions you would leverage to make this go-to-market (GTM) team successful.

Event marketing takeaways:

(ROI)? Are you going to build a community on Mighty Networks or Circle? Will you pop for the enterprise version of Zoom, and use mmhmm or Prezi video? How will you optimize your marketing, advertising, design, and public relations (PR) spending to make your events as successful as possible? Our advice is to be less reliant on software and more focused on "customer-centric" storytelling. Set up an Event Stack (see Chapter 15) with free trials for a test run event so you can pick winners who delivered on their ROI promise before locking in contracts.

CHAPTER 30

Questioning Frameworks Game— Costanoa Ventures

I n this interactive game, Jim Wilson recommended qualification methods like Demo2Win, Sales MEDDIC (Metrics, Economic buyer, Decision criteria, Decision process, Identify pain, and Champion), ACE (Activity, Concentration, and Effectiveness), wagon circling, and other top sales methodologies and discovery frameworks. Jim focused on a hypothetical startup he'd invested in within the construction vertical. Each contestant had the same core scenario with prospect personas and value props. So, isolating and equalizing the scenario leveled the drill's playing field.

Jim's deep understanding of sales discovery frameworks helped him drive explosive growth and exits at software as a service (SaaS) leaders like Merced Systems (Nice Systems), and Sumo Logic. In this mock simulation, the contestants pitch their platform to the VP of Field Operations for Skedulo. They need to ask open-ended discovery questions for 8 minutes to probe deeper into the issues and get to the root cause of challenges in the field the software can solve. (Peel the onion and conduct a root cause analysis.)

The goal is to practice an initial 5-minute discovery call, get coached, and teach it back. Jim teaches blended Discovery Frameworks like MEDDIC; they run back through the framework multiple times.

Rules:

Whoever best applies the reframe from Jim's discovery method wins per Jim. Ultimately, who dug deepest, uncovered pain (latent pain) better and tailored their value prop to inspire Jim to take action to buy.

> *Role play:*
>
> *Company: Healthworkers United*
>
> *Problem: They have reps in the field, and they are trying to manage schedules.*
>
> *Solution: Your company sells a Mobile Workforce Management solution (i.e., Skedulo).*
>
> *Buyer Persona: I am the VP of Field Operations.*
>
> *Goal—Ask me questions to uncover my problems, then explain how your product might solve the problem. Get me interested enough to take a second meeting and see a demo.*

GTM Lessons

There are so many acronyms for sales discovery, it could make your head spin. TAS (Target Account Selling), NEAT (Need, Economic impact, Access to authority, and Timeline), SCOTSMAN (Solution, Competition, Originality, Timescale, Size, Money, Authority, and Need), FAINT (Funds, Authority, Interest, Need, and Timing), BANT (Budget, Authority, Need, and Timing), and MEDDIC, just to name a few. No one will contest that asking practical discovery questions is the key to customer-centricity. Whenever there's a problem with marketing, Julia's response is, "Did you do a deep enough discovery?"

You need to listen to your market. We had Richard Harris on for a NEAT selling drill where he blew our minds with his ability to take discovery itself to easily 45 minutes just probing into the deeper underlying pains. Great GTM leaders do this, and you must embrace this way of thinking to unlock the total value of event topics, and what issues matter the most to customers you put on your virtual stage. Nine out of 10, the initial surface ideas and themes are not the real story.

Insightful Quotes

"Remember you're not trying to close a sale on a discovery call. You're trying to be memorable and make an impression on the prospect. The best way to do that, in my experience, is: to have good metrics. A metric is a number. I can tell you something is

fantastic, but if I give you a number behind it—a 54% increase— people remember numbers."

— Jim Wilson

"How do you respond to a zinger? Hey, can I have it for free? I'd love to use the product for six months, is that okay? Your competition said this. Repeat the question if you want to buy time to get your brain to click in to think about how to respond. Oh, I'm sorry, did I understand that right? Did you ask if you want to use the product for six months? And if you can, because you can feel the tension on Zoom, can you give me more clarity around it; is there more thinking behind it?

"Giving yourself 5 seconds or so gives you a chance to compose your answer. It's better to do a short 'proof of concept' based on your use case. Before offering it for free, we want to show you the different options and the ROI. Frame it back to—*it's about them*—and then use your best practices of how you believe others have evaluated your product as a way to frame the answer.

"You're better off NOT having slides. You're better off with conversation. The 'show-up and throw-up' problem. I think some of the worst discovery calls are when you get on and you've got a 20-slide overview of the company. People don't like that. What they want is back and forth.

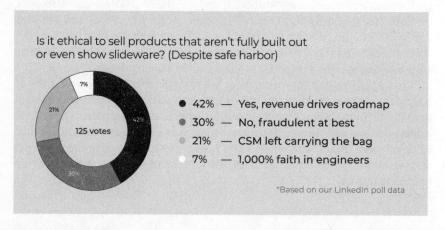

Is it ethical to sell products that aren't fully built out or even show slideware? (Despite safe harbor)

125 votes

- 42% — Yes, revenue drives roadmap
- 30% — No, fraudulent at best
- 21% — CSM left carrying the bag
- 7% — 1,000% faith in engineers

*Based on our LinkedIn poll data

"When we think about investing, we look at the whole package. We look at the founder and the background, and in many ways, founders with experience in sales and marketing have an excellent background because they know how to get to market. It's one thing to build a product. It's an entirely separate thing to figure out how to sell it. For those selling technical products, your best superpower as a salesperson is to say, 'I don't know' because it builds credibility and makes you real and human."

How customer-centric is that!

CHAPTER 31

Merger and Acquisition (M&A) GTM Game— CoachCRM

C ory Bray, Co-Founder of CoachCRM and ClozeLoop, is an entrepreneur par excellence, business strategist, and prolific writer of what will be nine Amazon books by this writing with the luminous Hilmon Sorey. He lays out this brilliant real-world go-to-market (GTM) scenario as follows in our game.

GTM Lessons

Fostering alignment between sales and marketing with a solid investment in RevOps takes time. You can't expect behavioral change overnight. The solution is to break down the silos and increase communication between cross-functional teams. Aligning key performance indicators (KPIs), objectives and key results (OKRs), and management by objectives (MBOs) can unite the fractured org.

According to Cory in a post-mortem, "I think a FAST focus on cross-selling is key. Build the playbook, roll it out, iterate, and COACH on what people actually do." A significant factor is arming the acquisition sales team with talking points or simple tracks. You're not going to integrate a new sales and marketing team, fully onboard them, and ramp them on the latest products

RedCo just purchased BlueCo for $50 million.

RedCo is a 500-person Series D tech company that has rapidly grown. They have traditionally been a powerhouse in their market. Everyone knows who they are. They have a complete executive team and have built a machine. They have every software tool under the sun, and most are used. However, growth has slowed recently.

RedCo has three products that are sold by three different sales teams. They are primarily junior sellers who live off of inbound. Leads are routed to the appropriate team based on the prospect's action, and the seller closes the deal and moves on to the next one. Well, the seller doesn't usually do so alone. Managers spend most days super-closing deals for their reps, which has scared off many top performers. Cross-sells are rare, and most sellers don't know much about the other two products.

BlueCo only had 50 people before the acquisition. Their CEO is a former chief revenue officer (CRO) of several high-growth companies, brought over the best eight salespeople he's ever worked with. Having an average of 25 years of experience, each of these folks hunts and closes big deals. All are above quota.

BlueCo had one marketing channel: events. They had no sales development team internally, but leveraged an external appointment setting firm that kept the sellers' calendars full. Customer relationship management (CRM) was sometimes a spreadsheet but usually held in the salespeople's heads or on their desk napkins.

The acquisition was exciting because all BlueCo customers could buy RedCo, and vice versa. However, the conflict has already started to arise:

- RedCo's product team wants to continue what they're building instead of focusing on integrations. BlueCo's sales team thinks that integration work is more valuable.
- RedCo's marketing team is concerned that BlueCo's employees (not just sales) frequently go off-brand during social posts and events . . . but these activities generate good leads.
- RedCo's chief information officer (CIO) wants to hire a consulting firm to do an assessment before touching anything revenue operations (RevOps)-related. Mostly everyone disagrees with this approach.

And the kicker, a large private equity (PE) fund has indicated that if the combined entities can double revenue in the next 18 months, they are a strong acquisition candidate. So they must move fast.

What should the new combined team prioritize? What should they ignore?

overnight. If they can speak somewhat intelligently to the value prop on calls, it can open deal flow for proper handoff.

CHAPTER 32

GTM Playbook Scenario—Redpoint Ventures

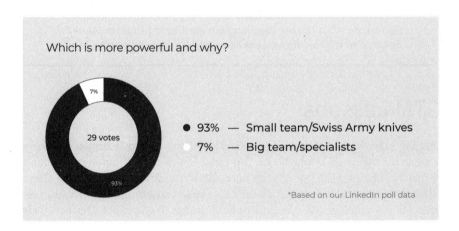

Which is more powerful and why?

● 93% — Small team/Swiss Army knives

○ 7% — Big team/specialists

29 votes

*Based on our LinkedIn poll data

Travis Bryant led sales at Front, Optimizely, and Salesforce. He's Partner, Founder Experience at Redpoint Ventures focused on enabling, empowering, and up-skilling entrepreneurs in portfolio companies. He focused his drill on building out go-to-market (GTM) playbooks and the power of a thorough ideal customer profile (ICP) and ideal prospect profile (IPP) definition exercise.

Scenario:

The company is at $750,000 annual recurring revenue (ARR)—15 customers at $50,000 average annual contract value (ACV). All founder-led sales so far, with one sales development rep (SDR) doing a combination of inbound qualification and some outbound prospecting. One growth marketer doing demand gen, website, and so on. One technical support individual does onboarding, support, and ongoing success management—one Ops person is responsible for analysis, tools/systems, and data across all GTM.

It's time to scale the GTM function. We have 15 happy customers, but we haven't taken the time to reverse-engineer how we got them to happiness. We need to hire a sales leader and build a customer-facing team, but we're not sure which roles to prioritize based on the customers we should focus on right now. We haven't documented our Ideal Customer Profile nor figured out the ideal path from Prospect->Happy Customer.

Challenge:

What steps would you take to build version 1 of the GTM playbook? How would you distill the learnings from the first 15 customers into a process that you can train a team to use and hold them accountable to?

GTM Lessons

Our big takeaway from our time with Travis was to take a design thinking approach to your GTM playbook. You need to get clear about your ICP and IPP to be effective. The granularity here and thoughtfulness in refining these attributes present a series of trade-offs. It's the same as building out a successful event. You can't please everyone or be all things to all people. "Narrow your niche," as Aaron Ross always says. Notice in the drill the impetus to "reverse-engineer" customer happiness. Once you win, why did you win? What is making customers realize real value and *impact*? Once you hold a successful event, analyze all aspects of it so you can rinse and repeat. A customer-centric event (CCE) can be so pivotal it even informs the product roadmap, which is another reason you should effectively roll out a vocal customer advisory board (CAB) like our partner Chili Piper.

CHAPTER 33

GTM Pillars Challenge—Edison Partners

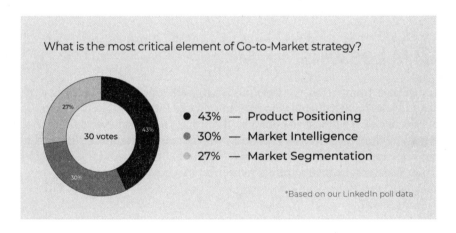

What is the most critical element of Go-to-Market strategy?

- 43% — Product Positioning
- 30% — Market Intelligence
- 27% — Market Segmentation

30 votes

27%
43%
30%

*Based on our LinkedIn poll data

K elly Ford Buckley is a General Partner at Edison Partners. She walked the top sales and marketing contestants from weeks 1 and 2 through a slide illustrating an end-to-end go-to-market (GTM) strategy for growth-stage companies. Then, she presented this scenario:

Company: BEACH, Inc., a B2B business with 150 employees, $25 million revenue.

Situation:

- Consistent grower, 45%–55% year over year (YoY) for the last three years.

- Ideal customer profile (ICP) is any mid-sized and large company; no vertical focus
- Single, direct, new-logo-focused sales team selling a single product; average deal size: $75,000–$100,000
- The pricing model has a single lever: users
- Best-in-class gross revenue retention, 96%; no difference between gross and net retention
- Recently raised $20 million Series B; primary use of proceeds: Accelerate growth through diversification
- New high-value product capabilities will be released soon

The Challenge: Describe how you would define and align the GTM for greater diversification to capture more value per customer (new and existing) for BEACH. Give at least one example per the following GTM pillars.

STRATEGY POSITION PLAN PROCESS PEOPLE

GTM Lessons

We learned from Kelly that account-based marketing (ABM) vendors don't want to take on bad clients who have misaligned internal GTM processes. To be effective with a robust solution like Terminus, you must have your house in order and the process defined. Plan to win and win by planning. "If Marketing is focused on an inbound strategy that's not aligned with target accounts while Sales is out whale hunting," objectives can be misaligned.

Quotes and Insights

You need alignment with your marketing and sales team post-events to capture the total value of the audience you generate. "Alignment creates acceleration." Don't "generate demand with the wrong customers" and "slow your sales process down." Misalignment can cause problems downstream, including "stickiness factors."

Kelly is laser-focused on aligning GTM teams at her portfolio companies. Kelly highlights "levers for growth and diversification. You might add one or two markets, new industries, and products to serve them and tailor the positioning to support them. What kind of investments do you need to make to drive the growth levers of the business? Consider your pricing and packaging. Diversify by adding a partner channel versus selling direct."

CHAPTER 34

Disruption and Product-Market Fit (PMF)—U+

There's no such thing as a disruptive idea. Customer adoption at scale is what creates disruption.

— Sean Sheppard

Challenge:

> *"What's the big problem that you're solving today?*
> *Who's the team? What's the market?*
> *What product are you offering in that market?*
> *What traction do you have to date?*
> *How are you different?"*

We loved the powerful simplicity of Sean Sheppard's venture capitalist (VC) round because it was a chance for a top seller and marketer to pitch their startup idea to an accomplished early-stage VC. You may know Sean Sheppard of U+, a 5× founder with three exits who is a go-to-market (GTM) philosopher and pragmatist with a penchant for Stoicism. You better have "traction" before barking up his tree. He's an angel investor and venture capitalist behind some of the biggest business-to-business (B2B) successes that sponsored our event.

When he went to crown the winner of the GTM Games, he decided to break our rules. And we couldn't help but let him. Not because we are pushovers, but because it "made sense." He declared a tie on the merits of the two contestants' delivery and the strength of each company's GTM. One award was for a Certified B Corp with an egalitarian mission, and the other for a C Corp.

In Sean's simulation, he highlighted five pillars that act as a GTM filter for the startups he invests in. But before that, he always asks, "what's the big problem you solve?"

Pillar I—Team

Pillar II—Market

Pillar III—Product

Pillar IV—Traction

Pillar V—Differentiation

Gabrielle "GB" Blackwell (Airtable) and Arthur Castillo (Chili Piper) did a tremendous job applying what they learned over the past two weeks switching lives (*sellers become marketers become sellers*). They implemented Sean's live coaching as they each presented how they'd approach the preceding pillars. The mission of the games worked. By going through the two-week intensive, the contestants learned hard skills they could already apply under the extreme pressure of pitching a VC.

Sean decided that GB's "Women in Sales Club" and Arthur Castillo's "Chili Piper" both won for their respective mission-driven and commercial aspects of GTM. GTM Games democratizes access to GTM strategy training for executives at all levels. Sean decided to make a difference with his coaching and change the game when he didn't have to. Instead of one GTM Winner, he went with a real-life scenario of magnanimously awarding funds to both a B Corp and a C Corp because he could. Change is a choice.

Thank you, Sean, for dedicating your time and brilliance to the event and helping us optimize a model where everyone wins. Gabrielle commented, "The whole experience was amazing. I've learned so much. To have had the opportunity to learn from Sean Sheppard today and also to be able to have two winners was phenomenal." And Arthur wrote, "I feel like you started me on my path to becoming a CRO [chief revenue officer]. The strategies and ideas made me realize how much I love this GTM function."

Quotes and Insights

"It always starts with a clear understanding and a very simple narrative around the problems you are solving. And if you can't explain that clearly, people can't identify with it, raise their hand, and say, 'yes, I have that problem.'

"We get too focused on our product and not enough on the problem. People don't care about our products. They care about their problems and whether or not they can be solved. Products are simply byproducts of trying to solve those key problems. Then, can you assemble the right kind of team with the right subject matter expertise in the appropriate roles necessary to solve that problem for an early cohort of customers? Because word of mouth is the fastest path to product-market fit (PMF). That word of mouth has to come from that initial cohort of customers where you have user stories before and after that can show the rest of the market that there is a problem and you are the right one to solve it for them."

What is the novel unique differentiator between you, and how do they solve it today, internally or alternatively?

There are two kinds of entrepreneurs. Those who have disruptive ideas that change the game and those who have practical ways of improving on the game.

Traction speaks louder than words.

Speaks volumes about the quality of the team.

Most successful founders have dealt with that problem and figured out how to solve it themselves. Until you walk a mile in the shoes of the customer, we don't really understand how deep that problem is. Don't write a single line of code until you know who your customer is. I don't care what you know. I care what you understand."

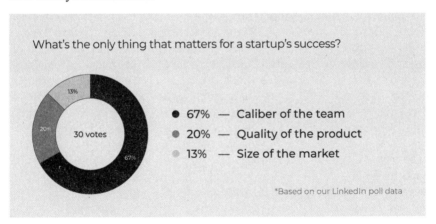

"Build something 100 people love, not something 1 million people kind of like." — Brian Chesky, Co-Founder & CEO, Airbnb

Stereotypically:

→ Marketing is easy.

→ Sales is easy.

→ Ops is easy

Or is it hard?

→ Product is hard.

→ Engineering is hard.

→ CEO is hard.

There's a mythology around the "GTM Natural." Perceptions that one can be a "natural" seller, marketer, or even a natural-born operations leader.

Maybe it is easy to just go through the motions of the role. But it's tough to be excellent in how you execute. Neil Patel writes, "Being an entrepreneur isn't for everyone. It often takes years of hard work, long hours, and no recognition to become successful. A lot of entrepreneurs give up, or fail for other reasons, like running out of money. Statistics show that over 50% of all businesses fail after five years."

Per Brian Chesky of Airbnb, getting the PMF is the hardest piece. Per Neil Patel, it's the investment of time, sheer amount of failure, and white-knuckled financial pickle. Marc Andreessen wins for the most provocative idea in this space. Excerpt from his famous essay in the archive "The Only Thing That Matters."

"Personally, we'll take the third position—I'll assert that the market is the most important factor in a startup's success or failure. Why? In a great market—a market with lots of real potential customers—the market pulls products out of the startup."

SECTION 5

Recession-Proofing Your Event Vision

CHAPTER 35

The Future of Events in a Socially Distant World

We know from chaos theory that even if you had a perfect model of the world, you'd need infinite precision to predict future events. With sociopolitical or economic phenomena, we don't have anything like that.

— Nassim Nicholas Taleb

In every event contract, there's a force majeure that frees up the parties if something like a hurricane, insurrection, flood, or fire happens. We've never seen a more volatile time in human history, so we write this potentially going into a recessionary condition after a pandemic kept boomeranging back. Hybrid, digital, and virtual reality (VR)-style events will become more and more the norm into the 2030s. We'll probably have to revise this book to account for the many new platforms and enabling technologies for events in the not-too-distant multiverse future racing toward us.

Building trust is about building affinity, shared vision, and sparking curiosity. If an event is dull and flat, it will repel even if the content is exceptionally well produced and seemingly high-quality. How many webinars have you been on that look like a million bucks, but you're so bored you can't help but multitask? Or it's so cringeworthy you spend the entire hour slacking colleagues like Siskel & Ebert, grappling to stay awake. It's like bad ads on the

Super Bowl. Sure they cost a king's ransom, but they didn't capture your attention more than your bucket of chicken wings. That's the same miss when you don't nail a customer-centric theme.

Executives are looking for ways to shatter the paradigm, see around the corner, and disrupt themselves. No matter what they will tell you, you need to believe us on this statement. You need to challenge conventional thinking and the status quo.

You should adopt a growth mindset of innovation to test new platforms like TikTok; experiment with virtual worlds, avatar-based event platforms, and new social networks; explore different formats; and ABC/I—always be creating/innovating.

The world of business-to-business (B2B) will look like a scene out of *Ready Player One* or *Minority Report* before we know it, transacting in virtual reality with our Oculus or HoloLens VR headsets to negotiate and close deals at the speed of light. Next-level growth hackers will find new and innovative ways to bring warm leads inbound. We could see a fundamental shift away from the pervasive *Moneyball* sales development rep-account executive (SDR-AE) model that has siloed outbound and inbound motions.

Future event concepts comprise hybridizing themes, category breaking, and genre-bending, focused on skill-building. There must be a way to train reps on skills 1:1, which Julia has built out with Hard Skill Exchange™ (HSE™). Welcome to a new marketplace that breaks the B2B cohort training model making hard skill-building and apprenticeship more like a gym where you can train on-demand with multiple experts.

Customer Experience Is the New Marketing/Salesperson

Phenomenal user interface/user experience (UI/UX) and design thinking applied to online digital experiences are what the work of Brian Solis is all about. There are tech limitations to what we can build to truly entice your best prospects and clients in a digital world, with digital events, within a two-dimensional Zoom call. At this writing, we hear rumblings that Apple will enter the fray with a VR headset, as Magic Leap, Oculus (Meta), and Hololens (Microsoft) have done. Once we inject more creativity into augmented reality/virtual reality (AR/VR) formats, it will allow us to express our ideas and make webinars far more interactive overall. The issue with this conceptually, though, is adoption.

It's likely, well into 2030, even toward 2050, that the majority of webinars will still look eerily similar to the Zoom, BlueJeans, WebEx, and GoToMeeting of yesteryear—not to mention these companies will innovate around the curve.

We'd like to see more ways to fuse multimedia elements, make it even more interactive; exert more manipulation over the image, video, sharing, and screen layouts; and go 3D holographic for collaboration. We need AI-assisted interactivity across the board. The AR/VR channel is compelling, but the jury's still out on when laypeople will adopt VR goggles to go into Metaverse.

Upon adopting our model, we see the future of events with your "customers" in the spotlight. The essence of an in-person event was an experience. You were willing to invest the hours and resources plus sacrifice family time to receive a priceless memory. While you can't provide drinks, pyrotechnics, swag, and booths in online events, you *can* take them to the next level by making them interactive.

Think about it: even when attending a keynote offline, you as a customer are in the spotlight too as you interact and network with top thought leaders. You get the intangible feeling that you're a part of it. The risk of Zoom Reality is you tend feel like you're in the shadows. Big online keynote: nothing happens—no networking, no discussions, maybe a question or two. Your voice and opinion are not necessary.

The Best Communities Happen When Your Users Build the Community with You

You never feel like Nike Run Club *owns* you, even running every morning. You are excited to be there. That this is Nike, your partner (versus a vendor), teaching you how to run better transcends a random ticker symbol driving revenue to a shoe company. You feel like you are part of a movement, holding the torch and creating something meaningful together with the brand. An equal part of the community vision, Nike's chief marketing officer (CMO) listens to you. It happens through an app (quantified-self movement for the win, sensors in your shoes or watch, soon glasses?). You have a chapter in your city, and although everyone can do what you do, you somehow feel important. Your status depends on how active you are in the movement.

The goal is not only to achieve this in communities but across all channels. Give customers the idea of what you're co-creating and let that idea evolve into something greater with your customers at the helm of creativity and collaboration. As a founder or CMO, you are KPI'd to impossibility, so you restrict the "freedom of movement" of customers and participants in your events. Why not take the event topic somewhere more expansive or in a different direction than what you initially wanted it to be?

We get it. You have to push this widget up a hill all day with a strict social media policy. You're avoiding chaos and "off-brand" career limiting moves. But we have news for you. Nobody wants to attend another webinar on "How to Automate the Sales Process with AI" except your competitors to steal your pitch. Didn't you cringe just reading that? Moderators feel forced to keep the talk track on a single topic. The moment someone says, "AI is not happening in B2B. It's fake AI," you block that person or don't let them lead that conversation to an objective, creative place of healthy debate. You're worried about the optics if your CEO watches it. Now it's sterile, controlled, and inorganic.

CHAPTER 36

Making Virtual Event Promotions Soar in a Down Economy

The '90s and early 2000s were the "I" decade. iPhone, the iPod—everything was about me. Look where that got us? In a terrible recession.

— Adam Neumann

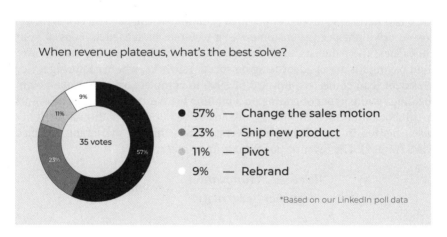

When revenue plateaus, what's the best solve?

35 votes

- 57% — Change the sales motion
- 23% — Ship new product
- 11% — Pivot
- 9% — Rebrand

*Based on our LinkedIn poll data

As we've stated in this book numerous times, if only you could "buy your way into the winner's circle." Julia came out of nowhere with her first event concept, which captured the attention of business-to-business (B2B) rapidly. The HYPCCCYCL GTM Games remains a smash hit created on the principles of this book. As of this writing, global travel is surging to such an extent post-pandemic, despite international economic pressure: humans are clamoring to get back "in person" again. The hybrid model is built to last.

We see a paradox with economic factors and events. Sure, there was a massive surge of virtual events, but "will it become irrelevant when the world opens back up?" Pandemics could come back, portends Bill Gates. You need to be ready with a digitally enabled strategy to capture audiences.

> *Customer-centric events (CCEs) create positive brand exposure and generate executive champions that position you favorably as the undisputed innovator in your industry.*

We used to write off the cost of flying our sales and marketing leaders to Barcelona to set up a booth for a week and fund a neon-lit DJ after-party with an "open bar" relative to the return on investment (ROI) of attracting millions of dollars from qualified prospects into your funnel. Now contrast that with presenting a webinar for a fraction of that price tag. Hold the paella! Virtual reigns supreme without any resultant travel and entertainment expenses from an in-person gathering going up in smoke. Virtual events make sense economically; you can spin them up within 10 business days and leverage basic technology like Zoom as a bulletproof foundation where attendees traveling off the grid with low dial-up speeds can make it.

There are ways to do virtual wine tasting events with a sommelier remotely and effectively, even shipping fruit and cheese. In a down economy, the customer acquisition cost per lead plummets. Suppose you calculate the cost to drive prospective customers to a webinar via feedback loops of your colleagues, the panelists, and your customers. In that case, it's much lower than paying for direct advertising on social networks, where acquiring a vice president lead could cost upward of $200 to complete an action like downloading a white paper or getting on a mailing list. You can produce the events in this book for under $500 per month and drive hundreds of thousands, if not seven-figures, in qualified pipeline versus indeterminate marketing qualified leads (MQLs). The revenue potential is up to relevance.

$$\frac{Relevance * Innovation}{customer - centricity} = Revenue$$

Customer-Centricity

It's critical to run lean even when the economy is booming, but these best practices will help you when dark clouds fill the economic forecast.

Event promotion ideas leveraging the butterfly effect:

1. Act as your own "sales development rep (SDR) team of one" using a sales engagement platform to send out personalized, targeted invites to attend and follow-up/drip-nurture.

2. Experiment with non-obvious platforms like calendar dropping; we highly recommend Chili Piper (partner) and WhatsApp messaging with Loom Video customized intros.

3. Consider a third-party SDR agency, appointment setter, or email lead gen house to blast out invites for you, like Veth Group.

4. Write engaging social posts and tag the participants to share.

5. Get everyone in your event to share promotions to their networks for downstream amplification.

6. Press release the local media on how groundbreaking the events are, including building a public relations (PR) strategy for the various niche-focused publications. Remember, customers can lead the charge here in our new model.

7. Build out a community on Dark Social with members, brand ambassadors, and volunteers

8. Get your tribe to badge their profile with your event community, which will create a ripple effect of visibility.

9. Make an in-kind trade with a gifting automation sponsor in return for exposure to send swag to your base to increase goodwill. Email them once received and ensure that they share on social. We send our biggest supporters and winners wine with the slogan, "B2B Boredom Remedy."

10. Emcee all your events to bring a charismatic, entertaining silver lining. Remember to talk only 10% of the time and keep quality interactions going.

11. Push all your video content to YouTube, then reshare it frequently through LinkedIn, Twitter, Instagram, Snap, TikTok, and Facebook and ask 20–30 supporters per day to spread those links.

CHAPTER 37

Bulletproof Lead Generation Year-Round

Instead of interrupting, work on attracting.

— Dharmesh Shah, CTO and Co-Founder, HubSpot

You can generate leads in a down economy just as quickly as in boom times. When the customers on your panel promote to their lists, you unlock what Reid Hoffman described as "networked intelligence." LinkedIn built a whole product around this for employee advocacy called Elevate, now LinkedIn Pages. Your weak ties become very strong because you can reach an exponentially larger audience through second- and third-degree connections spreading the word.

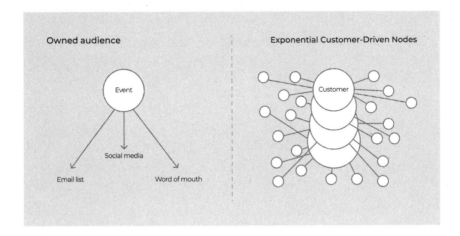

When you're a single vendor working on your "owned customer" file, tap into the downstream networks of ecosystem partners, sponsors, coaches, panelists, audience, and especially your customers. You can foster virality and pull all those networks toward you. You must take the traditional event promotional model on the left and turn it into a multi-dimensional electromagnetic pulse (EMP) on the right by activating and incentivizing your participants to share. Best way to do this? Design and innovation.

It's vital to grow your LinkedIn fan base as large as possible. Did you know you can switch your connect button to a follow button on LinkedIn? Also, by leveraging "Creator Mode," you'll have more visibility. Select the tags you share most. We feature favorites like #sales #marketing #gtm and #innovation. We built up 61,000 followers, and Justin was able to max his connections to 30,000. Our daily posting discipline to relevant social media channels about go-to-market (GTM) paid off over time. As you see, it greatly influenced the research into this book. As skeptical empiricists, we became our own analyst firm leveraging snap poll data to bring you never-before-insights first we pressure tested with the crowd. The source? All of you!

We reverse-engineered the LinkedIn algorithm, so if polls were trending, we exploited that, built out video highlight reels, or cut up custom GIFs moving at hyper-fast speed to stick way out on the feed. Dare to be different.

The starkness of the contrast black-and-white imagery stood out like lightning flashing against the darkness of a deep ocean night (our first sites always featured onyx water moving to symbolize infinite energy and creativity). We became a beacon of innovation and disruption in our tiny business-to-business (B2B) echo chamber of "blue Calibri" seemingly overnight—*by design*. Leads flooded our website as 50,000 visitors arrived rapidly to see what all the fuss was about.

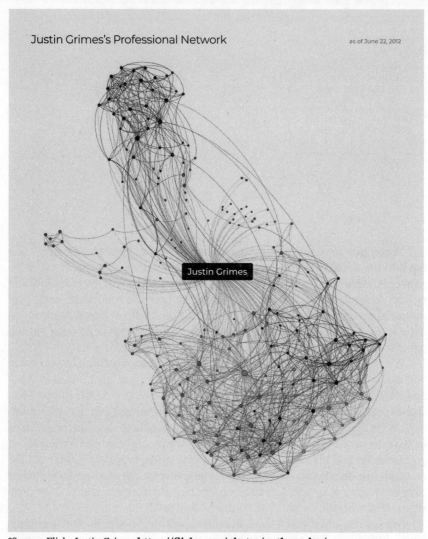

Justin Grimes's Professional Network

as of June 22, 2012

Justin Grimes

*Source: Flickr Justin Grimes **https://flickr.com/photos/notbrucelee/**

CHAPTER 38

Ecosystem-Driven Events

I don't care whether the technology is invented by our employees. I want to bring everybody's innovations into our ecosystem together.

— Masayoshi Son

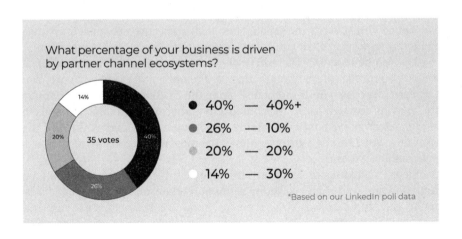

What percentage of your business is driven by partner channel ecosystems?

- 40% — 40%+
- 26% — 10%
- 20% — 20%
- 14% — 30%

*Based on our LinkedIn poll data

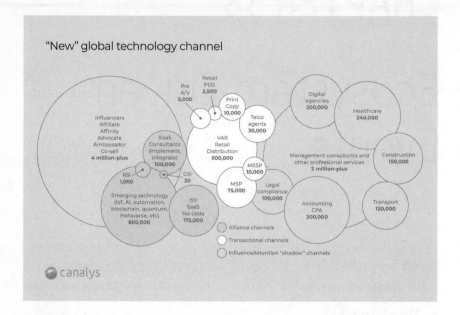

We are living in the "Decade of the Ecosystem." By 2030, 90% of business will be driven via the ecosystem, as predicted by Jay McBain, Chief Analyst at Canalys. It's going to be a similar mega-trend for driving events. We dismiss ecosystems as simply "partner channels." Do you have an extensive list of integrated partners? Imagine involving them all in an interactive, online virtual event and tapping into their respective networks to create a marketing halo effect of air cover that creates a virtuous cycle of "lead-sharing."

Jay also believes in "The end of the marketing qualified lead (MQL). If you talk about the future of marketing, you're not going direct anymore. You may earn one or two of 28 moments" along the customer journey. Customers are "moving through these 28 moments to gather the confidence to make a vendor selection without ever talking to a salesperson. That's over half the cases now. You must only involve sales in the most highly considered products and complex issues."

Steps to building an ecosystem-driven event: Pick a partner, decide on a mutual theme, and align marketing teams and sellers for optimal event distribution and amplification. Make the event about a collaborative use case and the value the integration unlocks to the customer. Feature a customer who's currently benefiting from the partnership to talk about success, results, and return on investment (ROI). Examples: Salesloft and 6sense, Outreach and Regie.ai, Metadata and Mutiny.

Jay goes on to share, "Out of the 14 spheres of influence that we track, events are one of the most important. Events are driven by vendors, distributors, the media, associations, peer groups, and others to bring together like-minded people and drive messaging, educational content, and the all-important human-to-human (H2H) interactions that sit at the core of influence."

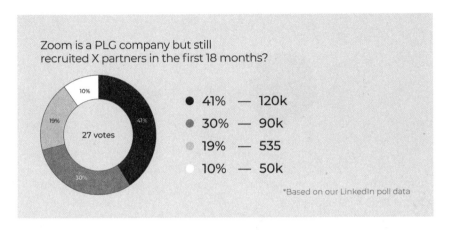

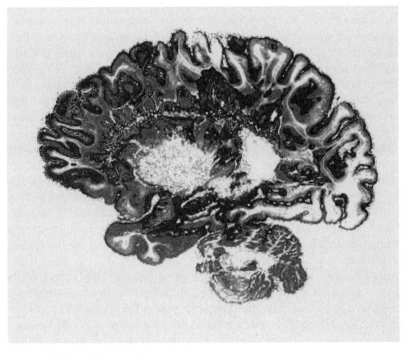

Source: NIH: public domain

Dunbar's Number comes from the measurement of nodes in the neo-cortex. It's a law that governs primate societies and a guideline for the size

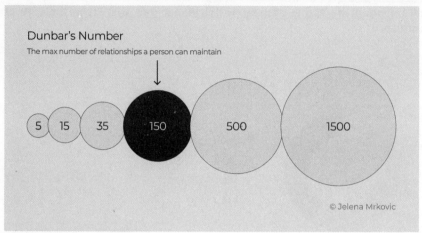

© Jelena Mrkovic, Wikipedia

of military divisions and Gore-Tex business units. It's also called the Rule of 150. Oxford evolutionary psychologist Robin Dunbar found the number of relationships we cognitively maintain. The human mind can comfortably recall about 150 nodes before getting hazy. When you think nodally, you can map an entire industry relatively quickly by locating the opinion leaders and key influencers with the highest follower counts and most influence and rattle their cages. Then event amplification and lead generation become metaphorically "rattling the nodes." If you vibrate those, the entire ecosystem moves.

Just like synaptic firings and impulses move in the brain, you must look at your social ecosystem. Good news travels fast. When something is exciting, innovative, and groundbreaking, everyone wants in on it. The irony of the world is that it's starving for content. Millions of tweets, likes, status updates, comment threads, and trillions of emails, and you're thinking, "What's the validity of my idea? It's all been done before." On the contrary, by staging something new that is a mash-up of other ideas, you'll become the lighthouse of your industry and make a splash with the media.

Our audience wants to be a part of the go-to-market (GTM) community to discover new tools for sales, marketing, and revenue operations (RevOps). They seek strategies, tactics, techniques, and unique blends for tech stack optimization. They clamor for various methodologies whether it's GTM strategy, strategic sales, account-based marketing (ABM), product-led growth (PLG), or human-centered design thinking applied to growth.

CHAPTER 39

Pivoting Your GTM in Recession with Events

Whatever there be of progress in life comes not through adaptation but through daring.

— Henry Miller

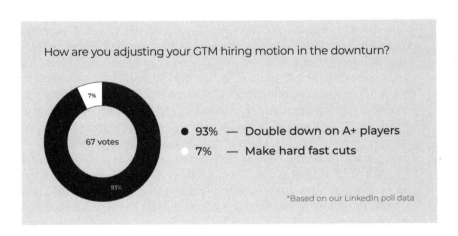

How are you adjusting your GTM hiring motion in the downturn?

7%

67 votes

93%

● 93% — Double down on A+ players
○ 7% — Make hard fast cuts

*Based on our LinkedIn poll data

Remember 2008. Your best bet was a commission-only sales role, as no one was hiring. Marketing leaders went back to corporate, took pay cuts, or worked for equity. Marketing budgets dried up, and positions became scarce. Cutbacks and layoffs ran red across the trades. Everyone had a second or third home mortgaged, and all the value deflated. Right now, renting and leasing will look attractive versus buying as software as a service (SaaS) companies move further to shore up capital expenditure (CapEx) and shift into operational expenditure (OpEx).

Where do events fit in? We've researched this one, so you don't have to. Nobody on LinkedIn talks about how to survive and thrive through a bear market. Here are some constructive go-to-market (GTM) strategies to combat the recession and transform it into a competitive advantage.

Based on 2000 and 2008, here we go with recommendations on a pivot:

1. **Spend:**

   – 80% of revenue comes from 20% of existing customers. Focus on re-tention and up-sell/cross-sell into your best existing accounts. Why not throw an event focused on expansion business? Bring your best custom-ers together in an environment where they can share knowledge. High-light new elements of your product roadmap or key up-sells/cross-sells that will help them outperform peers in a downturn. What can you pro-vide them to create a unique competitive advantage?

   – Stack rank your customers, scoring them based on various value met-rics. Whether you have 200 customers or 10, it's time to prioritize. Use a Ben Franklin style list or a weighted algorithm as your customer bell curve is asymmetrical. Who has the most upside? Where is your relation-ship the strongest? Where are you single versus multi-threaded?

   – You should institute a 90–120 renewal process with targeted quarterly business reviews (QBRs) to ensure you're getting ahead of churn and rec-ommending expansion upstream. What makes a great customer? Net Pro-moter Score (NPS) 10, Customer Satisfaction Score (CSAT) between 75–85%. A net revenue retention rate (NRR) over 100% is ideal, meaning you succeed in repeat sales, up-sells, cross-sells, and expansion. According to ChurnZero, "Net Revenue Retention calculates total revenue (including expansion) minus revenue churn (contract expirations, cancellations, or downgrades)." Example NRR cited by Jason Lemkin at SaaStr: Hubspot 90% NRR at IPO, 100% today, Zoom 130%, Asana 115%. Remember, we may be moving into a down economy where subscription business mod-els could feel pressure, but we're not cancelling our Zoom or Asana mem-bership anytime soon.

– Optimize your marketing mix to the bankable channels with the highest lifetime value (LTV) to customer acquisition cost (CAC) ratio. Look for good buys if cost per thousand (CPM) drops. Experiment with more-innovative, non-saturated channels for business-to-business (B2B) like TikTok. If ad costs spike, cut them depending on supply and demand market conditions. You may have to pull back advertising from Google, Facebook, and Instagram. Leverage a next-gen ad-buying automation platform like Metadata with algorithms that create efficiency and uncover audiences you wouldn't usually see. (Disclosure: they've been a GTM Games partner.) Now's the time to get creative with business-to-consumer (B2C) platforms that could be a diamond in the rough and have a high yield. In advertising your events, consider these factors.

2. **Teams:**

– Adjust your key performance indicators (KPIs)/tighten the qualification criteria of marketing qualified leads (MQLs). Are you accepting too many lower-level approver leads? Run account-based marketing (ABM) campaigns specifically targeted at director level and above. ABM has its counterpart in account-based sales development (ABSD) (hat tip to Lars Nilsson). How about considering account-based events? Hold an event with just your "dream" prospects on the panel.

– Refine *lead-routing*: Move off of a "Territory Model" or random round robins and get every quota-carrying rep and sales development rep (SDR) into shared Google Sheets. Assign no more than 200 named accounts per SDR so they can synchronize with account executives' (AEs') ongoing outbound activity, pulling back inbound in a flywheel motion aligned to your optimal targets. Tailor and throw events targeted by vertical or even baskets of similar accounts. Remember, we will see an explosion of mergers and acquisitions (M&As), and companies leaving the public markets to go private. Ordinarily, these contraction points are a negative leading indicator, but in this market, it's an excellent trigger to engage prospects.

– Calibrate your quotas to sell more but improve commission rates; sales are worth more now due to the "time value of money." Improve margins and cut stock keeping units (SKUs) with low margins.

– Explore (up to) a 20% services mix, but don't go past it to hurt valuation when things bounce back. Usually, we'd never recommend offering "services" as it can lower your "forward-multiple" of valuation, but right now, cash is "king, queen, and ace," so monetize every avenue you can.

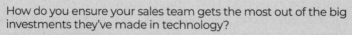

How do you ensure your sales team gets the most out of the big investments they've made in technology?

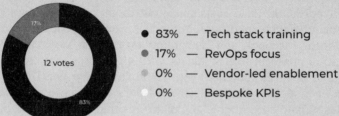

12 votes

- 83% — Tech stack training
- 17% — RevOps focus
- 0% — Vendor-led enablement
- 0% — Bespoke KPIs

*Based on our LinkedIn poll data

– Bolster your outbound sales training and optimize tech stacks. It's mystifying to see companies increasing their headcount to prepare for the crunch without investing in training and tool sets to up-skill their teams. Drop one head count and pour that into training and tools. Answer these: are your SDRs the sharpest point of the spear with high buyer acumen and product knowledge? Can they surface latent pain effectively on first calls and peel the onion? Highly unlikely. Are your AEs strategic enough? Are they using "Solution Selling," "Value Selling," or "Challenger Selling" frameworks to progress business by understanding the political power base or conversely, leaving money on the table with endless pilots, free trials, and plummeting annual contract value/total contract value (ACV/TCV)? Concurrently, are you making them dial a phone one at a time versus ConnectAndSell (CAS) (disclosure: sponsor), which can do 1,000 dials per day with 20+ live connects versus 3–5? We'd hope you'd invest in call recording and sales engagement platforms to automate outbound touch cadences like Outreach and Gong (disclosure: sponsors).

– Boost equity on key people. Employee retention is paramount right now. You can give out more stock and change your vesting schedules for new hires. Understand motivation, whether that's the stock allocation or bumps in base salary. Letting your employees innovate can boost retention even more than compensation, so allowing them to apply this book fully will actually help you retain them.

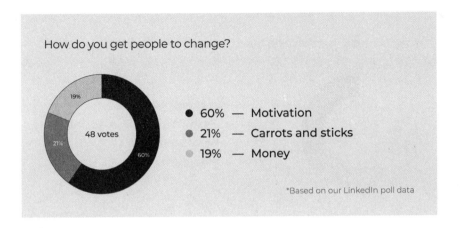

How do you get people to change?

48 votes

- 60% — Motivation
- 21% — Carrots and sticks
- 19% — Money

*Based on our LinkedIn poll data

3. **Data management:**

– Invest in data enrichment and revenue operations (RevOps), and clean up your database customer relationship management (CRM). We've already been shocked to see cuts in the RevOps layer as there are economic jitters. Our whole mission is to align sales and marketing through go-to-market (GTM) cross-training. RevOps is the bridge, the glue, that unifies these two warring functions (factions?!) at long last through the prism of integrated software, metrics, analytics, and dashboard. It's penny-wise and pound-foolish to slash this crucial role.

You need to invest in platforms like Syncari (disclosure: sponsor) to clean up your data and sync your disparate systems in real time into one cohesive data model. Most CRM data is up to 50% error-prone. Going to market with messy account history, duplicates, ghost objects in your CRM, and trying to generate accurate pipeline reports and forecasts is nearly impossible. On that note, many major REV Tech SaaS players have released forecast solutions this year. Per Seth Marrs at Forrester, you don't want your reps manually inputting CRM data—that should all be auto-captured so you can free up selling time (dismally low below 40% industry average) and improve guided selling.

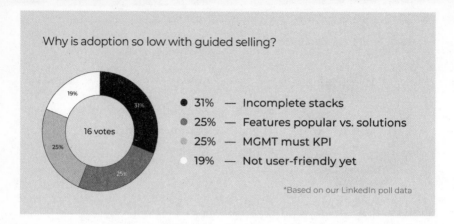

Why is adoption so low with guided selling?

16 votes

- 31% — Incomplete stacks
- 25% — Features popular vs. solutions
- 25% — MGMT must KPI
- 19% — Not user-friendly yet

*Based on our LinkedIn poll data

– Verify your data quality, purge bad records, dead opportunities, and noise in your back end. There are third-party RevOps shops that do this work as well as Virtual Assistants. Get your house in order and clean up your act.

Regarding orchestrating events, there's nothing worse than bouncing 30% of your event invites from a bad CRM email "house file." To gauge the effectiveness of events, you need custom fields in your CRM that show the source so you can tie each experience back to revenue. The best way to get buy-in for a future customer-centric event (CCE) is to show the attributed pipeline downstream.

LeanData is a phenomenal platform for this. Downstream pipeline and positive revenue impact from an event can continue from six months to two years, so be meticulous about storing that data in your CRM and watching for source attribution. In simple terms, that interactive event you held on "Top 3 Revenue Intelligence Trends" last March is where the VP of Marketing first came into the funnel on your latest seven-figure, two-year deal closed.

4. **Sales:**

– Flip value props from revenue growth to "cost-cutting" verbiage when communicating to your prospect base. We all go to market with various value props, but the one-note commonality is typically *drive revenue*, and not even *profitably* up until the recession. Attracting net new customers or retaining/expanding customers will be based on containing, cutting, shifting, and optimizing costs. Run a meeting similar to when the coronavirus hit, where you redraw your ideal customer profile (ICP) around a cost-cutting value prop. See if that changes your targets and how you stack rank your existing customer base to grow. Your value props on your websites, events, and themes should all change to reflect this new demand type.

– Don't price cut. Lock in multi-year contracts; you may even need to increase your pricing. Again, money is worth more now than it was six months ago. Cash up front gets weighted over monthly payments, PAYG (pay as you go), or quarterly and bi-annual terms. While we're not advocating deep discounting, you'll have to institute price increases based on record inflation, interest rate hikes, employee demands for salary, and supply chain issues. Go to market with a price increase and leverage this sense of urgency as the impetus to get a multi-quarter or multi-year lock-in from your existing customer base. Make it a value-driven incentive and guarantee to grandfather them into the previous pricing regardless of the economic roller coaster.

Events are a great sounding board to understand how your customers are doing. They're a proving ground wherein intimate non-public (but not confidential) information is shared in a safe space. You don't want to promote your price cuts or start to be the bargain basement player, but create event themes where return on investment (ROI) calculations and stories are shared to help improve NPS and expand your revenue streams on an efficiency metric for growth. You want your customers to see you as a cash register instead of a cost center, which is often a significant challenge in SaaS. The monthly subscription rate is so often seen as "burn" or operational expenditure (OpEx) versus the upside revenue it's throwing off—return on investement (ROI).

5. **SWOT Analysis – Strength, Weakness, Opportunity, and Threat:**

– Are any of your competitors losing customers, and can you poach them? As we covered, the top trigger event is a "job-relationship" change per Craig Elias. If your competitors are slashing budgets and failing to provide the white-glove service they once did, there could be high levels of churn now in their customer base and within their sales and customer success management (CSM) team. Savvy players like you can swoop in and provide high service levels, customer-centricity, and a consultative approach. David can conquer Goliath here and win over some lighthouse "dream" accounts with this approach in the deluge. A rising tide lifts all boats, but all the rocks appear when the tide goes out.

– Are new competitors rising and undercutting you? You need to be just as careful with upstarts or companies that are "war chesting" by saving up a ton of cash for a rainy day to be more nimble and undercut your pricing and business model. Pooh-poohing the competition just drives your customers into their arms. Your solution is to add incredible value and frequently meet your customers in quarterly business reviews (QBRs) to check their pulse. Multi-thread with robust connectivity at the C-Suite, C-to-C, ensuring your CEO, COO, CFO, and co-founder are friendly with theirs. Best way to bring those roles under one roof? A virtual event.

For every preceding scenario, there's an event tie-in. Opportunity cost is high for not bringing your best prospects and customers together to be reminded of your value. Your value prop moves from effectiveness to efficiency in the recession in a Peter Drucker sense. Build and execute GTM plans that position your product as a solution they couldn't possibly live without. Find creative ways to evangelize your platform from the lens of how customers still gain incremental value by implementing it. In a recession, the biggest thing to remember is that you must do the opposite of your instincts, as everything is pulling back. Paradoxically, you need to be more hands-on, reach out, and communicate more. Put on your founder hat and CEO of your territory and begin fire fighting. Pre-empt churn and ensure customer happiness by understanding what's going on with your best customers. What defines your best business may change as well as your ICP. Overinvest in data strategy and RevOps to maintain a technological edge.

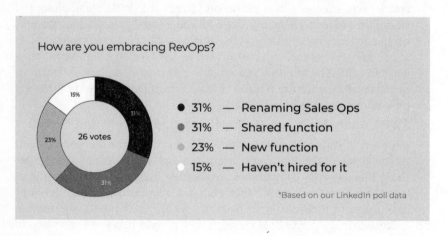

How are you embracing RevOps?

- 31% — Renaming Sales Ops
- 31% — Shared function
- 23% — New function
- 15% — Haven't hired for it

26 votes

*Based on our LinkedIn poll data

CHAPTER 40

Reinventing Your Reinventions

There are no rules. That is how art is born, how breakthroughs happen. Go against the rules or ignore the rules. That is what invention is about.

— Helen Frankenthaler

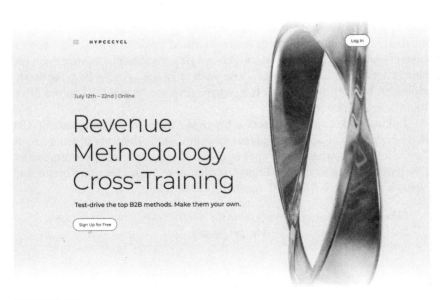

HYPCCCYCL

For year two of our hit series, we introduced a new concept to the industry called "Revenue Methodologies Cross-Training." The idea was to identify and then feature all the various methods for sales, marketing, and revenue operations (RevOps) in a competition to see which is the most powerful, almost like Ultimate Fighting Championship (UFC) showcases mixed martial arts. Traditionally, marketing has always had more subtle methods, whereas sales is more accustomed to giving its methods fancy names. What if we could include new go-to-market (GTM) motions in the event mix and highlight which ways are more potent by cross-training them? Leaders with strong opinions can try to prove what's most effective by drilling judged by visionary venture capitalists (VCs) like Sean Sheppard (U+) or Mark Roberge (Stage 2 Capital).

Marketing is strategy. There are way fewer marketing strategies than sales-authored approaches to selling. In the sales world, the methods can tend to be lighter-weight acronyms that are situational, mixed, and match. It's exceedingly rare to see a software as a service (SaaS) company enforce one framework. We often see 20 disparate sales methods living in a company because it's all about who sells better. Marketing is heavily dependent on the GTM strategy and alignment with your sales, customer success management (CSM), product, and CEO's vision.

Marketing is so dependent on other departments that it's extremely rare marketing would lead the company. There's far less space for experimentation with deeper models, sure you can AB test the site copy and header tag (H1) button "yellow or green." As a marketing department, you're almost one mechanism that drives a certain strategy, it's more GTM than marketing techniques in its essence. Sales is methodology and marketing is GTM. In our research we only found four or five codified marketing methods because there are few (if any) individual quota-carrying marketers. Because even the team is not quota-carrying, there is no push to create as many bespoke methodologies. Marketing becomes the passive revenue channel way more often than the active player in SaaS.

Talking with some customers is the best way to get out of a plateau. Get on the horn and call some attendees and begin asking them about what trends they're following, what other types of events they attend, which communities they participate in and why. Brainstorming new angles for your brand and events is what our WRKSHP™ seminars are all about.

> *"The real voyage of discovery consists, not in seeking new landscapes, but in having new eyes." —Marcel Proust*

What Do You Do When Things Go Wrong?

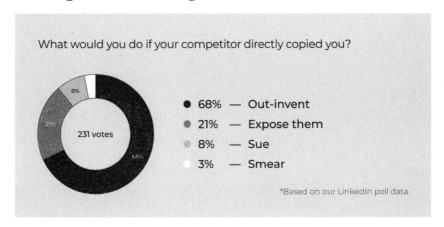

What would you do if your competitor directly copied you?

231 votes

- 68% — Out-invent
- 21% — Expose them
- 8% — Sue
- 3% — Smear

*Based on our LinkedIn poll data

We've weathered everything from a sponsor trying to upstage us (live on our event!) to a competitive community copying us right down to the font, colors, and our core GTM Games event theme. They even stole the main messaging off our homepage and put it on theirs. Then members came to our games and promoted their community with the identical value prop. Shenanigans!

You just have to keep calm and carry on out-innovating the competition. You can't let competitiveness eat you. Jeff Bezos says it best here: "If we can keep our competitors focused on us while we stay focused on the customer, ultimately we'll turn out all right." Always exhibit sportspersonlike conduct. There's not enough time and money to enforce your copyright, trademarks, or unique idea on the copy shops that will endlessly spring up. Keep your head down and run like hell. You'll stand out in the industry if you stay grounded and execute.

Focus on innovation is paramount. Never react. Gandhi put it best, "An eye for an eye makes the whole world blind." Unleash your inner Banksy, Frida Kahlo, Van Gogh, Monet, Amelia Earhart, Renoir, Mozart, Marie Curie, Jimi Hendrix, or Steve Wozniak.

Here's to the crazy ones, the misfits, the rebels, the troublemakers, the round pegs in the square holes . . . the ones who see things differently—they're not fond of rules. . . . You can quote them, disagree with them, glorify or vilify them, but the only thing you can't do is ignore them because they change things . . . they push the human race forward, and while some may see them as the crazy ones, we see genius because the ones who are crazy enough to think that they can change the world, are the ones who do.

—Steve Jobs, 1997 [RIP]

CHAPTER 41

What's the Future of Events?

© Luca D'Urbino 2022

You'll notice we didn't cover much about hybrid, in-person, plus virtual online audience events. Our definition of *hybrid* is thematic regarding mash-ups, formats, cross-functional, and cross-training concepts. The 2020s have seen a flock of black swans so far! There is no doubt that remote, hybrid, and fully digital events are here to stay. We will also see some of the first forays into business-to-business (B2B) for Metaverse as we approach 2025 and 2030. Zoom will continue to dominate as the central platform of choice based on "ease of use," fidelity with various internet signals, and mass adoption.

At this writing, travel has exploded worldwide, breaking records with thousands of flight cancellations and delays. We can only imagine the level of disruption had this happened during the latest San Francisco mega-conference.

Pre-pandemic, those events were so packed that they were bringing in cruise ships to extend hotel capacity.

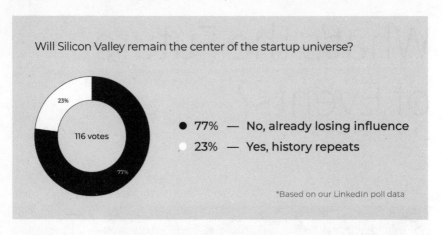

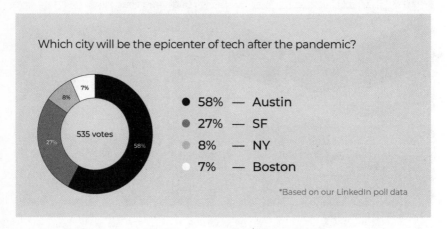

Here are our **top 11 futuristic predictions for events**.

1. Customer-led events reflect Customer-led growth (CLG)—tracking this trend. Simply put, your customers drive the funnel as evangelists at the heart of your go-to-market (GTM), public relations (PR), events, and sales/marketing funnel. Your customers are the star of the show! Keep your eyes peeled on ecosystems too. Shout out to Jay MacBain and Allan Adler.

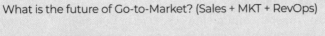

What is the future of Go-to-Market? (Sales + MKT + RevOps)

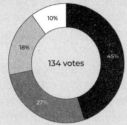

- 46% — CLG (customer-led growth)
- 27% — PLG (product-led growth)
- 18% — Inbound/Demand Gen
- 10% — Outbound/automation

*Based on our LinkedIn poll data

2. You will see booths at trade shows where attendees don augmented reality/virtual reality (AR/VR) headsets to communicate with attendees at simultaneous events in other cities through the metaverse. We will see analog, digital, and metaverse components of live events blending into a hybrid with the panelists sporting Magic Leap, Oculus, HoloLens, or new headset form factors from Apple.

3. You will be at a live event, and the speaker will dial in from Metaverse, a jet, another country, and possibly a colony on Mars or the international space station.

4. Artificial intelligence (AI) will continue to play a massive role in the social networking aspect of events. Mark Sylvester of Alias | Wavefront Technologies (a pioneer in early 3D motion graphics) built introNetworks as an early visionary of algorithmic matchmaking during a live conference. One of the most exciting aspects of virtual events is the ability for the system to ingest all the profiles on the registration list, suggest matches, and even match attendees up in real time. "Where did you source this deal that just closed, Kevin?" "HYPCCCYCL matched me during a game."

5. Empathy, democratization, and access will come from technologies that flatten the barriers to entry for online networking. This breaks down cultural barriers, invisible geopolitical walls, and socioeconomic silos to foster an enablement experience. The best knowledge is free. As Shakespeare said, "All the world is a stage." A metaphor for freeing the world's social enclaves and hidden educational resources for the entire

population of Earth to enjoy equally. Marc Andreessen predicts college could cost $1 million soon.

6. In contrast, super-premium elite events akin to a digital "yacht party" will crop up with outrageous ticket prices, waiting lists, and a speaker roster at Elon Musk or Jeff Bezos level. It will no longer always be safe, practical, or carbon-neutral to file into jets and head to Switzerland or California to take these in—God forbid.

7. We will see a renaissance of interactive cohort training, coursework, and the return of massive open online courses (MOOCs), which failed because they were ahead of their time, just like Google Glass. Universities like Stanford, colleges and higher ed everywhere are getting into the virtual training game. Incubators, accelerators, and founder education are all going borderless and classroom-less.

8. Marketing, sales, and revenue operations (RevOps) technology will merge into alpha-uber platforms (hat tip to Mary Shea of Outreach and Seth Marrs of Forrester—thanks for the Foreword). As artificial intelligence, AI/ML (machine learning), and natural language processing (NLP) jump the proverbial shark, it's at last possible to automate 70% of manual tasks and bring all these functions into one room and central source of truth. This aligns well with the customer-centric theme in this book and those organizations.

9. Developing new interactive skill-building exercises like the ones highlighted in this book will be necessary to train and effectively enable the next generation of workers. We need to up-skill the labor force quickly because most of the skills college kids learn these days will be obsolete within 5 years. IBM research shows skills have a half-life of 5 years and technical skills just 2.5.

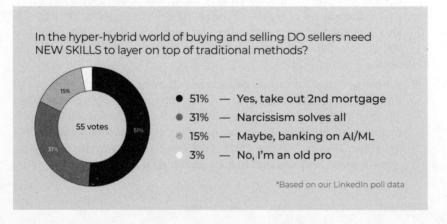

In the hyper-hybrid world of buying and selling DO sellers need NEW SKILLS to layer on top of traditional methods?

15%

55 votes

51%

31%

- 51% — Yes, take out 2nd mortgage
- 31% — Narcissism solves all
- 15% — Maybe, banking on AI/ML
- 3% — No, I'm an old pro

*Based on our LinkedIn poll data

10. We may see a day when a top sales leader has never met a live customer. An ominous prediction and antipathetic to the clarion call in this book. We believe all GTM positions should get in front of the customer face-to-face often. The point is the technology for events, video conferencing, and training will get so good—think Holodeck on Star Trek—that physically meeting in person will no longer be a barrier to entry. Witness the new executive comfort level with six- and seven-figure deals fully remote without ever meeting the salesperson. At this writing, we've never met 99% of our event participants in real life (IRL).

11. 2D is moving to 3D. We all remember the princess hologram in early sci-fi movies. We've got to break out of the silo of the 2D zoom reality into 3D. The new digital whiteboards in our Event Tech Stack section and technologies like mmhmm allow you to powerfully manipulate the visuals, but we're thinking about this in a meta context. There's a scene buried in antiquity where Socrates walks through the picturesque hills of Athens near the Parthenon, training his budding scholars with the Socratic method. Wouldn't it be incredible to recreate this in a VR metaverse experience? Imagine walking through the Galapagos Islands with the top 25 leaders in global innovation as they have lively discourses with you from the safety and privacy of your home with VR goggles. We will undoubtedly see more technologies that look like holograms and holographic AR make appearances in our live meetings with new holographic broadcast tech in the works at the time of this writing.

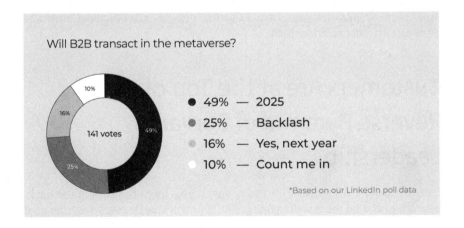

Will B2B transact in the metaverse?

141 votes

- 49% — 2025
- 25% — Backlash
- 16% — Yes, next year
- 10% — Count me in

*Based on our LinkedIn poll data

It's a brave new world, so use this technology wisely and for the good of all humankind. Like the internet, you can utilize virtual reality for good or evil.

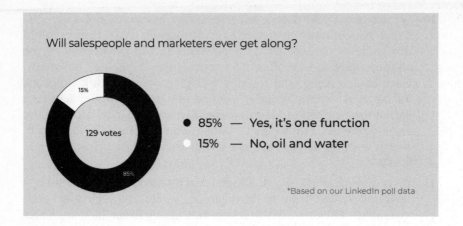

Fine

That's our book! You made it. I'm sure you picked it up and thought, "How could they possibly write a book this long about such a simple subject?" Da Vinci said it best, "Simplicity is the ultimate sophistication."

The big thing to realize is that the medium changes, but the message stays the same. This book is long on the quality of ideas and short on technology jargon. We hope your crucial takeaway is to focus on storytelling, innovation, creativity, and customer-centricity. As you utilize new technology stacks and experiment with hybrid models, we believe you must consistently seek to disrupt yourself, innovate your virtual events, and stay laser-focused on transforming customer relationships.

Customers Are at the Top of the Reverse Pyramid of Servant Leadership

Treat them well, bring them into your opera, give them the keys to the backstage area, and let them write your script. You will shatter every revenue goal you have if you follow this simple formula.

The customer is your platform, and ideas create movements. Join us for Events 3.0.

—*Justin & Julia*
Los Angeles and Palermo, Italy July 4, 2022

GTM Games RECORDINGS: To unlock the ultimate vault of B2B simulations, log in to **HYPCCCYCL.com**. Access the complete event archive of over 100 GTM Games with 100+ top thought leaders and venture capitalists (VCs) in B2B. Simply badge your profile in your work history and reach out to us. Add: Member, HYPCCCYCL—HYPCCCYCL is an invite-only, professional community where top B2B revenue leaders cross-train their GTM skills with VCs.

SPONSORSHIPS: Reach out to us if you are interested in sponsoring our events, and we will share a prospectus highlighting sponsorship packages, audience demographics, and referenceable partner return on investment (ROI). We are always looking for top B2B companies with software as a service (SaaS) products to feature *as the drill*, plus speakers, coaches, contestants, and VCs, so please reach out or send them our way.

Appendix I: WRKSHP™ Examples

FLYYT-X

https://hypcccycl.com/agency/flyyt-x/
Daring, Optimistic, Provocative
Behind the hype

Challenge

The parent company of FLYYT-X, ConnectandSell (CAS), has a calling technology that is so powerful that often people disbelieve the results are real.

We came up with a spin on their Flight School and were looking for ways to make the idea as disruptive as possible. Instead of calling field salespeople to participate in tests of the software, CAS wanted to pull the market to them with a competition-style event.

#hypcccycld

We immediately isolated the disruptive nature of a space mission theme versus Top Gun. The client could showcase their technology by holding gamified calling events while pulling ideal customer profiles (ICPs) into their ecosystem.

Instead of flights, caller astronauts would take missions that reflected rocket stages. These stages are also the steps of a client's signature process to act as an educational vehicle for the adoption of the product.

For a wow factor and additional gamification hooks, we proposed creating a custom cryptocurrency called FLYYT-$, allowing participants to purchase additional experiences.

Salesborgs

https://hypcccycl.com/agency/salesborgs/

Futuristic, Aggressive, Cyberpunk
Behind the hype

Challenge

How do you take a business consultant that has 6,000 competitors and build the most savage business-to-business (B2B) brand + community ever to make them stand out in the crowd?

Justin Michael is a sales consultant who wrote a book on technology quotient (TQ). In the book, he talks about becoming a Salesborg, which is seller meets cyborg.

He was struggling to drive consistent retained business and get his community to grow. By trying to be something to everyone, he struggled attracting the ultimate ICP.

#hypcccycld

To disrupt the conventional Salesborgs brand approach, we built a gamified TQ test, the first-ever of its kind. The mechanic is a viral feedback loop that perpetually delivers testers back to the website to keep attempting to pass the test and get a higher score. This drives consistent book sales and lucrative consulting work from a C-level audience.

The community is now an exclusive experience that commands the attention of the industry.

Justin's new brand presence dominates the category of revenue operations (RevOps). His work is taken seriously by industry analysts.

Appendix II: Go-to-Market (GTM) Templates

Checklist to Hold a Customer-Centric Event (CCE)

- Are your customers the stars of your event, not just watching but competitors, judges, and coaches?
- Do you have a colleague who can direct while you host to keep the customer's viewpoint in mind?
- Do you have a Zoom package enabled for webinars?
- Do you have special effects? Try Prezi Video or mmhmm.
- Do you have a diverse speaker pool composed of various backgrounds and levels?
- Have you built onboarding docs, media kits, and graphics so your attendees can cross-promote?
- Have you set up a LinkedIn event (or are ready to *restream* to several platforms at once) and asked your fan base, colleagues, family, and friends to spread the promotions?
- Do you have a shared event calendar to make it easy for everyone involved to get alerted?
- Do you have a custom Zoom background graphic for all participants?
- Do you have a structure for the hour call that lays out the intro, challenge, Q&A, and so on, almost like modules?
- Who hosts break-out sessions if your event is multi-track, like an all-day virtual conference?
- Has your theme been done before? Is it a mash-up of at least two or three other themes to make it innovative?
- Do you have a Facebook and LinkedIn page, Instagram and YouTube channel, and TikTok as spokes established to amplify your LinkedIn hub?
- What is your social media posting schedule before and after the event? Did you build a social media marketing (SMM) doc?

- Do you have an editing resource or DIY way to cut your highlight reels to post to video?
- Do you have an ad strategy or third party ad agency? Have you built out ad copy and graphics?
- Have you equipped your sales development reps (SDRs) (or third-party lead gen shop) with post-event scripts for call follow-ups?
- Have you built voicemails, video follow-ups, email sequences, and LinkedIn InMail templates?

SPEARS: Hyper-Short Emails

How not to do it:

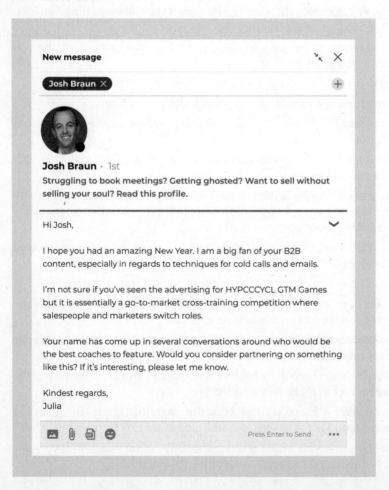

How to do it:

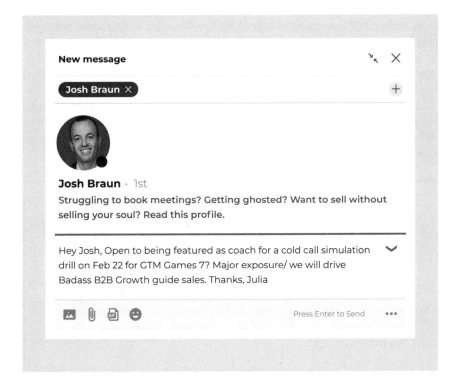

How not to do it: With traditional messaging, it can take hundreds of back and forths to build out the buzziest event, get skeptical coaches to participate in something unknown, and pull in an audience.

How it's done: The Justin Michael Method™ (JMM™) applies to all business-to-business (B2B) communications. Sure it's blunt, but respecting someone's time, getting straight to the point, and leveraging social proof out of the gate are the gift that keeps on giving.

First, you want to optimize your mobile-responsive email communication because 50% of what you send to prospects gets opened on a smartphone. Second, when you reduce your emails to under 50 words, that's when the magic happens.

Check out these eye-opening stats from Lavender:

– 70% of emails get written at or beyond a 10th-grade reading level.

– 5th-grade writing gets 50% more replies.

– 50-word emails have a 65% higher chance of getting a response than 125-word emails.

We can tell you that three-sentence emails process in 3.3 seconds. Multi-paragraph emails take 11 seconds to read and trigger fight or flight.

The basic idea is to make an email look like a text message or ad unit. I know your chief marketing officer (CMO) will wince at this idea, but open rates immediately shoot up past 60%, and then the other lever to pull is from the heuristics we talked about earlier—fear/pain, emotional resonance. Try linguistic innuendo to the tune of: "a similar company was stressed out about, challenged by, tearing their hair out," and so on.

Hey, {{First_Name}}—Thanks for coming to SQLfest. Any initiatives to allocate budget toward [blank] in 2022? I have a product that may be able to [reduce risk, reduce spend, increase revenue, etc.]—[pain point]. If this is on your radar, should we set something up Q4? Thanks, J&J

"SPEARS" framework frequency is revolutionary in creating a "swarm of bees" effect—making an assertive seven touches over the first 72 hours after an event! Watch closely, our fellow Honey Badgers:

> *First, let us settle a debate over other "less effective sequence/cadence methods" widely* en vogue. *Running a prospecting sequence Day 1, Day 3, or Days 1, 2, 8 is less effective than a consecutive Day 1, 2, 3. Why?*
>
> *Waiting a full six days makes you appear "sneaky" like that news-letter nobody signed up for. Prospects think, "Why are you SPAMMING my email when I didn't opt-in?" Hence, you get so many "take me off the list."*

In the JMM™—Day 1 contains a strong subject line (under three words like *growth*), email under 50 words—three sentences max, bumps back up on Day 2 with simple "thoughts?" and again on Day 3 (with imagery), so it's only one thread. You've left up to a couple of VMs + LI connected during that time. Then you stop on Day 4. Then it repeats fractal holographically.

2022 Sequence/Cadence Overview

Day 1: Call, Voicemail, Email (Triple)

Day 2: Re: Email 1 (Reply Bump), LinkedIn blank connect

Day 3: Reply Bump with a visual, ghost call

Day 4: Nothing

Day 5: (Triple), LinkedIn

Day 6: (Reply Bump)

Day 7: (Reply Bump), ghost call

Day 8: Nothing

Day 9: (Triple)

Day 10: (Reply Bump)

Day 11: (Reply Bump), ghost call

Day 12: Nothing

JMM™—SPEARS—Email Structure

Subject line: <relevant info bit> + <key word>

Greeting: Hey, <<Name>>—

Sentence 1: <<mention event - relevant info bit>>, curious if you're open to discuss <<specific outcome related to key word>> strategy?

Sentence 2: <<lookalike customer>> uses us to <<achievable outcome>> by (x% or $x).

CTA: If it makes sense, when can we hop on a zoom?

Examples:

Hey, Jim—Dug your judging for our event. Noticed your time at Acme; they're a current customer using us for outsourcing the SDR function— wanted to go over some similar ideas with you. They were able to gener- ate 30 solid leads in a 1mo period. If it makes sense, when is good to jump on a call? Thanks— JM

Hey, Glen—John Doe set us up on LI after K8 Jam—Acme saved $7.5MM in OpEx by calling our API for <<thing you do>> in various workflows— Beta Corp likes us too. If this makes sense still, how does your calendar look? Thanks—J

Results from the crowd:

"Every meeting so far has come from a Reply Bump."

"Response rates went way up, and negative replies went slightly up. What also shot up? Referrals and meetings set."

Keenan Yoseph glows, "I've never had a sequence that booked me meet- ings. I only had luck with one-off hyper-personalized touches. I created industry-specific sequences, modeled my approach 100% after the JMM™, and went from booking 0 meetings through sequences to booking 2–3 per week. My open rates are 82–100% and average around 90%. Some of my reply rates are double digits. I've only put 51 prospects through the sequence since creating them two weeks ago. This is just my first iteration. I cannot imagine what hap- pens as I continue to optimize."

Getting attendees:

Hey, Tim—Ever thought about attending an event where CROs get judged by SDRs on cold calling? Talk soon—Julia

(continued)

Re-engaging attendees:

Hey, Tim, Thanks for coming to our "No Pitch" Contest. Curious what you'd change about it? [opinion heuristic]

Why it works: The first SPEAR email is under 25 words. For the second, everyone has an opinion/is dying to share it, which consistently garners a fantastic response rate.

When prospects go dark and ghost you:

Could you have the *courtesy* to point me in the right direction to who handles <<function>> over there?

Why it works: The principle of congruence—hat tip to Dr. Robert B. Cialdini. People want to be civil, so they help you when you hold them accountable.

Voicemail template:

Hey, Jim—Justin Michael from Acme Corp 917.232.2164—Great to see you compete in the ad targeting game Thursday. I have a product/service that's relevant to your work; do you mind if I tell you a bit about it? We helped Acme and Beta get a 36.5% revenue lift via ad fraud mitigation that's algorithmically derived by our team of 17 data scientists. I have some ideas to apply this solution to Your Corp. Again, Justin Michael at Acme 917.232.2164. I'll follow up with a quick note. Thanks!

Why it works: You leverage social proof and a cliffhanger about more ideas you'll share once they find time with you. You put the phone number at the front and back as this is part of a COMBO Prospecting "triple" where you call, leave a voicemail and send an email in under 90 seconds. (Hat tip to Tony J. Hughes & Lee Bartlett)

A brief note:

Here's the exact sequence template we use across clients and is plug-and-play. It works (for the most part) every time. Not many people use this, and you'll stand out in the inbox. We haven't made a sequence like this public. Many of our LinkedIn updates hint at something like this.

A bump email is in reply to the original subject line. So each cluster has a primary email and two bumps that go with it. The bumps are pretty flexible; this is just a sample.

The concept maximizes the propensity for the original message consumption. You're getting to open another loot box every time it gets bumped. That's why the bump messages are sparse. You're directing them back to the original message in the thread.

Your open rates on the main spears will go through the roof. By the way, a *spear* is simply a short, compact three- or four-line email that focuses on customer outcomes, social proof, and conversational but professional and authoritative language.

Event Follow-Up Sequence

Cluster 1

Day 1: Email 1 subj: growth + Ad Olympics

Hey, {{First_Name}}—Couldn't believe at the last minute you got voted off on our event. Curious if you're open to chat re: [blank] strategy? [Customer] achieved [outcome] in [timeframe] with us by [process]. If it makes sense, should we set up some time to chat? Thanks—JWD

John Denver/Company / ### ### ####

Day 2: Bump

Hey, {{First_Name}}—Any thoughts?

Day 3: Bump

What do you think of the implications of this diagram? [insert Venn diagram]

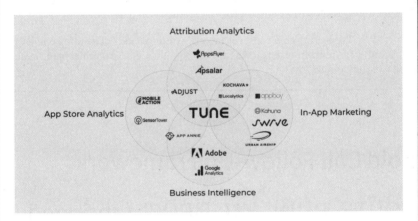

The Venn diagram should always be the second or third bump email on your first spear in the cluster. You should even vary this as you're firing. Maybe every other contact gets *thoughts* first, with the alternates getting Venns first.

They would have seen this thing if they had opened your emails like a UFO hovering on the horizon. Suddenly, their friends at work are getting blasted with it. You're trying to get them to talk to each other about you.

Cluster 2

Day 5: Email 2 subj: innovation

Hey, {{First Name}}—Any initiatives to allocate budget toward [blank] in 2022? I have a product that may be able to [reduce risk, reduce spend, increase revenue, etc.]—[pain point]. If this is on your radar, should we set something up Q4? Thanks—JWD

(continued)

Day 6: Bump [customer quote]
Day 7: Bump
[visual, case study, screenshot, etc.]
Day 9: Email 3 subj: reduce risk

Hey, {{First Name}}—Have you heard [current event] [pain point]? What steps are you taking to ensure your grounds are covered? P.S Would love to show some of the recent work we have done for companies to avoid these situations. Lemmeno! 🫙

Day 10: Bump
[gif/video]—Recommended gif creators: **getcloudapp.com** or **gyazo.com**
Day 11: Bump [customer quote]
Last Ditch
[Reply to Cluster 1] Break-up options

1. Knock-knock—gate is closing. . .

2. Have you given up on securing your systems? (ref: Chris Voss)

3. Favor, could you please have the courtesy to point me at the team that handles this? (inspiration: Cialdini congruence)

P.S.: Try pairing cold calls/voicemails within seconds of sending emails 1, 5, and 9 for maximum engagement (see complete cold call/voicemail breakdown that follows).

Cold Call Follow-Up Framework

ROUTE–RUIN–MULTIPLY™ (abridged for events)

"Noticed that you attended our event on _____ topic. What did you think? (pause) Just curious . . . Who's in charge of your _____ strategy?" (ROUTE)

I am.

"Oh, what do you normally use to do ___ x process?" (RUIN)

Acme.

"They're great. How's that working out for you?" (validate)—pause—(Uncover pain)—polarity shift. Essentially, keep listening until they ask you, "Wait, what do you do?" [convey interest]

"Why don't you plug us in alongside what you're already using to multiply the effectiveness of your _____ existing solution _____?" (MULTIPLY)

After the event happens, how do you re-engage your potential customers? How do you build a proper flow for that?

To discover much more, simply DM us for the JMM™ templates.

Tailored for Event Follow-Up:

Hey, Jane Smith?

Hey, Justin Michael from HYPCCCYCL

Just curious, what were your thoughts on the GTM Games event you attended last week? How would you improve it? (opinion heuristic)

Or:

Just curious, do you think the drills we did were realistic to your challenges?

Yes

Curious about what tech you're currently using to solve those? (RUIN)

Everyone wants to give an opinion. Look at the thousands of Amazon reviews on a pair of blue jeans—not kidding. Calls to action should always be a pattern interrupt, and never about your product or getting a meeting. That's too salesy and obvious.

RRM—Cold Call Framework (full script)

Cold calling isn't dead. Not by a long shot. If done right, it can be your secret weapon for filling your pipeline. Few still call. You'd be surprised because being over-reliant on sequencers is a crutch. Sure, there might be industries where it converts better than others. But you didn't get in sales to hang up the towel on a whole channel, did you?

Try this and watch your pipeline truly grow. What you're about to read has been honed over two decades. Word for word. Sentence by sentence. So if you're satisfied with your current results, delete this. Throw it away. Please. But if you'd like to get a taste of finally cracking the top of funnel (TOFU) on the phone . . . this is it. Introducing the Route-Ruin-Multiply (RRM) and Route-Ruin-Rip (RRR) methods.

The first three heartbeats determine everything:

1. Whether you get hung up on.
2. Whether you get routed or not.
3. Get told to pound sand, or . . . .
4. Get to the next step in your script.

ROUTE-RUIN-MULTIPLY

STEP 1: INTRO

Say the prospect's full name—go for the pronunciation even if it's hard. (Dale Carnegie heuristic) *Is this Nancy Kowalczik? Koh - wal - chik*

Yes

Hey, it's Justin Michael from Acme Corp.

STEP 2: INTRO

Noticed that you attended our webinar on Marketing Automation. Just curious.... Who's in charge of your CX strategy?

Why, what's this about?

I have some CX tech but don't want to waste your time . . . just curious who heads up CX, does that roll up to you?

Yes

STEP 3: RUIN (PEEL THE ONION)

How do you do that now? Do you handle it internally or work with a third party?

OPTION 1: Oh, we actually build internally . . .

Oh, did you choose to do that or someone there before you? OR

How long did it take you to build it out?

OPTION 2: We already have a vendor.

Makes sense—who do you use?

[Won't Disclose] Can't say.

Oh, interesting . . . what do you like about them? [Then shut up.]

[If they name the vendor] It's Beta Corp.

Beta Corp is great—how's that working out for you? [pregnant pause . . . wait]

Get the prospect talking about the status quo.

Customer replies, **We don't do it at all.**

Doing nothing is a choice; validate it.

Always validate the status quo; agree, and make them right. "Agreement" is the greatest pattern interrupt of all—sellers always debate.

If they surface pain, peel the onion with open questions.

NEVER address pain by spoon-feeding your solution, feature function, or benefits.

The essence of the RUIN step is once they start talking about why their decision or indecision is right, they invariably move across the emotional spectrum from positive to negative, surfacing pain.

It seems unlikely this would happen, but it's the greatest reverse psychology breakthrough discovered from tens of thousands of calls.

When you get a PAIN—peel the pain.

Never meet pain with a bandage; never bandage the wound. Instead, twist the knife. Be Columbo versus Marry Poppins's "spoon full of sugar."

Customer says, **We love Beta Corp mostly, but the customer service is pretty weak.**

WHAT NOT TO DO: spoon-feed

Our customer service is excellent. (Blather on about YOUR solution.)

WHAT TO DO:

"Oh, that's interesting; why is customer service interesting/important to you?" (Answer a question with a question to go deeper toward the pain/latent pain.)

> **"Well, their CS team is based in Australia, so we need to wait one day to get a ticket answered. Not an issue except at the end of the month when we charge credit cards, customers can't refund for 72 hours and go ballistic." [pain]**

"Oh, no! What happens then?"

> **"It's costing us millions in negative NPS scores. It lights up Google and G2 Crowd with negative reviews spilling blood on Page One."**

"Oh, your customer service is an issue. What would happen if you fixed it?"
"Honestly, I calculated that we would reduce churn by 15%, adding 3 million in ARR."

STEP 4: MULTIPLY

"Look, Nancy—don't change what you're currently doing (frictionless)—plug us in alongside Acme Corp to multiply the effectiveness of your current solution."

Other good verbs for Multiply:

Turbocharge

Force multiplier

Spike

Boost

You want to position "augmentation" over "rip and replace"—remember, they're likely locked into a heavy multi-year SaaS contract, so you'd be DOA to suggest a rip out.

ROUTE-RUIN-RIP (RRR)

Buyers of IT products and services can often only transact with one vendor at a time. Same with something like custom relationship management (CRM) or sales engagement platforms (SEP).

Route-Ruin-Rip (RRR) is a "pitch later" framework and when you *do* pitch, leverage a solid full-value prop to differentiate why you're better. The time delay on when you pitch will increase your propensity to convert.

Personalization—3×3 research works well—3 facets of personalization in 3 minutes or even 30 seconds. We call this Synthesis or Hyper-Personalization.

Personalization Stacking

Scan their LinkedIn profile, Twitter, and a quick Google search and tie any three points together. "Right brain, left brain" is best—always include something logical with something emotional to stimulate emotion and reason.

> *"Noticed you went to Notre Dame, majored in Applied Statistics, and won 30 under 30."*

Better would be to tie their Ernst & Young "Entrepreneur of the Year" award back to a facet of their agile software development team approach.

> *"Hey, Nancy—Noticed you got the 30-under-30 as an entrepreneur; it reminds me a lot of our founder who had a similar award and cracked into the IT world at a young age like you."*

Be relatable, tying personalization to relevance. Use "personalization stacking" to mention multiple points in the email or call.

TONE: DMV Approach + Air Traffic Control

Neutralize your voice with "non-hunger" like it's the Department of Motor Vehicles (DMV) counter or you're directing air traffic at the airport. The less emotion and more down tones, the more control.

When you're getting hang-ups in the first three heartbeats, you're not down toning, and sounding like you work at the DMV = non-salesy is the key.

When RRM fails . . . you're not following the preceding nuances, or the word "charge" is too combative. Ask the top script differently when you hit the R over and over . . .

What's This About?

Instead of "Who's in charge of your IT strategy?" Second time ask:

Who heads up your IT strategy?

Who's responsible for your IT strategy?

Who's the appropriate person on IT strategy (speak with finesse)?

Who's responsible for decisions on software for your IT strategy?

Caution

- Keep your listen-to-talk ratio always at 80/20 or better.
- Do not skip prematurely to RUIN or MULTIPLY—reps do this because they're impatient.
- Go back to ROUTE over and over and over again until DM is confirmed.
- Never start pitching until you hit the POLARITY shift (remember, they trigger the pitch by a desire to hear it).

Why don't traditional permission-based opener (PBO) phone approaches work like "the reason for my call . . ."?—you interrupt and spotlight yourself versus the prospect speaking. You disagree and overcome objections versus agree and lower friction/build trust rapidly.

Traditional scripts are Kung Fu, whereas RRM is Aikido. You're interrupted, and within 3 seconds, the caller is getting you to confirm your exact name pronunciation (Dale Carnegie, the most beautiful sound in the human language). Then immediate relevance (references the event you attended or something extraordinary you did in it), your power (what you do), and then gets you to open up to them about your latent pain.

Callers must remove all the friction and recoil from the call to eliminate "prospect resistance." (Hat tip to Mike Bosworth.) Speed to trust quantum leaps.

Warning: In 2007, with this technique, Justin started to close deals fully on the first call. In the 2020s, there are 11+ decision-makers involved in a buying decision, so getting a solid referral or "closing for time" is your best bet aka landing the meeting (the first commitment).

Signs You've Done This Method Right

1. They ask you for time on your calendar!
2. They suggest or ask permission to bring multiple stakeholders.
3. Deal velocity speeds way up—show rates move to 90% plus for meetings.
4. Call time balloons over 10 minutes, but sales cycle length comes down under 45 days.
5. Your post-event lead conversion percentage goes through the roof.

Classic Cold Call Way

1. Interrupt.
2. Don't let them talk (one-way firehose).
3. Pitch your product.
4. Persuade, convince, argue.

New Way

With RRM, the spotlight is on the prospect, not yourself, and you're agreeing, listening, and peeling the onion the whole time—it's never been done in 20 years.

Rules

Strive for 85/15 even 95/5 listen-to-talk ratio. You're talking way too much if you ever go above 50%.

Wait for the POLARITY shift—keep asking onion peeling questions until they ask:

Wait, what do you do?

Wait, can you do that?

What's your name again?

What's the company called?

Vampire Rule—you must wait for them to desire knowing what you offer. Prospects must invite you "over the threshold."

Venn Diagram Templates

Venns are a flux capacitor moment because complex symbols like this unlock the brain at 60,000× words. So it's like hitting all 27 touches, per Outreach's new research, and it's possible to get a meeting even on the first try.

The best question to ask when you send a Venn in a "bump" email is:

"What are your thoughts on the implications of this diagram?"

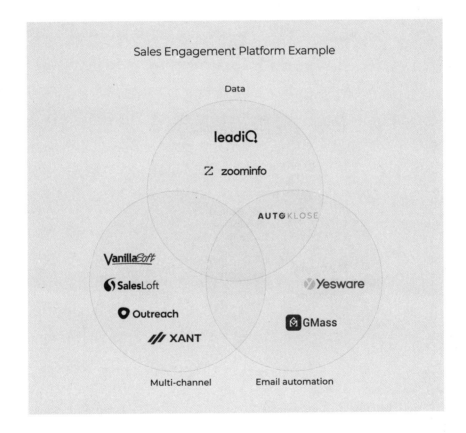

Why it works: Your prospects are in consideration and buy cycles with many of your competitors simultaneously. If they can't understand your solution with words, the competitive logos trigger their selective awareness (ref: Craig Elias), and get them to respond and say, "Wait, are you like vendor X?" Visuals like this are worth 60,000 words. So many companies are afraid of broadcasting competing logos into the prospect base, but chances are, if they've done a Google search, they're already talking with them. Start differentiating yourself ahead of Google and G2 crowd competitor searches.

Be "first in" and the Craig Elias "emotional favorite" so you can write the rules on the RFP upstream. We get this response all the time, "Wow, perfect timing, we were just looking into a solution like this." That's when you know you've won!

Venn Examples:

The Genius of White Rabbit Intel

>75% of SDR's missing quota
>85% of AE's not achieving 75% of quota
(Becc Holland)

Prioritized Leads — Maximize Production — Hyper Precise (Micro-niching)

Current Pipeline

Zero Cannibalization — Always Sell Hot

Controlled Explosive Scale

Nurturing Future Pipeline — Consistent Over-Target Performance — **Strategic Partner Pipeline**

Partnering w/ Customer — 10x in Pipeline

Zero Competition — Frictionless Pull-Through

Coverage — Loaned Credibility

Pipeline not a sewer — Maximize wallet share

WHITE RABBIT

Credit: Marcus Cauchi & Rob Turley

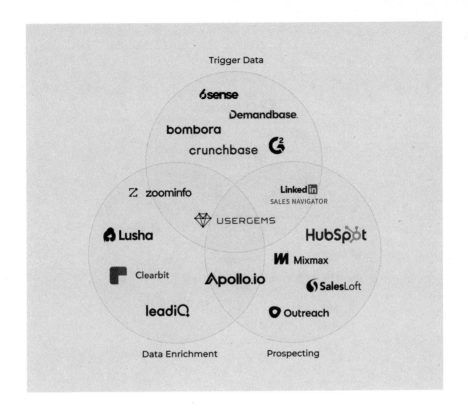

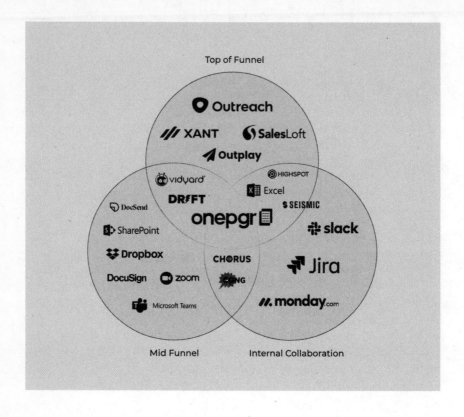

Acknowledgments

Oren Klaff, Belal Batrawy, Gerry Moran, Ryan O'Hara, Steve Richard, Josh Braun, Bryan Elsesser, Mike Bosworth, Sean Sheppard, Sydney Sloan, Kyle Lacy, Sangram Vajre, Brad Smith, Scott Leese, Anthony Iannarino, Kevin Dorsey, Rosalyn Santa Elena, Lars Nilsson, Abby Orlosky, Jennifer Smith, Brynne Tillman, Mary Shea, PhD, Alice Heiman, Chad Nuss, Jake Dunlap, Seth Marrs, Doug Landis, Amir Reiter, Stephen Pacinelli, Scott Barker, Marcus Cauchi, Marcus Chan, Mario Martinez Jr., Anita Nielsen, Jordan Henderson, Jim Wilson, Jeremey Donovan, Rob Peterson, Darryl Praill, Leore Spira, Todd Caponi, Roni Green, Kathleen Booth, Jay McBain, Dave Boyce, Eric Quanstrom, Megan Bowen, Justin Welsh, Wes Bush, Daniel Berger, Chaniqua Ivey, Jennifer Allen, Susan Whittemore, Matt Hersh, Brooklin Nash, Julie Hansen, Sarah Brazier, Jason Widup, Gerry Hill, Shawn Sease, Gabrielle Blackwell, Scott Ingram, Kelly Ford Buckley, Samantha McKenna, Shruti Kapoor, Stu Heinecke, Ben Kipnis, Jorge Soto, Leslie Venetz, Josh Braun, George Brontén, Jorge Soto, Joe Caprio, Sarah Brazier, Alexander Kesler, Mike Bosworth, Latané Conant, Ashleigh Early, Kevin Dorsey, Scott Barker, Richard Harris, Aaron Ross, Guru Chandrasekaran, Shari Levitin, Matt Heinz, Viveka von Rosen, Carole Mahoney, Chris Beall, David Hoffeld, Sangram Vajre, Max Altschuler, Victor Antonio, Carole Mahoney, Sammi Reinstein, Holly Xiao, Jed Mahrle, Shari Levitin, Jake Dunlap, Rajnation, Cory Bray, Travis Bryant

Index